The Campus History Series

ANDERSON UNIVERSITY

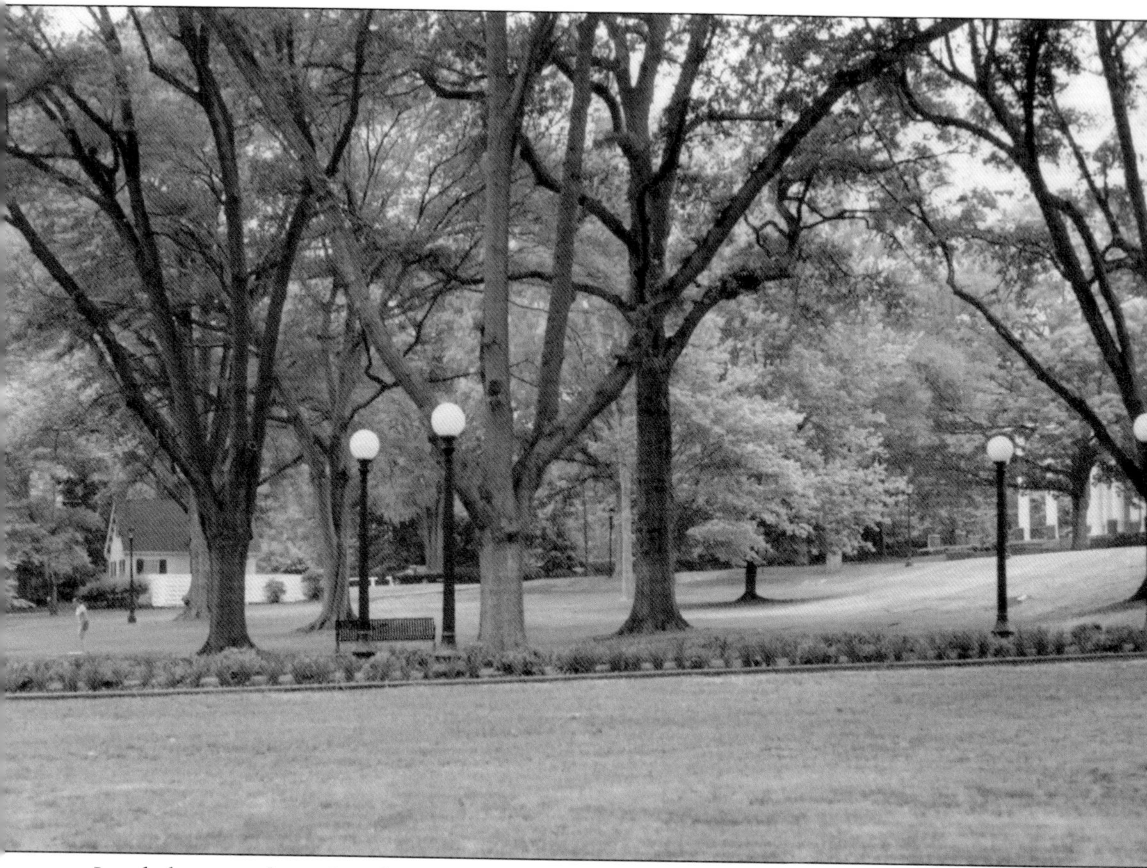

Lovely lawns and stately oaks greet visitors to Anderson University. These 6 acres, sometimes referred to as the "sacred six," have been a part of the historic view since its construction in 1911 and 1912. Because of its importance, this part of campus has been included, along with several of its original buildings, on the National Register of Historic Places since 1998. Acting as the setting for various campus activities ranging from the opening celebration for students in August to the closing ceremonies of graduation in May, this special space continues to be at the heart of campus life as Anderson University celebrates its centennial anniversary. In honor of every Anderson University alumnus—past and future—Pres. Evans Whitaker, with the blessing of the board of trustees, permanently designated this area as the "Alumni Lawn" on the occasion of the university's centennial. (Courtesy of the Anderson University Archives.)

On the Cover: Escorted by chains of flowers, graduates process down the stairs in front of the Merritt Administration Building on their way to the commencement ceremony. (Courtesy of the Anderson University Archives.)

The Campus History Series

ANDERSON UNIVERSITY

JOYCE WOOD

ARCADIA PUBLISHING

ISBN 978-0-7385-8715-8

Published by Arcadia Publishing
Charleston, South Carolina

Printed in the United States of America

Library of Congress Catalog Card Number: 2010934155

For all general information, please contact Arcadia Publishing:
Telephone 843-853-2070
Fax 843-853-0044
E-mail sales@arcadiapublishing.com
For customer service and orders:
Toll-Free 1-888-313-2665

Visit us on the Internet at www.arcadiapublishing.com

This book is dedicated to all those who contributed their time, talents, and resources towards the nurturing and preservation of God's project of this institution so that it would survive and flourish to His glory.

Contents

Acknowledgments

Any project of this type is never a "one-man show," and this is particularly true of this centennial overview. Enthusiastic support has been so generously supplied by so many, which include the following: librarian-archivists Anne Marie Martin and Brenda Dubose (retired), as well as student assistant Bethany Wade; Professor Emeritus Pat Mulligan '57, who provided invaluable assistance even though located in Turkey; Wendy Richardson, who supplied pictures; Doug Davison, who gave technological assistance; and Dr. Dave Korn, who supplied photographs and the index. Though taking the risk of leaving out someone, quite unintentionally, the list of contributors of information, pictures, ideas, and encouragement begins by including library staff members Kay Maynard and Kent Millwood; Pres. Evans Whitaker, Provost Danny Parker, and Dean Woods (vice president of Institutional Advancement), who all gave invaluable administrative encouragement and support; Annie Wharton and Rev. Leon Smith '59; faculty and staff members Dr. Beverly McAdams, Dr. Margaret Wooten, Beth Friend, Linda Clark, Rosemary Howlin, Barry Ray, Bradley Orr, Brenda McKee and Dennis McKee, and Mary Weinmann Long; and those in athletics, Chad Nelms, Randy Jones, Nancy Simpson, and former athletic director Bobby Beville. Unfortunately, we could not use all of the submissions, but picture contributions were deeply appreciated, and we would like to thank the following: Dianne Brown, Marion Mandrell, Dr. Brena Walker, Pat Mulligan, Margaret Hicks, Dr. David Perry, Claudia Boles, Elizabeth Nix, Daryl Iverson, Kristie Cole, Dr. Teresa Jones, Dr. Conny Palacios, Dr. Richard Williamson, and Dr. and Mrs. Mark Hopkins. Betsy Johnson of the Pendleton District Commission, curator Allison Hinman at the Anderson County Museum, and archivist Jane Poster at the South Carolina Baptist Convention provided gracious assistance. History major Luis Audelo contributed research time, and Sanford University student Matt McEniry donated vacation time. The editors at Arcadia, Maggie Bullwinkle and Lindsay Harris Carter, provided needed support in the process.

Any errors should be attributed to me rather than the generous assistance of my sources. To each and every one, my heartfelt thanks. Above all, to the God whose project is this university and the people who have been part of its past, make up its present, and will fill its future, I offer this account of His gracious hand at work in many lives.

Unless otherwise noted, all images appear courtesy of the Anderson University Archives.

INTRODUCTION

Anderson College was originally built on the rural edge of the textile and commercial town of Anderson, South Carolina. Incorporated in 1833, the city was founded around a central courthouse and named after Revolutionary War hero Robert Anderson. By 1900, the county had become a transportation, trade, and textile center at the forefront of the development of new public technologies, such as electricity supplied by the dam at Portman Shoals and transportation via an electric rail system. Active as well were leading women in the community, who conducted drives that raised funds to build Anderson's first hospital and attracted the Carnegie Foundation to support the building of a library. In 1910, the newly created chamber of commerce led a fund-raising effort that accumulated $100,000 in pledges, which were used to revive the tradition of higher education for women in Anderson. This led to the building of Anderson College. When the buildings neared completion, the funds to finish and furnish the college were again raised by those same women, who desperately wanted to see the doors open to students without further delay. Since the start of classes in September 1912, the institution has remained an integral part of the Anderson community. Today Anderson University has become a top-tier comprehensive university in the South and has garnered recognition as one of the 2010 "68 Up and Coming Universities in America" by *US News & World Report* and one of "America's 100 Best College Buys" by Institutional Evaluation and Research, Inc.

Pastor-presidents, those who oversaw its growth as a denominational baccalaureate institution for women, guided the early years of the university. The onset of the financial difficulties of the Depression enabled a gifted new president, Dr. Annie Dove Denmark, to chart a new course, making it a two-year junior college that admitted men as commuting students. The late 1950s was a new era of growth. At this time, additional facilities were being built, which included the following: a library, the first men's residence halls, a student center, and a teaching center. By 1990, the long-term aspiration to return to baccalaureate status had become reality. By 2006, Anderson became a university and launched several graduate programs. As this remarkable institution embarks into its second century of achievement, the university's story as a vibrant contributor to a growing region is recounted in this book.

One

Founding and Early Years

In the years between the American Revolution and the Civil War, one of the marks of the rapid growth of the new nation was a dramatic increase in the number of institutions providing higher education. In noting the part played by Baptists in the movement, Baptist historian J. Bradley Creed called it a cottage "industry" because of their role in fostering numerous educational institutions. The first president of the Southern Baptist Convention and an instrumental founder in 1825 of the South Carolina Baptist Convention, which he served as elected president for 28 years, Rev. William Bullein Johnson was among the Baptist leaders in the expansion. His dream went further than the more conventional schools envisioned at this time; his dream was such a school for women. The earliest schools for women were called "seminaries" and were places where they were trained as teachers, the only respectable occupation for single women. Just a handful of such schools existed when Johnson founded the Johnson Female Seminary in Anderson, South Carolina, in 1848. Later known as Johnson University, it moved into a new building. The university did not survive the founder's death and the onset of the Civil War.

However, the dream did not die. At the beginning of the 20th century, the leaders of Anderson revived the dream of a women's college in their community, which reflected their civic pride and desire to show that Anderson indeed was a progressive, growing community that was reaching "to a certain level of respectability on the social index," according to Creed. With a newly organized chamber of commerce leading the way, the community leaders gathered pledges totaling $100,000 for the creation of a college for women and obtained the contribution of 32 acres near railroad tracks, which were important in the transportation of students. As generous as the community had been in its gifts, the amount given was insufficient to keep the dream going. The leaders approached several denominations asking for support of the college. The South Carolina Baptist Convention, though slightly hesitant since it was already supporting three other colleges in South Carolina, agreed in November 1910 to support Anderson College. The state legislature ratified the charter on February 14, 1911, and construction began on the first three buildings that year. Construction was completed the following year, with classes starting on September 18, 1912. Anderson College remained a four-year baccalaureate institution for women until 1929.

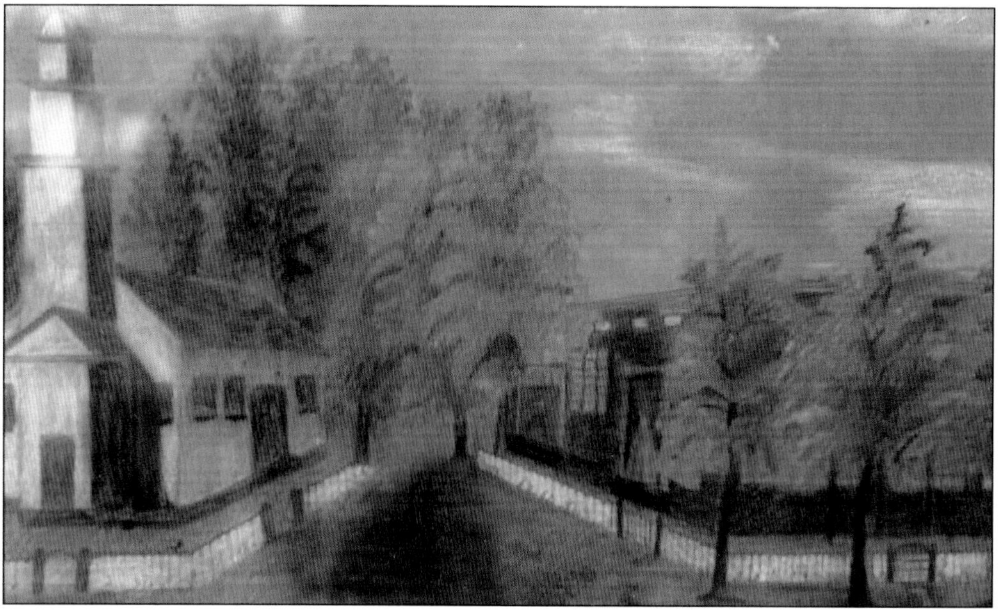

Johnson Female Seminary, founded in 1848 by Anderson citizens Daniel Brown, J. P. Reed, and Stephen McCulley, was named for Rev. William B. Johnson, a prominent Baptist minister and educator. J. S. Murray became the first president. This painting is a hand-drawn illustration of the first building. Plaques in either side of the entrances, located between the Merritt Administration Building and the dining hall, identify individuals remembered for their service to Johnson Female Seminary and succeeding institutions. Those listed are Mary E. Daniel, first principal; Gen. Lewis Malone Ayer (1821–1895), president of Anderson Female Seminary from 1881 to 1888; and Claudia R. Murray, teacher at Johnson Female Seminary. (Courtesy of Dianne Brown.)

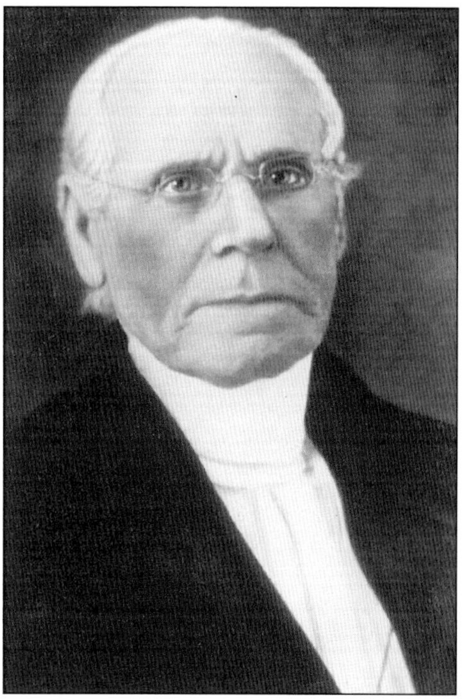

William Bullein Johnson (1782–1862) was prominent in Baptist endeavors in South Carolina and was a leader of the effort to create the Furman Academy and Theological Institution in Edgefield; Furman later moved to Greenville. Prior to serving as the first chancellor of Johnson Female University, he also served as the first principal of the Greenville Female Academy. In 1858, due to poor health, he moved from Anderson to Greenville to live with his daughter Ann, wife of Col. G. F. Townes, and her family and died in 1862. He is buried in the churchyard of Anderson's First Baptist Church, and his home still stands on Morris Street in Anderson.

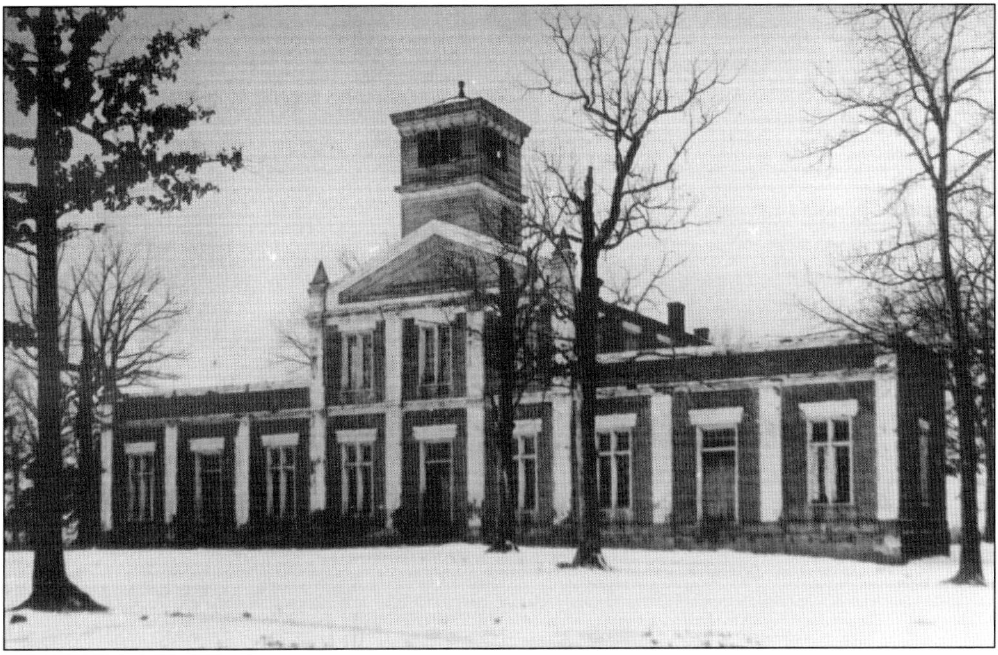

The seminary became Johnson University when it moved to a new building in 1852. Five years later, it had about 600 students who followed a challenging curriculum, which included calculus, Latin, and Greek. Literary talents were exhibited through publications such as *Le Bas Bleu*. The Civil War led to its closure in 1863. The main building became the location for the Confederate treasury and printing press until 1865, when Union troops destroyed the presses and used the buildings as the headquarters for the 1st Maine Infantry. Their departure saw the return of educational uses of the buildings by the Carolina Collegiate Institute, followed by the Patrick Military Academy in 1889, which was when this photograph was taken. The Patrick Military Academy closed in the 1920s, and the buildings subsequently have been razed. (Courtesy of Pendleton District Commission.)

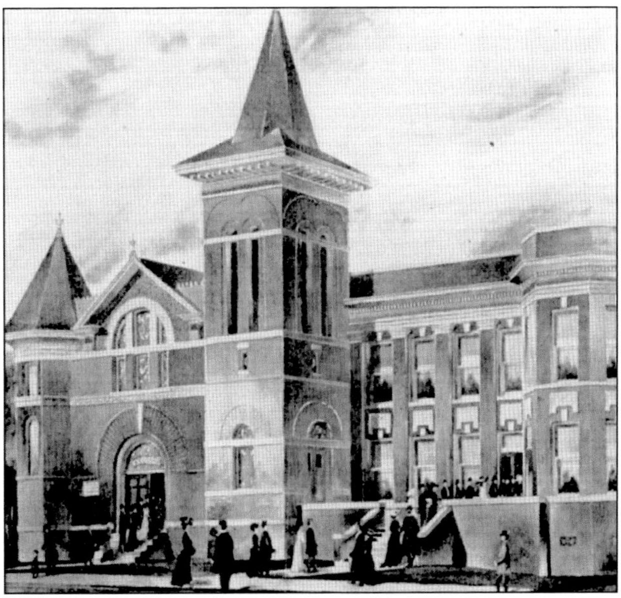

The First Baptist Church of Anderson, seen in this 1912 view, was closely tied to educational efforts in Anderson until well into the 20th century. The earlier schools had close relationships with the church, since Baptists made up a significant portion of the local residents. It has been called the "mother church" of Anderson College because of the ties between the two institutions. Some of the first presidents of Anderson College, John F. Vines, John E. White, and interim president Cort R. Flint (1957), were also pastors at First Baptist. For many years, the graduation baccalaureate services were held there.

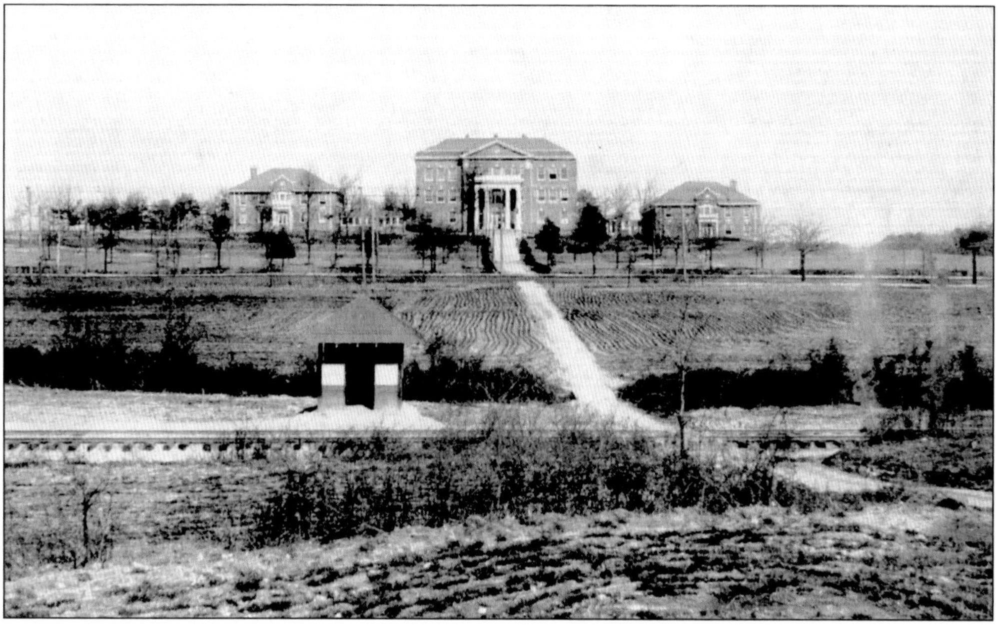

One of the earliest known photographs of Anderson College was taken in 1914. In the foreground is the shelter for waiting students to catch the electric streetcar. The architects who were selected by the board of trustees included Wheeler and Stern of Charlotte, North Carolina; Joseph H. Casey of Anderson; and Shand and LaFaye of Columbia. Richard S. Ligon gave the path that allowed students to walk to the railroad shelter to the college in 1923.

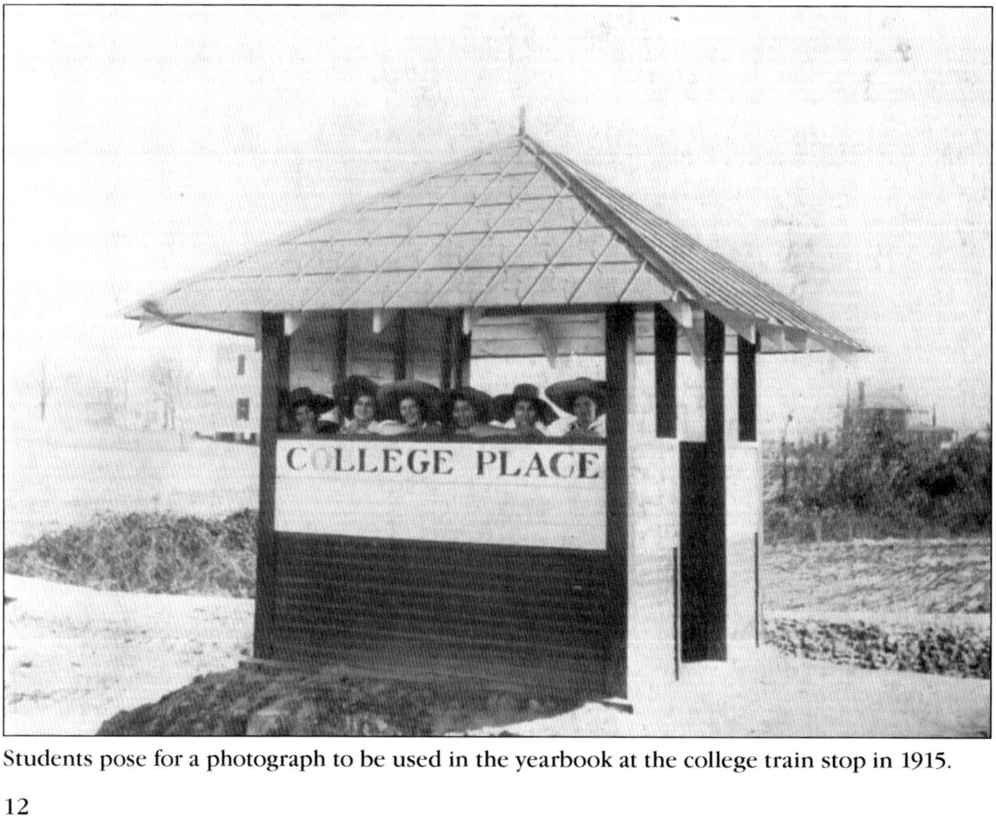

Students pose for a photograph to be used in the yearbook at the college train stop in 1915.

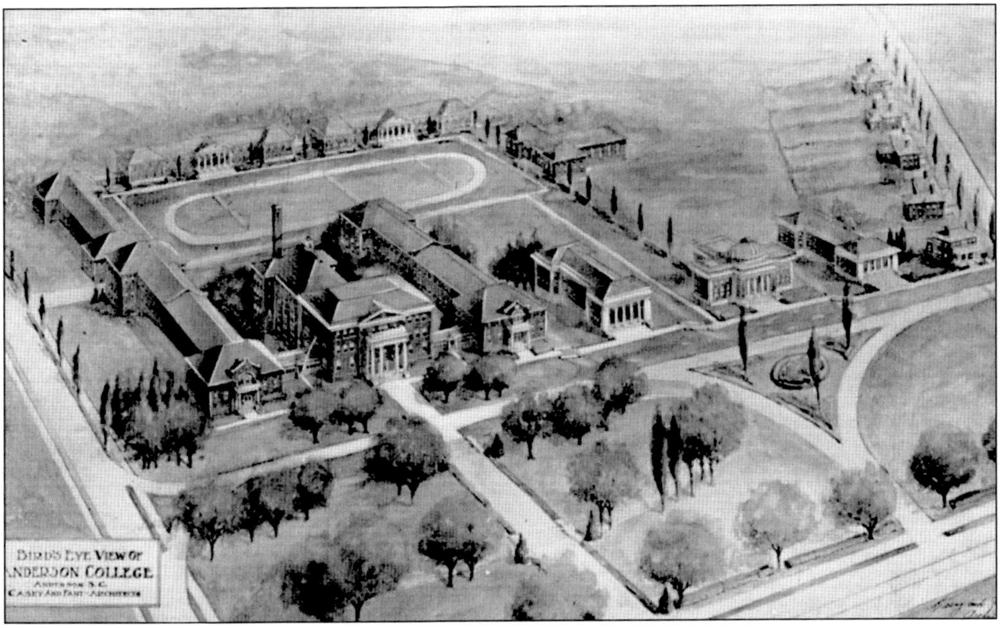

In 1917, architects Casey and Fant envisioned a future for Anderson College's campus that evoked a quadrangle design in this drawing, which was reproduced in the 1918 Anderson College *Bulletin*. The existing buildings are clearly seen. The architectural firm became Fant and Fant, for brothers Reece and Charles Fant, and was the most frequently used design firm for a large number of the buildings on campus for many years thereafter.

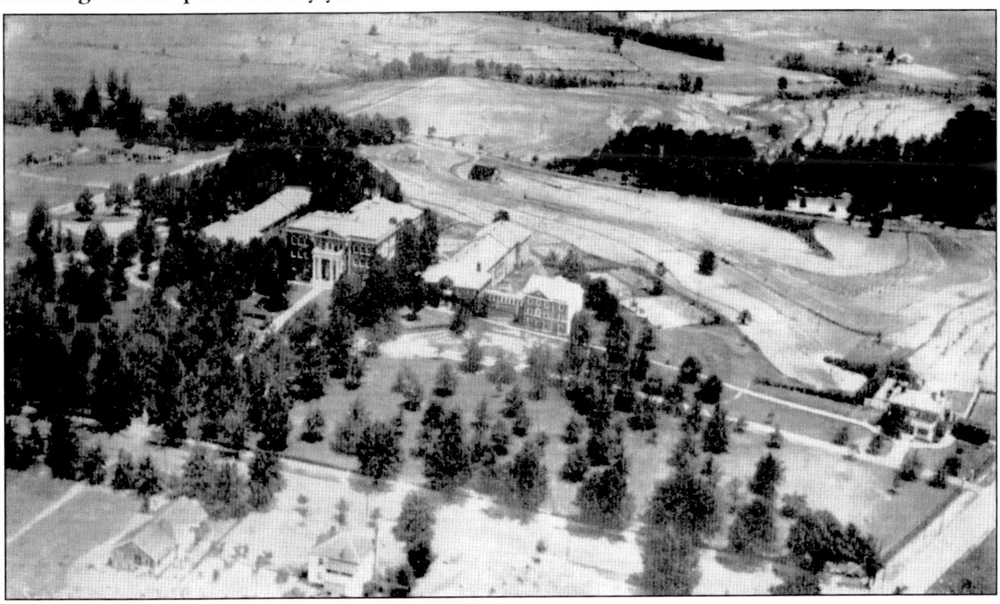

This aerial view of Anderson College comes from the 1927 Anderson College *Viewbook*. The agricultural landscape where the college was built is clearly visible, as are the first houses along the street that was once called "East Boulevard," which has now been shortened to Boulevard. In 1916, the *Bulletin* proudly noted that there were "three avenues of asphalt from the city center, which is just a mile away." The railroad, a major economic lifeline of the community, parallels the front of the campus.

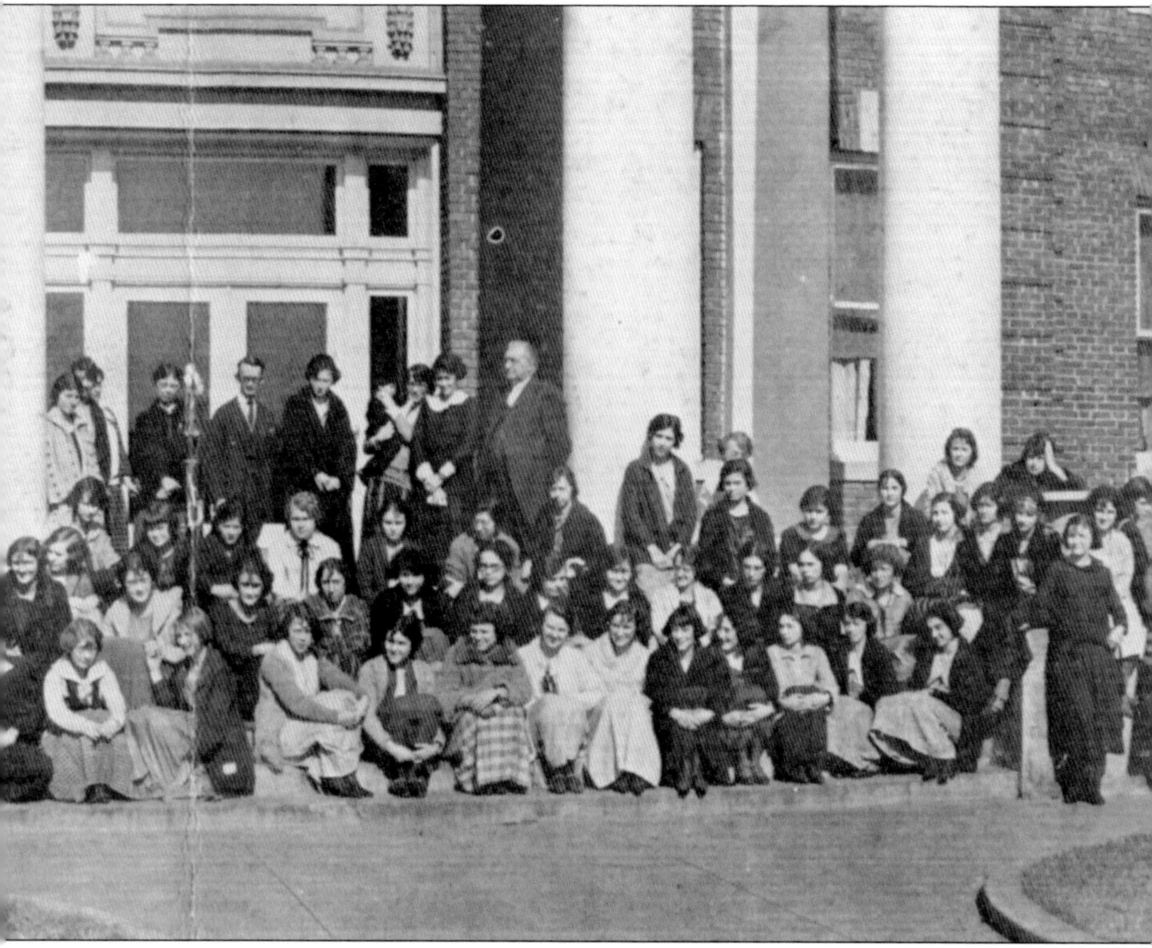

Labeled "A Part of the College Family," this group photograph of the students, faculty, and staff members in the 1920s shows the successful effort to create a close family atmosphere at the

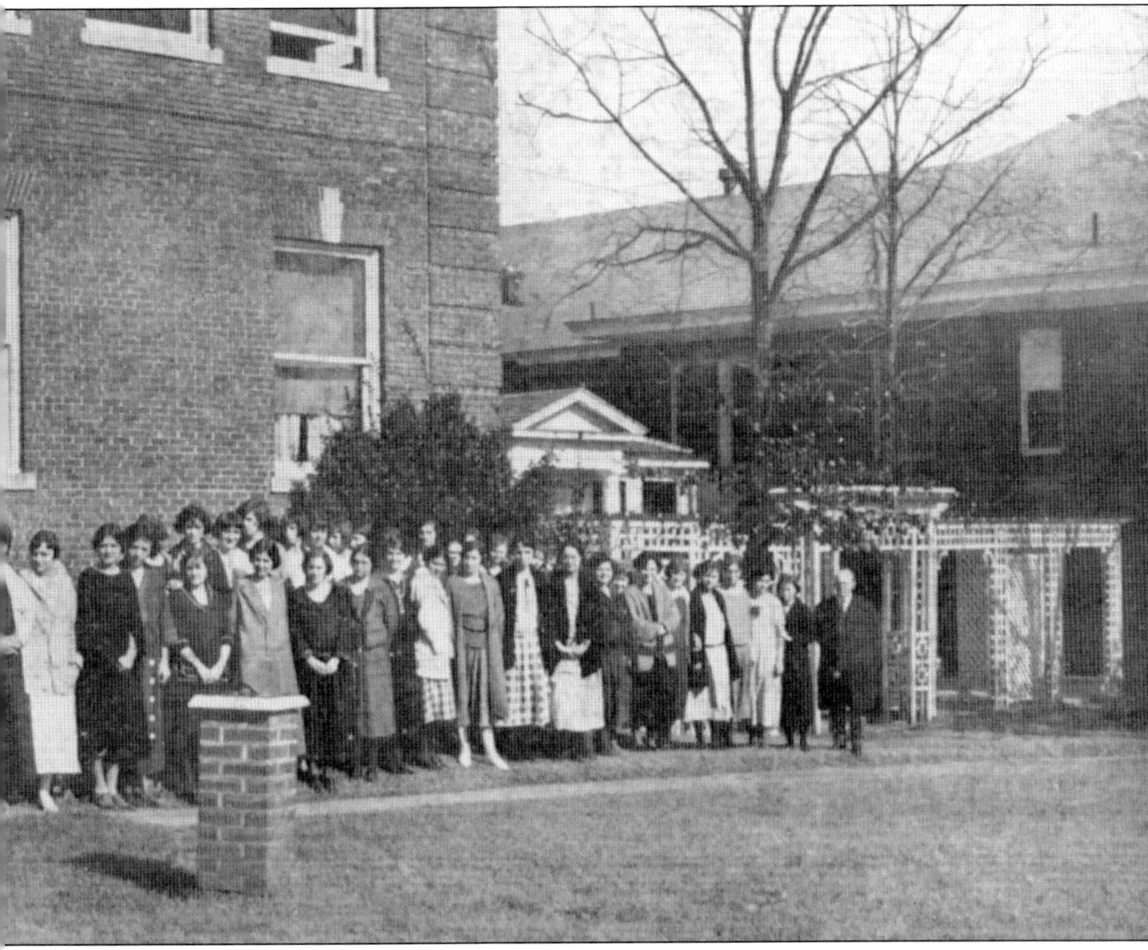

new college. The sundial, a gift from the class of 1916, graced the front entrance area of the Administration Building for many years.

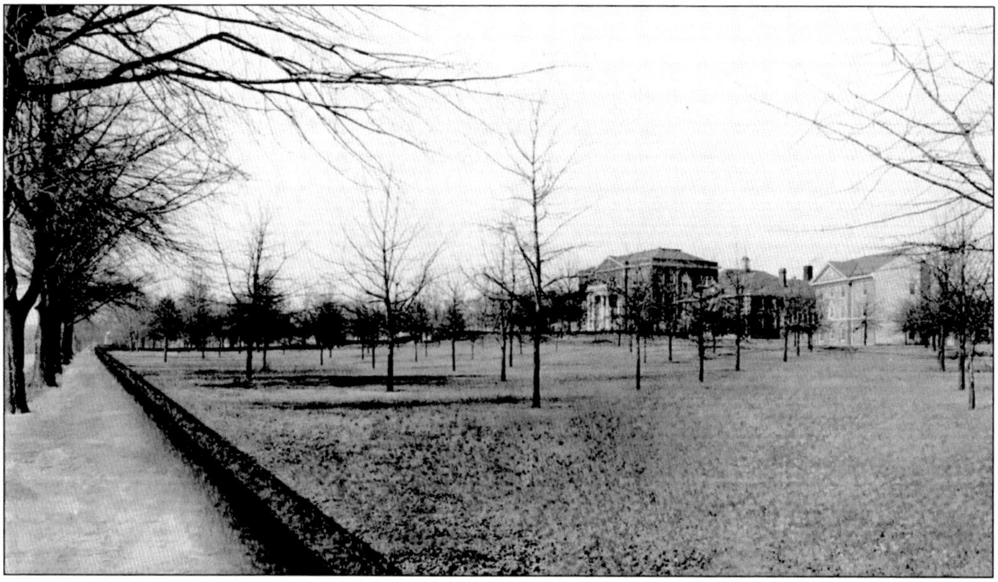

Taken during the middle of winter, this view of the campus shows the expansion of the core campus, which included three buildings. The original two residence halls were expanded, and a third was built in 1918. A home for the president was added by the time of this photograph, which was printed in the 1927 *Viewbook*.

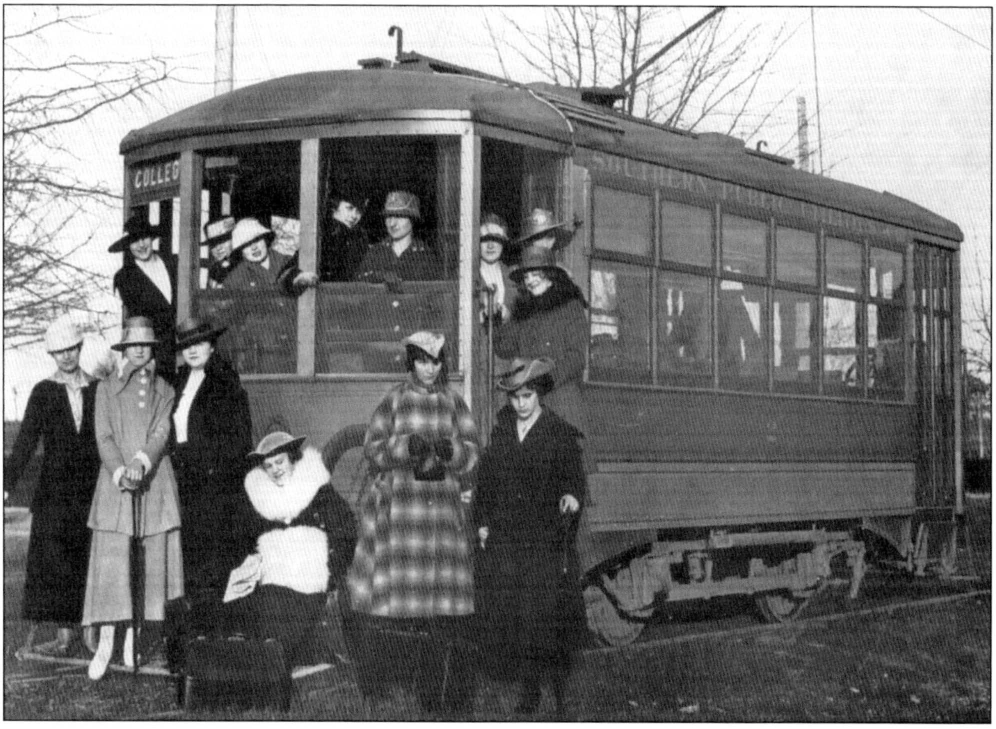

A train car served as a sophisticated stage for a 1917 *Sororian* yearbook photograph. This photograph depicts the very modern connections available to students who were often located some distance from the school. One of the reasons why Anderson has gained the nickname "Electric City" is because of its access to the electric train service on the Piedmont and Northern Electric Railroad.

Two

Leadership and Accomplishment

Anderson College owed its survival and success to the quality of the leadership and support that it received from its inception. These individuals, highly varied in background, preparation, and contributions, shared a deep commitment to education, a strong sense of mission, and a dream of a progressive future for the community. Equally imbued was a sense of dedication and service to humanity and to the Lord. In the 1840s, these individuals included community leaders such as Daniel Brown, J. P. Reed, and Stephen McCulley. Rev. William B. Johnson, W. J. Ligon, Gen. Lewis Ayers, and Col. John B. Patrick helped in the mid-19th century. G. M. Tolly, A. M. Carpenter, and other members of the Anderson Chamber of Commerce continued the vision into the beginning of the 20th century.

Originally the focus of all efforts was educating women of the region, which was a progressive concept for the day. A leading force for the community development was epitomized by the Anderson Ladies College Association, which worked tirelessly to complete the details involved in preparing for the opening of the new institution. Another critical component was the strong faith of the residents in the region, particularly those churches and individuals that made up the South Carolina Baptist Convention, which had continuously supported the institution's mission and vision and its unrelenting resolve to survive and flourish.

Among those who best personify the "Anderson University Spirit" and its combination of leadership skills, academic excellence, faith, perseverance, a pioneering spirit, and a commitment to missions and the improvement of the human condition was Dr. Annie Dove Denmark, who became president in 1928. She was the dean of women when the institution faced a crisis that nearly led to the closing of its doors and was later selected to become president. She was the first woman to hold such a position in the history of South Carolina higher education. She supervised the transition from a four-year women's college to a two-year coeducational junior college in 1930, which made it one of the first schools in South Carolina to adopt this new educational format. Dr. Denmark promoted the cause of Christian higher education, which made her a much sought-after speaker in pulpits and community organizations. Her retirement in 1953 ended the longest tenure of any president in Anderson University's history to date.

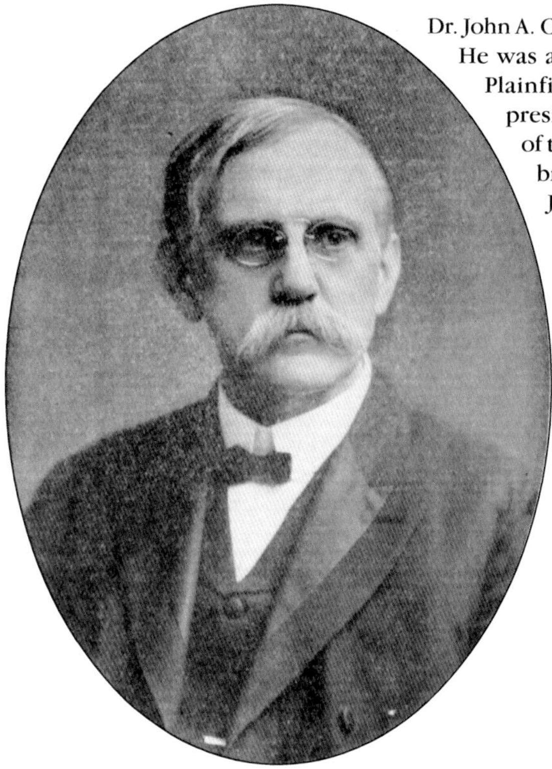

Dr. John A. Chambliss (1912–1913) was the first president. He was a 72-year-old retired Baptist minister from Plainfield, New Jersey, who came as a part-time president and English instructor. A past editor of the *Baptist Courier*, his distinguished career brought great prestige to the new institution. J. K. Breedin, who was hired in 1911 to supervise the construction of the school, did much of the actual organizing work for the new college. As dean of faculty, Breedin created the curriculum for the first classes in 1912–1913.

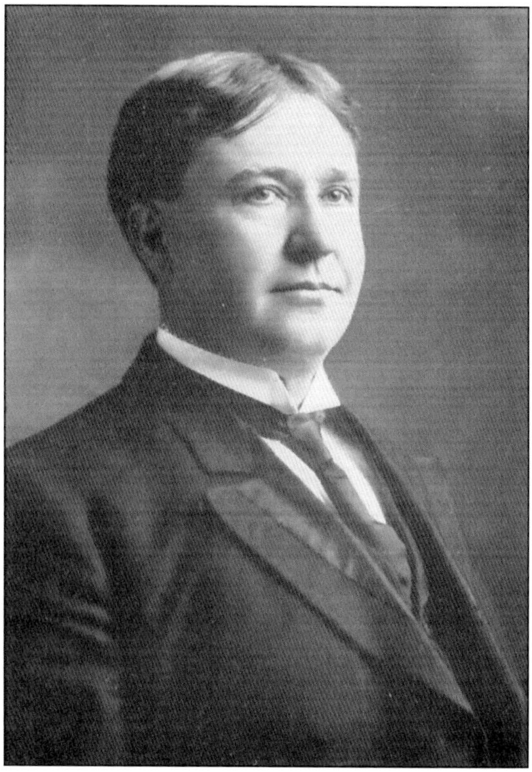

Dr. John F. Vines (1913–1914), who served as president while also serving as pastor of the First Baptist Church Anderson from 1908 to 1915, was born in Jonesboro, Tennessee, and graduated from the Southern Baptist Theological Seminary in Louisville, Kentucky, in 1902. He had served churches in Chattanooga, Tennessee, and Elizabeth City, North Carolina, before coming to Anderson. An enthusiastic supporter of the new college, he cemented the close relationship between church and college that lasted many years.

Dr. James P. Kinard (1914–1916) was a professor of English at Winthrop College when he came to Anderson College as president in 1914. The previous two office-holders had been part-time in the position; Dr. Kinard was the first to hold the position full-time. Financial problems proved daunting, and he returned to Winthrop College in 1916 and became its second president.

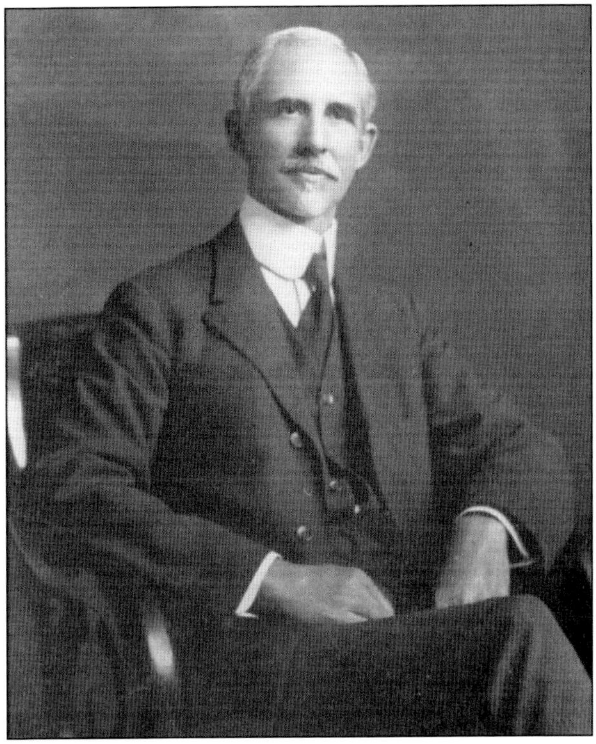

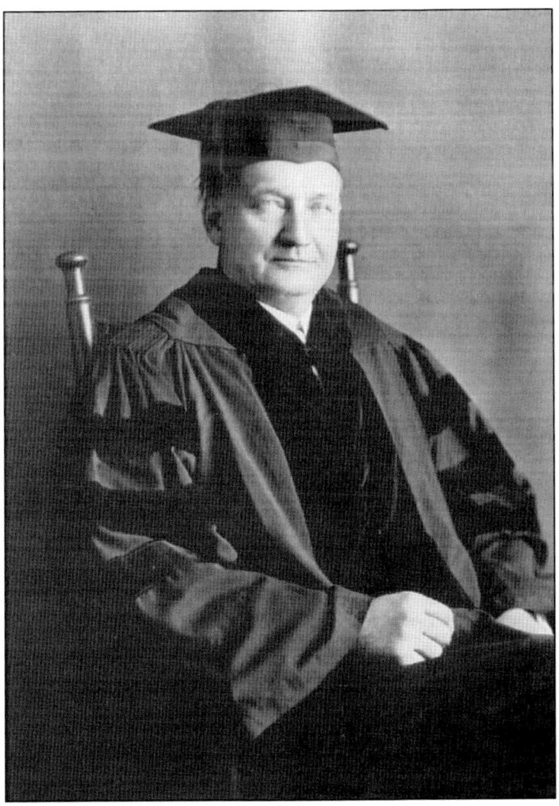

Dr. John E. White (1916–1927), author and pastor, received his degrees from Wake Forest and Baylor Universities and held a variety of positions at churches in Georgia and North Carolina and at the University of Chicago. He came to Anderson in 1915 as pastor at First Baptist Church. He became president of Anderson College at a time when it was in financial difficulties and nearly closed. He helped keep the doors open by obtaining a $50,000 loan from a friend in the banking business. At the President's Chapel Hour, his addresses covered a wide range of topics from literature to religion. Many of his sermons were collected by then faculty member and later president Annie Dove Denmark and published in 1932 under the title of *White Echoes*.

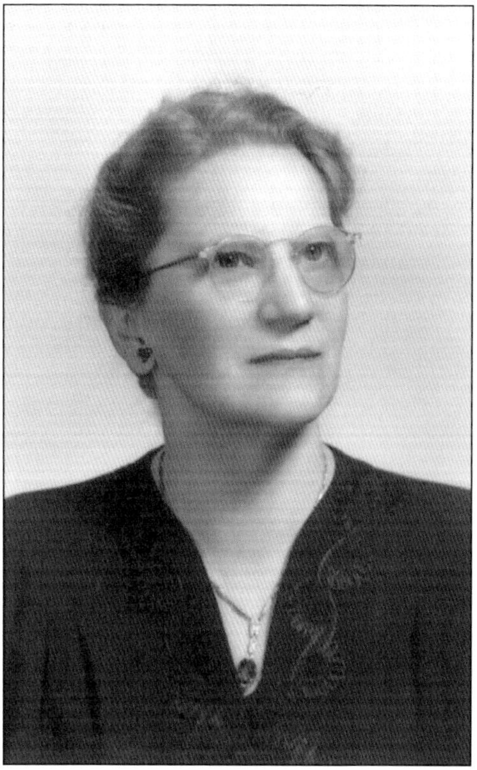

Amidst fears the college was about to close, Dr. Annie Dove Denmark (1928–1953) became president. Her inauguration on February 14, 1929, initiated a new tradition for Anderson College, Founder's Day, which celebrates the date of the chartering of the institution. She earned a piano certificate from Meredith School of Music in Raleigh in 1908 and then held several teaching positions before she came to Anderson College in 1917. In 1925, she became dean of women, and she accepted the position as president in 1928. She was awarded an honorary doctorate of letters from Furman University in 1941. Her leadership guided the college through a strict financial regimen that allowed the inherited $60,000 college debt to be paid in full by 1938. Additionally, she served as president of the Southern Association of Colleges for Women\, and as vice president of the Baptist State Convention. Since February 1944, outstanding graduates are inducted yearly into the honorary Denmark Society. She was selected for membership in the Anderson County Hall of Fame at the Anderson County Museum in 2004.

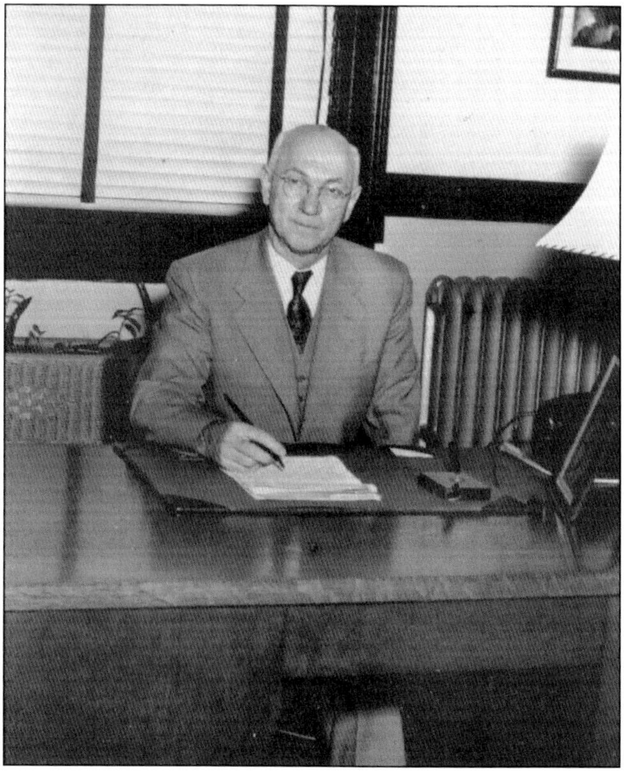

Dr. Elmer Francis Haight (1953–1957) was born in Washington, D.C., and educated at Furman, Tulane, and the New Orleans Baptist Theological Seminary. Before he took the position at Anderson, he had been a chaplain and a professor at Furman University and at New Orleans.

Dr. John Edward Rouse (1957–1973) took office when the future of the college was in doubt and effectively turned its path into one of growth and progress. A graduate of Andover Newton Seminary, Boston University, and Furman University, he came from the First Baptist Church of Laurens. He successfully opposed those who wanted to close the school or move it to Charleston. He actively and personally recruited students and funds. By the time he retired in January 1973, the college had added 10 buildings and had made extensive renovations on the existing buildings. The student body had grown from fewer than 200 students to around 900. He had raised hundreds of thousands of dollars, opened a new chapter in the relationship of the college with its community, and, above all, achieved the long-coveted accreditation by the Southern Association of Colleges and Schools in 1959.

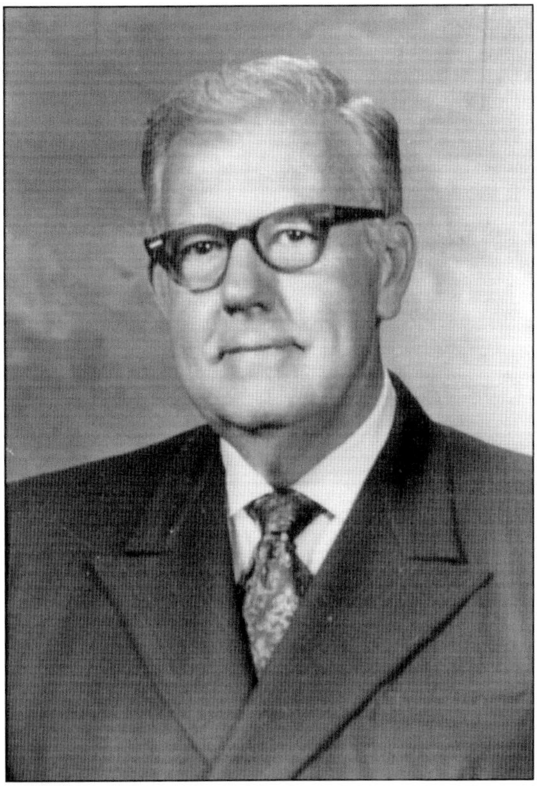

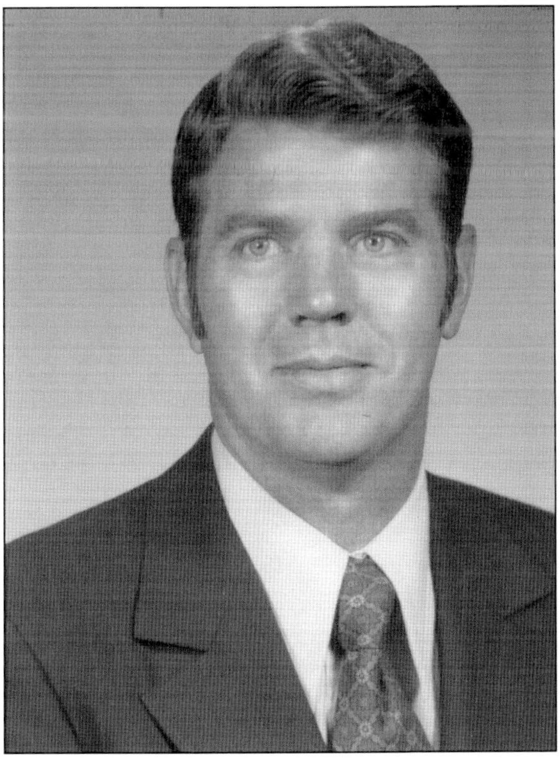

Dr. Cordell Maddox (1973–1978) came to Anderson College as executive vice president in 1971 before becoming president. The college continued to grow during his administration in the areas of enrollment, programs, and facilities. The athletic program reached the national stage during his term. The women's basketball team won the National Junior College Athletic Association national championship for four years in a row from 1974 to 1977. He also shepherded the school family through the aftermath of the tragic accident in April 1977 that saw the loss of coach Max Grubbs and all but two members of the tennis team. He left Anderson to accept the presidency of Carson-Newman College in Tennessee in 1977.

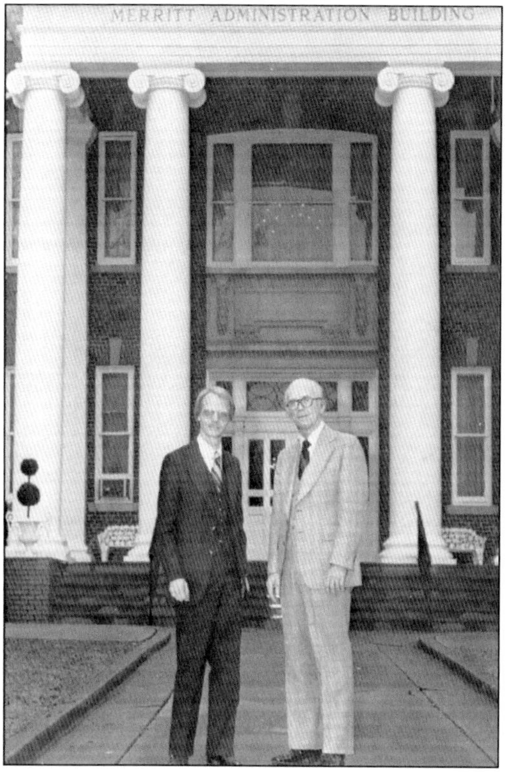

Dr. Ray P. Rust (right) was inaugurated as president in May 1978. He came from Louisiana and left to fill the position of executive director of the South Carolina Baptist Convention in 1981. Dr. Paul Talmadge (left) came from North Greenville College to serve as academic dean in 1969. He also filled in as interim president in 1978 and 1981–1982. In 1988, he moved to North Greenville College as president.

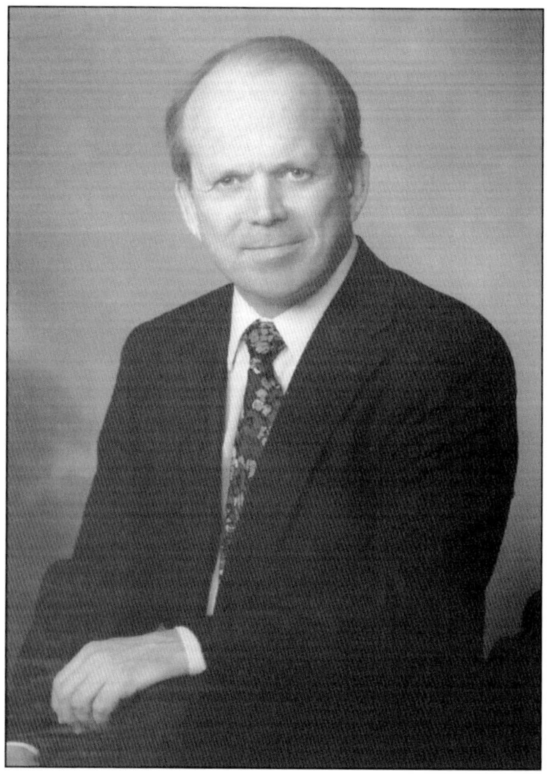

Dr. Mark L. Hopkins (1982–November 1994), a graduate of Southeast Missouri State University and Missouri University, had been president of Elgin Community College in Elgin, Illinois, prior to coming to Anderson. The first phase of the Rainey Fine Arts Center was completed under his administration, as were the construction of additional residence hall space and the expansion of the athletic program to include table tennis and baseball. He also led the move back to the status of a baccalaureate institution. He and his wife, local artist Ruth Hopkins, remained in Anderson, continuing their support of the college. Dr. Henry L. Ashmore (1994–May 1995), who had retired from Armstrong College in Florida, served as interim president and ensured the future of the college by capable shepherding through another difficult financial period.

Dr. Lee G. Royce (1995–2001), educated at Vanderbilt University, previously served as vice president of Belmont University. At the time of his arrival, Anderson faced significant financial challenges. His wife, Rhoda, was a faculty member in the English department. Dr. Royce's tireless and creative leadership helped the college not only survive but to thrive as it continued to expand programs and facilities. He inaugurated a redesigned evening college for adults, which is known as ACCEL. Under his leadership, enrollment increased significantly, and the institution constructed its largest residence hall, the Village. Dr. Royce left Anderson to become president of Mississippi College. Following his departure in 2000, Dr. Graham Hatcher, vice president for Academic Affairs, provided leadership in the interim until the new president was chosen.

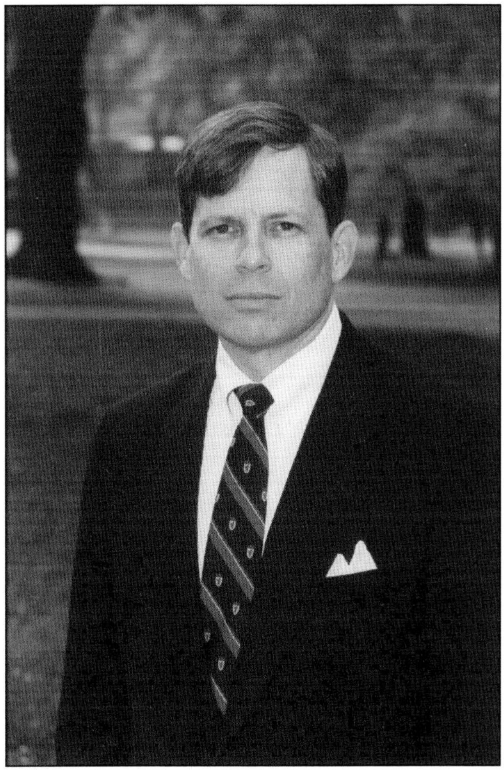

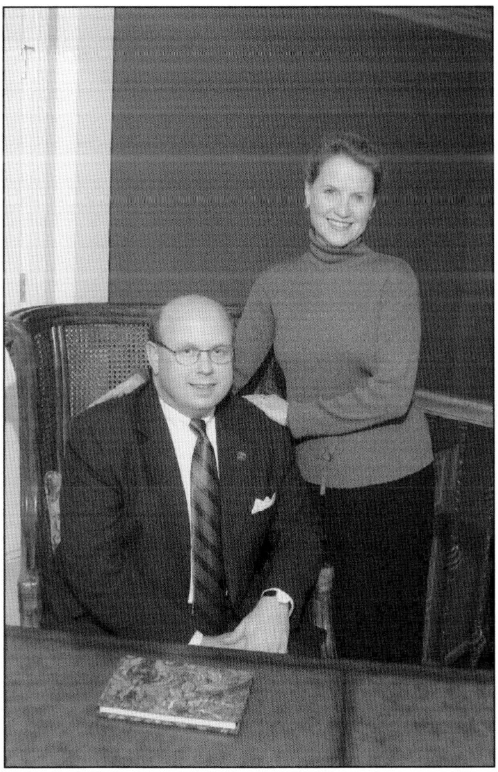

Dr. Evans P. Whitaker, a graduate of Vanderbilt University, became president in 2002. He had served three universities previously in both teaching and leadership roles, including vice presidencies of Wingate University and most recently Belmont University. He also became the first Anderson president to be a trustee of the institution's primary accrediting body, the Commission on Colleges of the Southern Association of Colleges and Schools. He is pictured with his wife, Diane, who also has been active in the campus's cultural, enrollment, and student service activities.

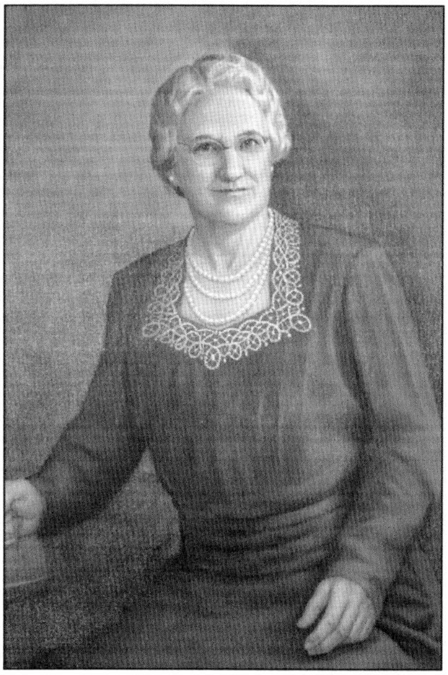

Dr. Olga Valeria Pruitt began her education at Winthrop College and then went to the Women's Medical College of Baltimore before completing postgraduate work at Johns Hopkins. The only woman in a field of 108 candidates for the state medical board examinations, she came to Anderson in 1911 with her brother Harrison Pruitt, also a doctor, and became the physician for Anderson College from 1911 to 1955. She was also professor of hygiene and physiology. Her heroic efforts during the 1918 flu epidemic greatly helped the community and kept the college open without the loss of a single student's life. One of the first female physicians in the Upstate, she died in 1970 at the age of 85. She was inducted into the Anderson County Hall of Fame at the Anderson County Museum in 2004. Her nephew, Dr. Basil A. Pruitt Jr., continues the medical tradition by serving at the University of Texas Health Science Center in San Antonio as clinical professor of surgery and holding the Dr. Ferdinand P. Herff Chair in Surgery.

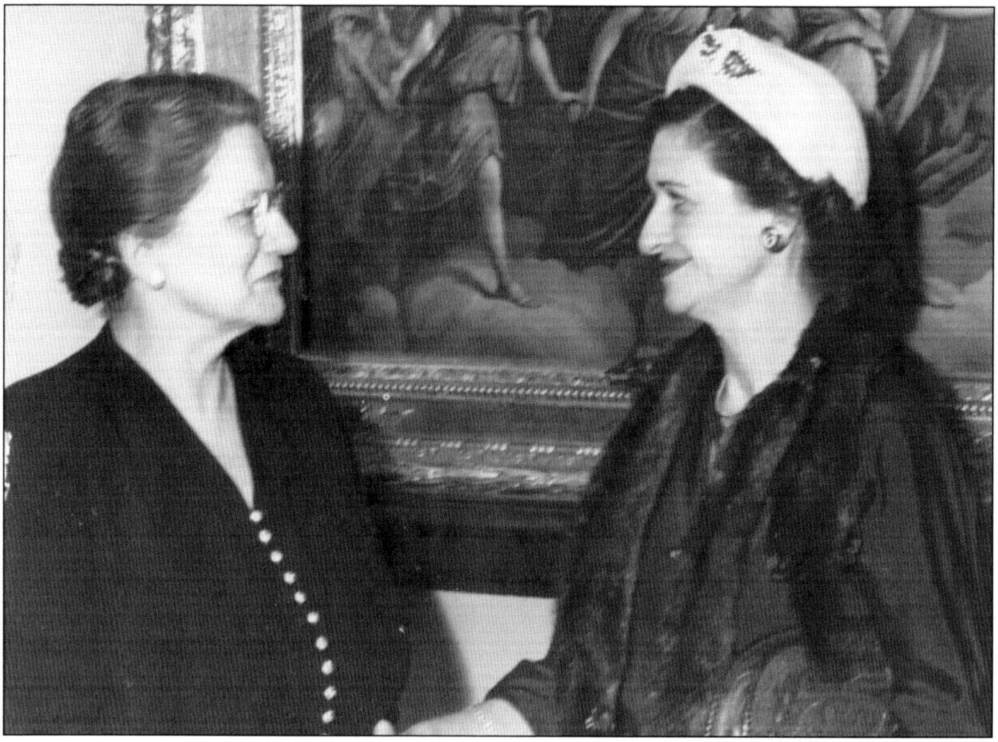

Pres. Annie Dove Denmark (left) is shown greeting Gladys Atkinson Johnston '23, wife of Gov. Olin D. Johnston. Johnston's support of her alma mater was evidenced in many ways, such as serving on the board of trustees, addressing the May commencement in 1943 and the February Founder's Day programs in 1953 and 1971, and providing the leadership gifts that enabled the building of the Johnston Memorial Library in 1956. She received the first Anderson College Alumni Service Award on May 10, 1970. The painting behind them is *Aurora* by Guido Reni. It hung in the Merritt Parlor for many years and was a gift from Grace Cronkhite, former head of the Department of Music.

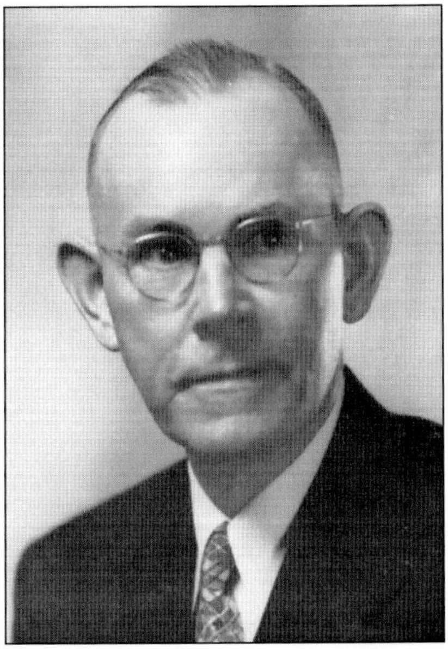
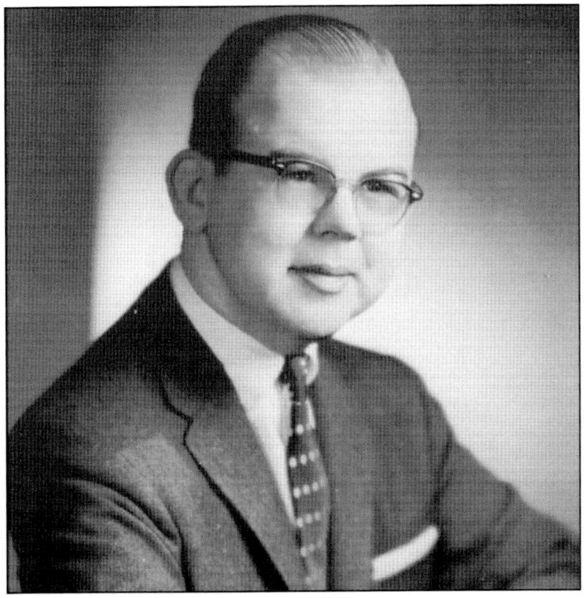
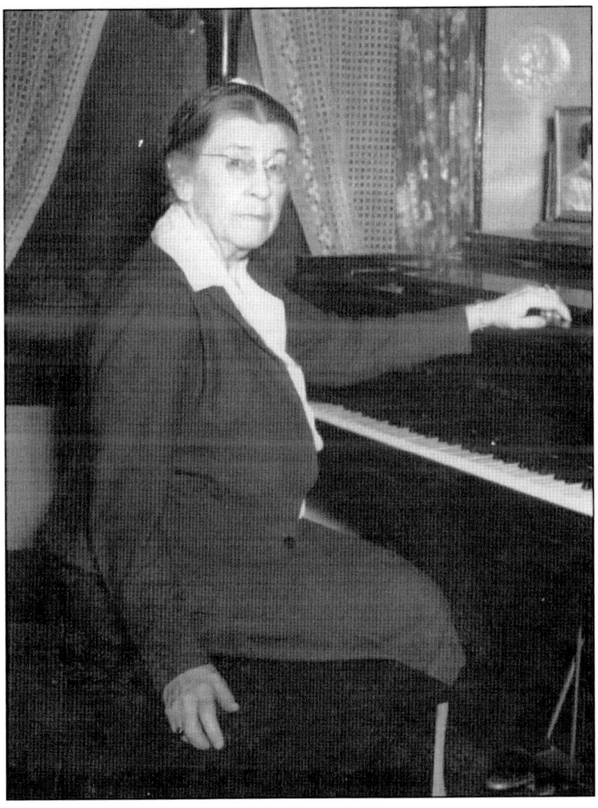

In the top left photograph is Webb von Hasseln (1915–1962), teacher of modern languages and the violin. In the top right photograph is his son, Henry von Hasseln (1946–1982), teacher of history and social sciences. Pictured above is Grace Louise Cronkhite, dean of the Department of Music from 1917 to 1953. Her nephew was the nationally known pioneer broadcaster Walter Cronkite. All three teachers are examples of the excellent instruction provided students over the century.

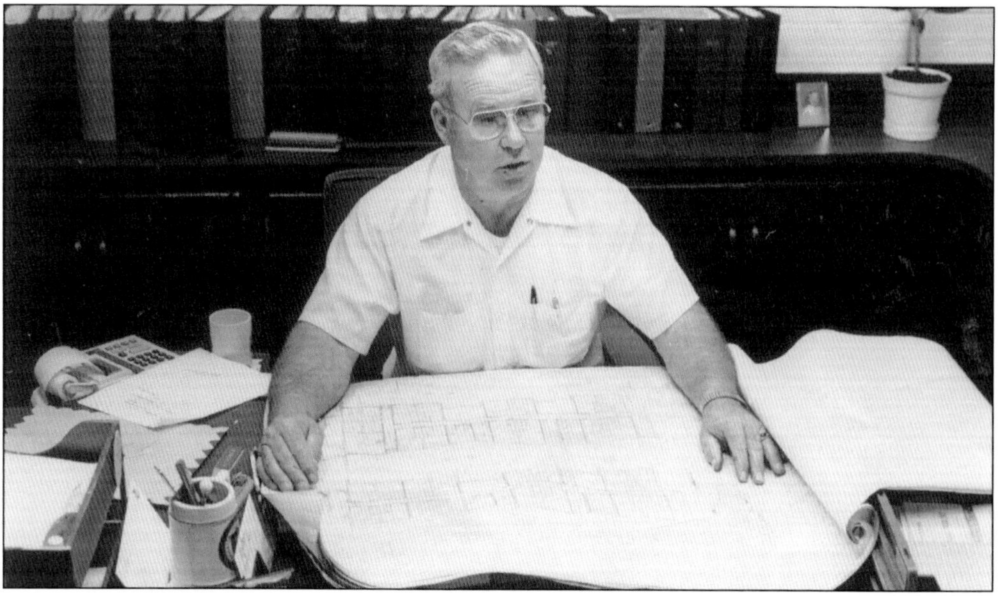

Following his retirement from the U.S. Air Force in 1973, Olin Padgett became head of the maintenance department. He worked in the day and completed his coursework with evening classes, graduating in May 1976. He became the second director of the Physical Plant, following Calvin McKinney, who was the first superintendant of buildings and grounds.

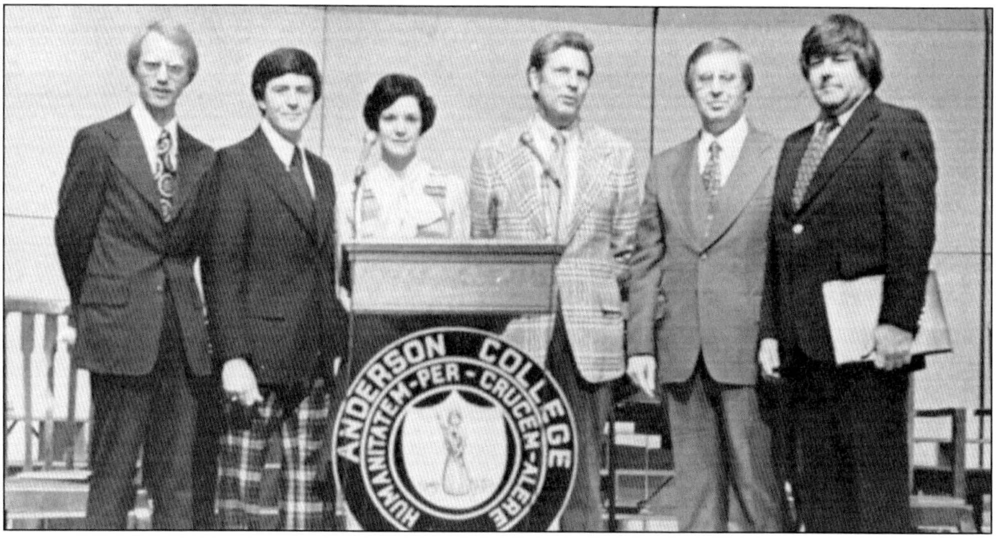

Anderson College benefitted from the talents of many different administration, staff, and community members over the years. Christian Emphasis Week in November 1977 is an example of such a beneficial gathering. Dr. Paul Talmadge, on the far left, was dean of academic affairs. Second from the left is Sanford (Sandy) Kidd. He served as chaplain and later as the director of the Counseling Center, working from 1974 to 1994. Third from the left is Kidd's wife, Sue Monk Kidd, who shared her experiences as a nurse and as a missionary in Kenya on that occasion. Her nationally known writing career was launched by a creative writing course at Anderson College, taught by Dr. Frances Mims. The remaining members of the platform participants are, from left to right, Dr. David Lockard from the Southern Baptist Mission Board, Rev. Jack Causey, and Rev. Sidney Hall, who was the Baptist campus minister at Clemson University.

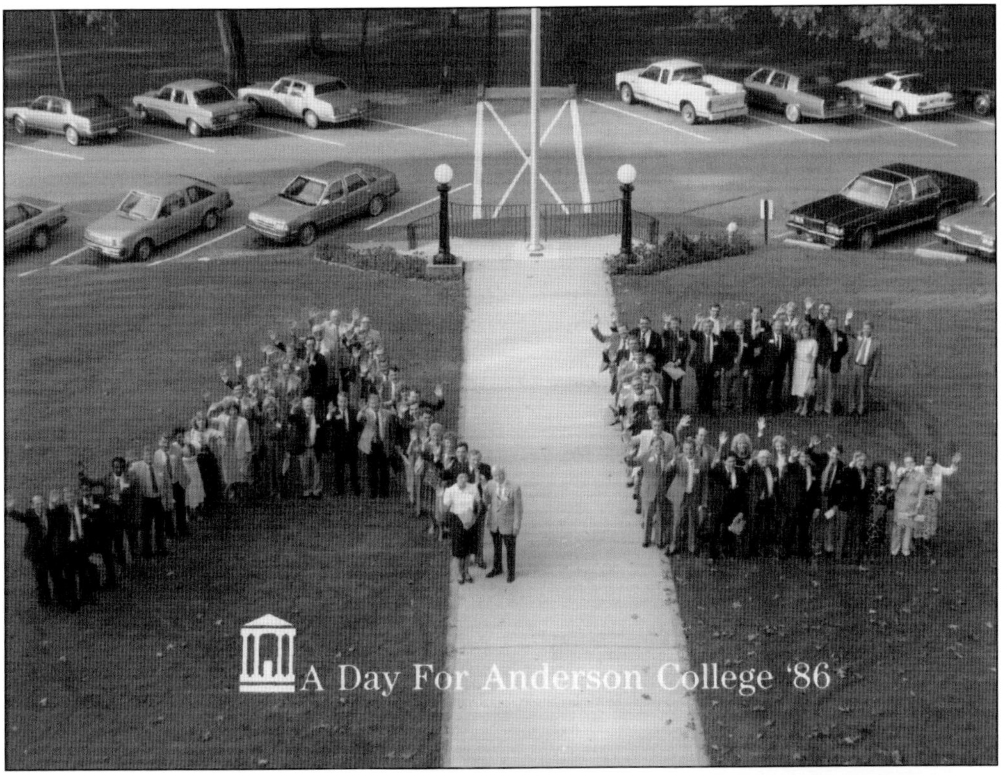

The common thread from its founding continues with "A Day For Anderson College" in 1986. The volunteers posed for this distinctive photograph, which was taken on the front walkway of the campus.

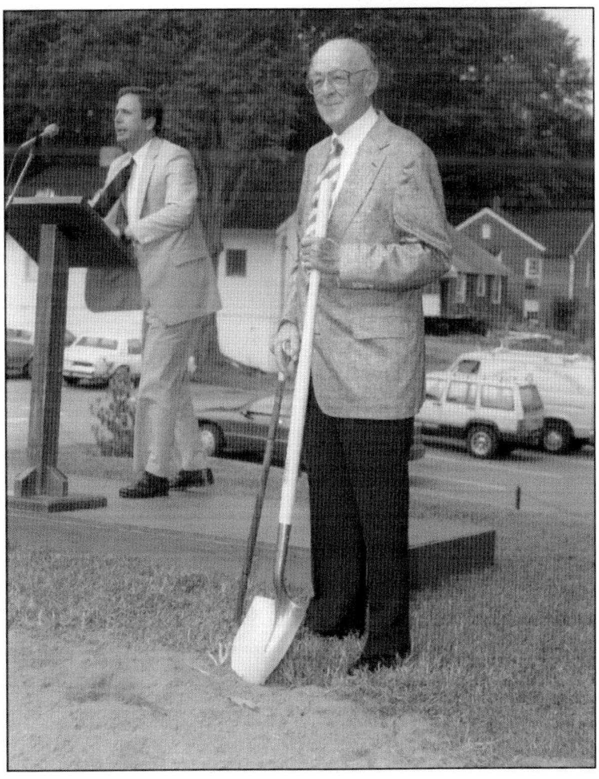

A devoted friend and benefactor, Dr. John F. Rainey, is shown here wielding the golden shovel on September 2, 1992, at the ground-breaking ceremony of the second phase of the fine arts center, which was named in memory of his wife, Callie Stringer Rainey. At the podium is R. Dean Woods '73, vice president for Institutional Advancement.

THE WHITE HOUSE

WASHINGTON

January 24, 1983

Dear Dr. Hopkins:

Thank you for your efforts to keep America on the road to economic recovery.

This Administration is dedicated to encouraging local initiative and response to best meet the needs within our communities. I am gratified to find that many innovative responses, like Anderson College's offer of education to the unemployed, with arrangements for deferred payment of tuition.

Anderson College is to be commended for this display of faith in our people. Yours is an investment in our Nation's future which can motivate educational institutions nationwide to effectively meet their own challenges.

Once again, thank you and all best wishes for success.

Sincerely,

Ronald Reagan

Dr. Mark Hopkins
President
Anderson College
Anderson, South Carolina 29621

In January 1983, Pres. Mark Hopkins and student Camilla York went to New York to be interviewed on the NBC *Today* morning show by cohost Jane Pawley. York was 1 of 85 students enrolled in an innovative program called College Education for the Unemployed. At that time, Anderson County had a 14 percent unemployment rate. The program allowed unemployed adults to "study now, pay later." The idea caught the attention of Pres. Ronald Reagan, who sent a letter "commending the college" shortly afterwards.

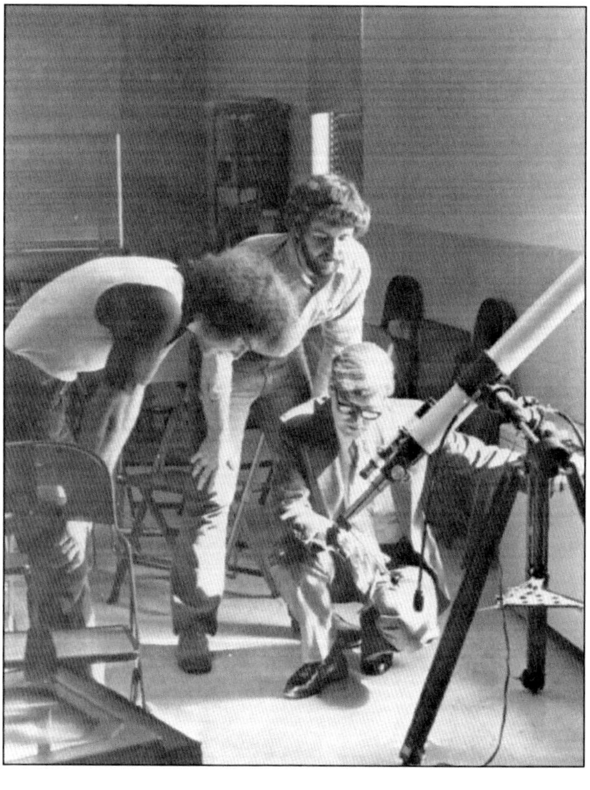

Pictured is Terry Tritt, whose freshman astronomy course in 1977, taught by Prof. Robert Fries, launched his successful and internationally known career in thermoelectric materials research. He went on to receive a doctorate in physics from Clemson University, which is where he now teaches. While he continued his education at Clemson, he and his wife, Penny, lived in Rouse as residence hall supervisors. Dr. Tritt, Professor Fries, and fellow student Marty Cooke (far left) are pictured studying sunspots.

The Distinguished Alumni Gallery inductees from 2009 were, from left to right, Gary T. Bailey '01, chief financial officer for the New Image Group of Ware Shoals, South Carolina; Alphaeus B. Anderson '05, producer and founder of ABA Ministries and musician, Music2ChangeU Records of Easley, South Carolina; Linda B. Gambrell '62, distinguished professor of education for the Eugene T. Moore School of Education, Clemson University; Jill A. Strickland '94, artist and owner of Strickland Fine Art of Anderson; Jeffrey L. Deal '74, physician and biocultural anthropologist and director of health research for Water Missions International of Charleston, South Carolina; and President Whitaker.

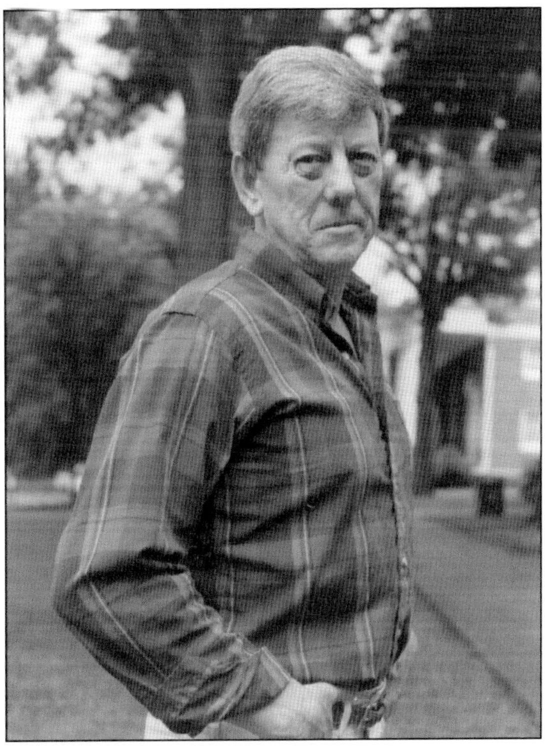

Actor and writer Hoke Howell '50 came back to his alma mater for a visit on Alumni Day 1987. He achieved national prominence from the 1960s to the 1990s. Other Anderson students who achieved national prominence include novelist Gwen Bristow (1921–1922) and screenwriter James Lee Barrett (1949–1950). Bristow's best-known publications are *The Jubilee Trail* and *Celia Garth*; Barrett wrote scripts for productions such as *Shenandoah* and was inducted into the South Carolina Academy of Authors, which was founded in 1986 at Anderson College.

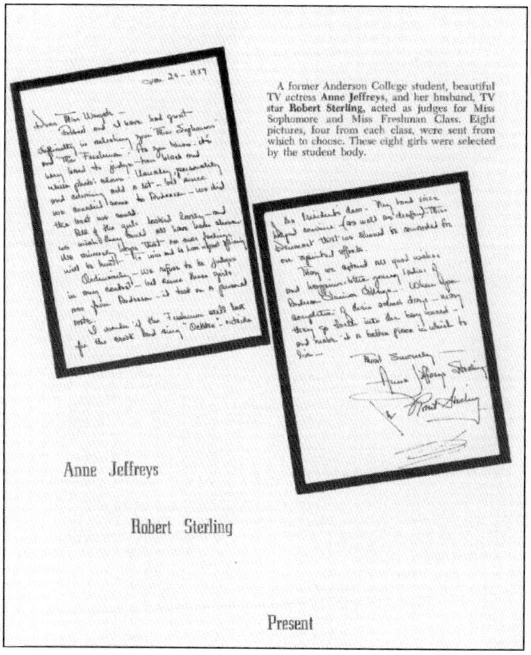

The wife of actor Robert Sterling, Anne Carmichael, whose stage name was Anne Jeffreys, was a 1941 voice graduate of Anderson College. Her film career began with musicals in the 1940s and then moved to Broadway and television. She was the last dancing partner filmed with Fred Astaire and now has a star on the Hollywood Walk of Fame.

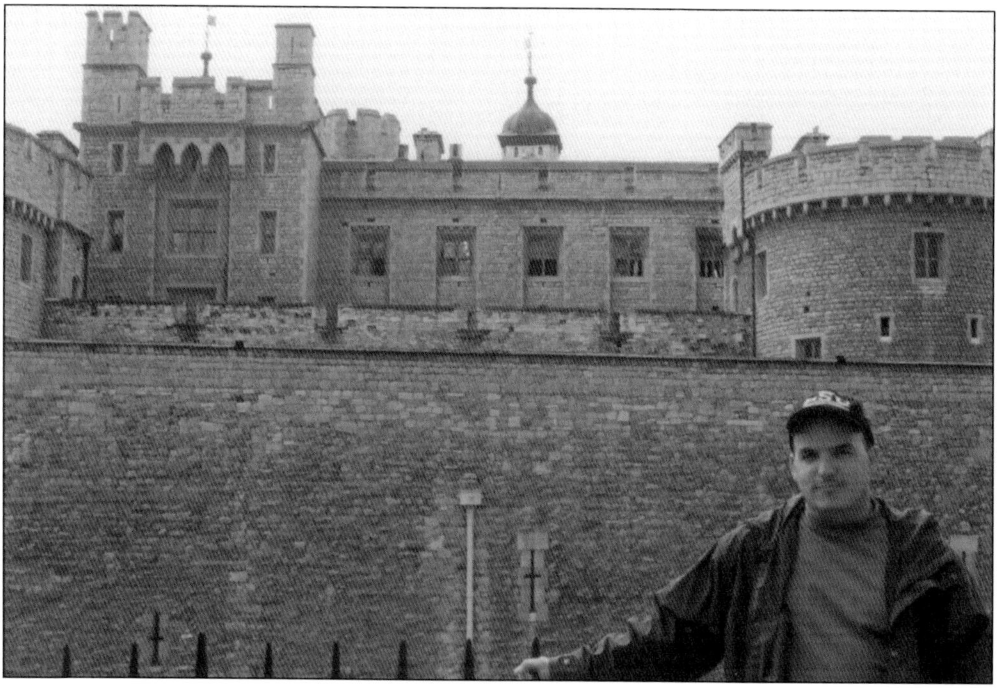

Pictured in front of Windsor Castle in Great Britain in 1994, Michael R. Boles was a commuting student from 1988 to 1994 who lost his life in a tragic accident. His name now graces the Michael Boles Excellence in Teaching Award, created earlier by Academic Dean Melvin G. Hipps. Recipients are selected by a faculty and student committee and presented at the May commencement exercises. The first recipient was Patrick Parker Mulligan on May 8, 1993. The award was later named for Michael and accompanied by a gift from his parents, David and Claudia Boles. (Courtesy of David and Claudia Boles.)

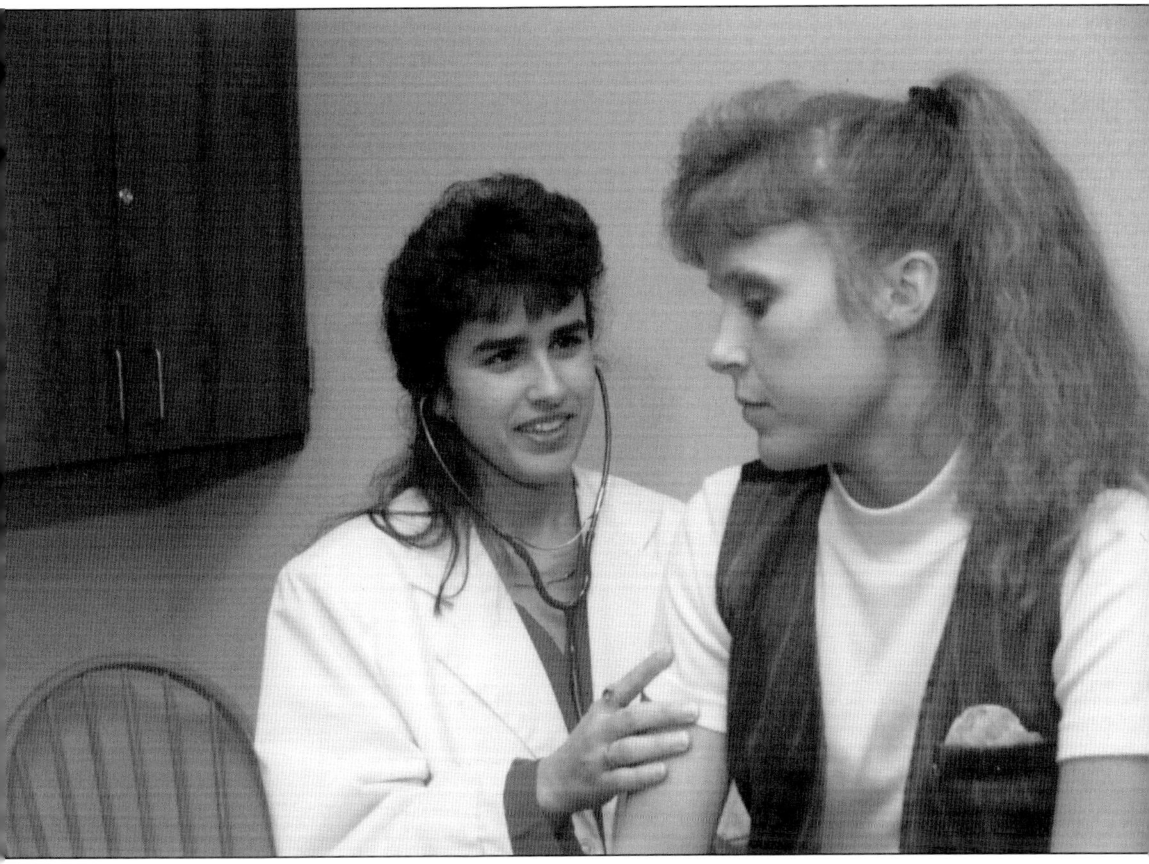

Brazilian-born Cacia Soares Welch was a member of the first baccalaureate graduating class in 1993 with a degree in liberal studies. She earned her M.D. degree from the University of South Carolina and then went on for further study at the Mayo Clinic.

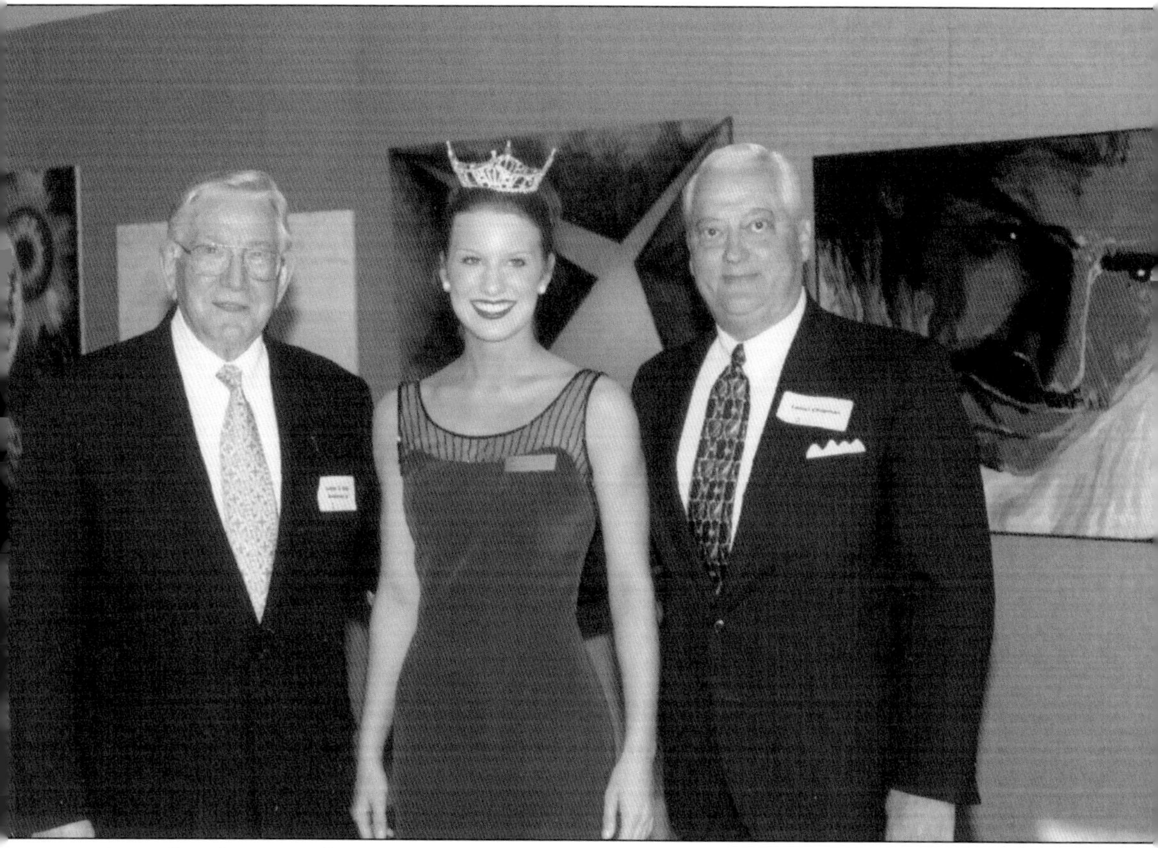

Several Anderson students have combined their intellectual skills with their talents and poise to win beauty contest titles. Melanie Wilder, pictured center, was the first to enter the Miss South Carolina pageant as "Miss Anderson" in 1998. Two board members and longtime institutional friends and supporters are on either side of her—Judge G. Ross Anderson Jr. on the left and Laniel Chapman on the right. Two graduates have been crowned Miss South Carolina, Kristie Greene in 1994 and Angela Michelle Hughes in 1996.

Three

Buildings and Grounds

The site for the college was located on a small rise on the outskirts of Anderson near a rail line, in an area that had once grown cotton. All of the original architecture is neoclassical in style, with the majority of the buildings designed by the architectural firm Fant and Fant. Like many schools, one of the advertising points for Anderson College was its healthy location and the beauty of the surrounding area, a characteristic of such schools noted by historian J. Bradley Creed. The original site included 6 acres on the front campus that were planted with trees, creating a leafy park that remains an iconic part of the campus to this day. From the original 32 acres contributed in 1910, the campus grew to 50 acres during the administration of Dr. James E. Rouse and 68 acres at the beginning of the 21st century. Under the leadership of Pres. Evans P. Whitaker and the board of trustees, the campus grew to 271 acres in 2008 with the gift of 125 acres from John and Marie Pracht and the purchase of 77 acres that comprises the old county fairgrounds of Anderson. The front campus has been listed as part of the Boulevard Historic District and on the National Register of Historic Places since 1998.

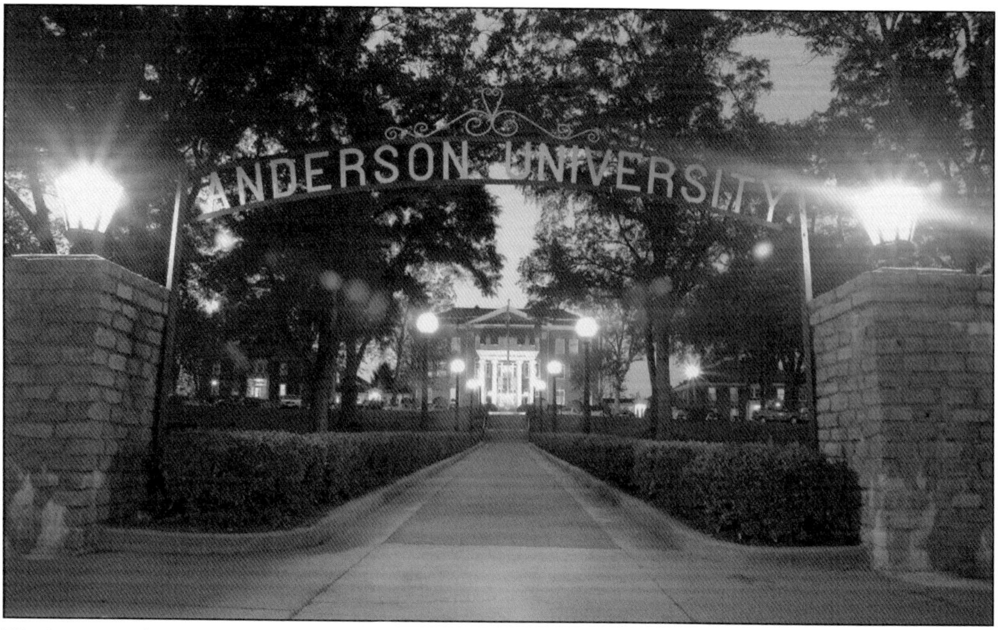

The Merritt Administration Building has served as the heart of the campus since the doors opened for classes on September 18, 1912. Originally known as the "Administration Building," it housed offices, a formal parlor indicative of the era, a dining hall, and a kitchen on the first floor; a library, practice rooms, and an auditorium that held 800 people on the second floor; classrooms and laboratories on the third floor; and a steam heating plant and laundry in the basement. It was renamed the Merritt Administration Building in 1976 following the gift of $100,000 from the Arthur H. Merritt family for refurbishment of the building. In 1977, a gift of $250,000 from the estate of Arthur H. Merritt's wife, Dona R. Merritt of New York City, provided for extensive renovations.

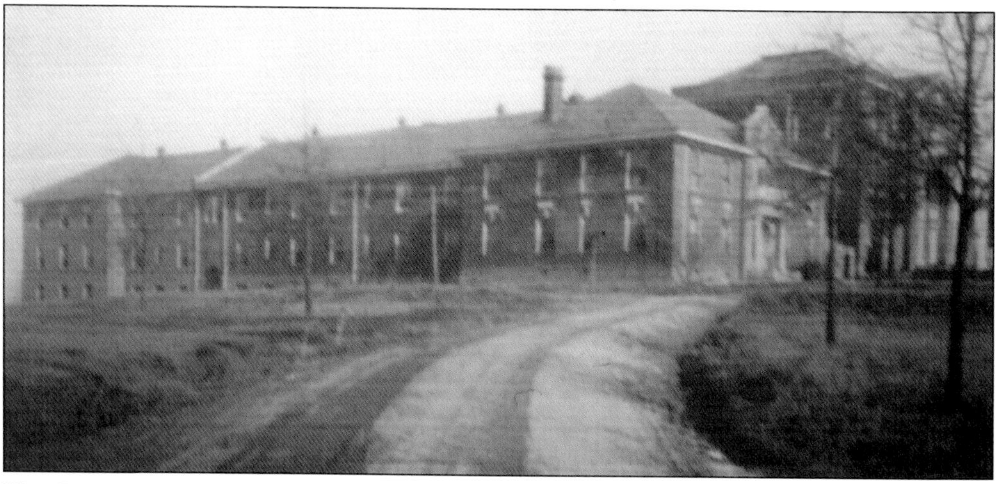

West Dormitory was part of the original construction in 1911. An addition was made to the rear of the building in 1917. It was renamed Denmark Hall in 1966 in honor of Dr. Annie Dove Denmark, who lived in the apartment near the entrance during her years as president of Anderson College. It was extensively renovated in 1986. It is connected to the Merritt Administration Building by an original colonnade, which features a fireplace that was donated as the gift from the class of 1923. In this chimney, a Yule log was burned for many years as part of the campus Christmas celebrations. A loggia or patio was added as a gift from the class of 1919.

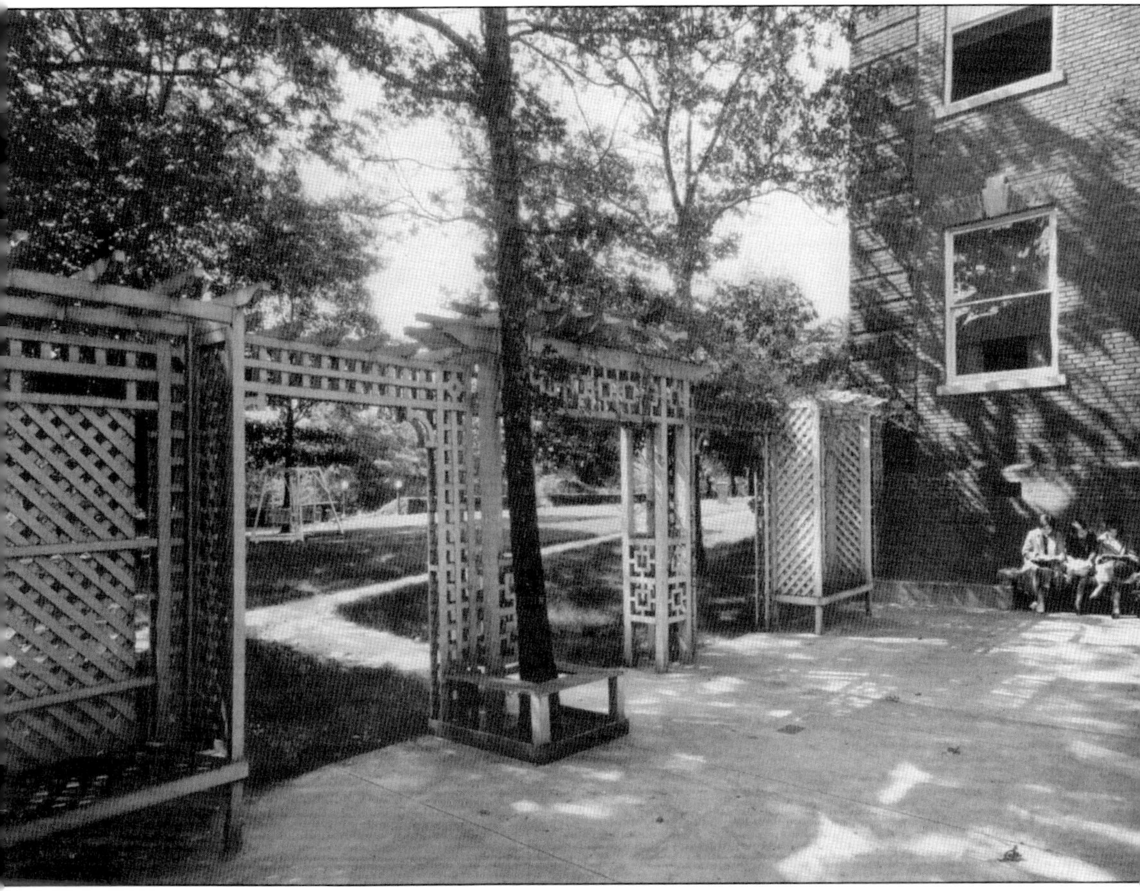

Pratt Dormitory was also connected to Merritt by an original colonnade, which provided seating space; an outside loggia or patio was donated as a gift by the class of 1920. Similar to the Denmark patio, an elaborate lattice-work screen at one time provided some privacy for students enjoying the outdoor seating area, as seen in this 1926 photograph.

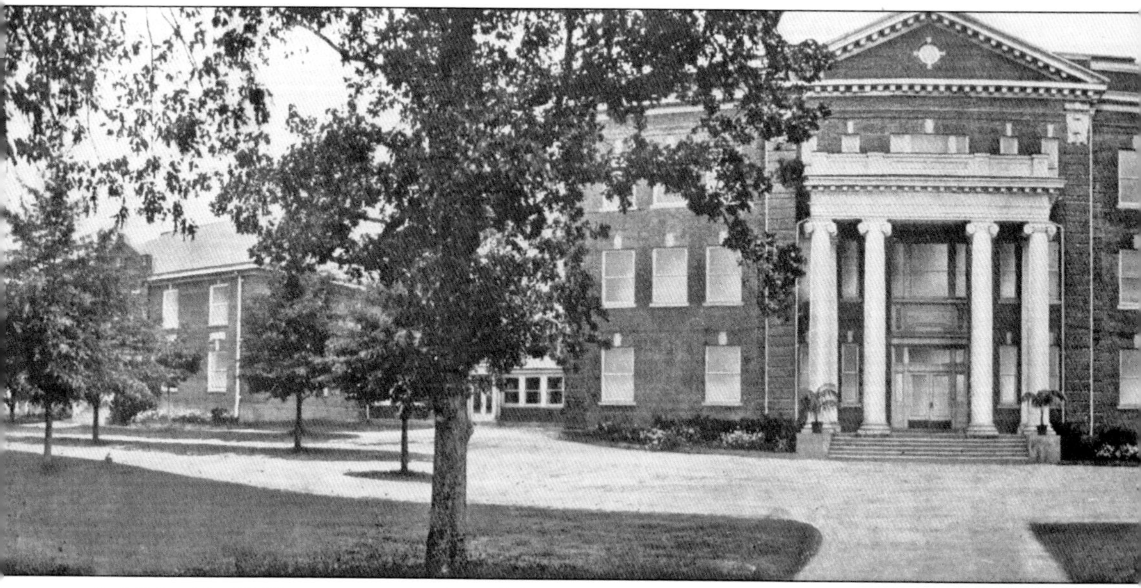

Published in 1916, a panoramic view of the campus includes the Administration Building, both the West and the East Dormitories, and, in the distance, the newly constructed president's home. The joggling board under the trees is an interesting early feature of the campus. The swings are not yet in evidence. East Dormitory, on the right, was also part of the original construction in 1911 and, like its twin, connected to the Administration Building by enclosed walkways that

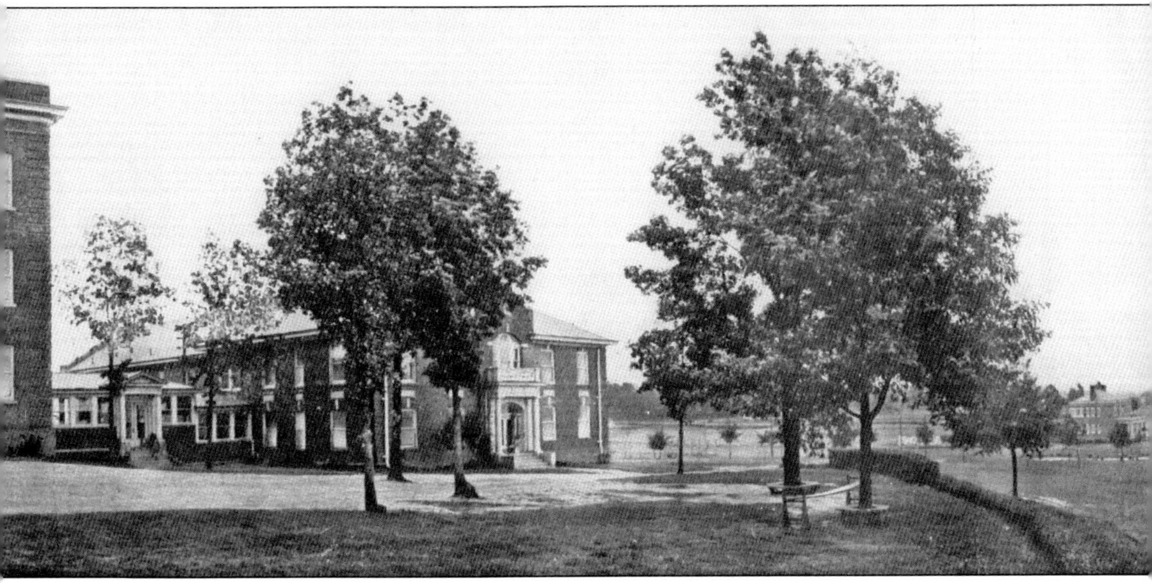

provided seating space as well. It was expanded in 1917 and renovated in 1988. It was renamed Pratt Hall in 1966 after Dr. and Mrs. R. N. Pratt. Dr. Robert N. Pratt taught the Old Testament from 1922 to 1926; his wife, Gertrude, taught expression and speech from 1922 to 1930 and was dean of women from 1931 to 1947.

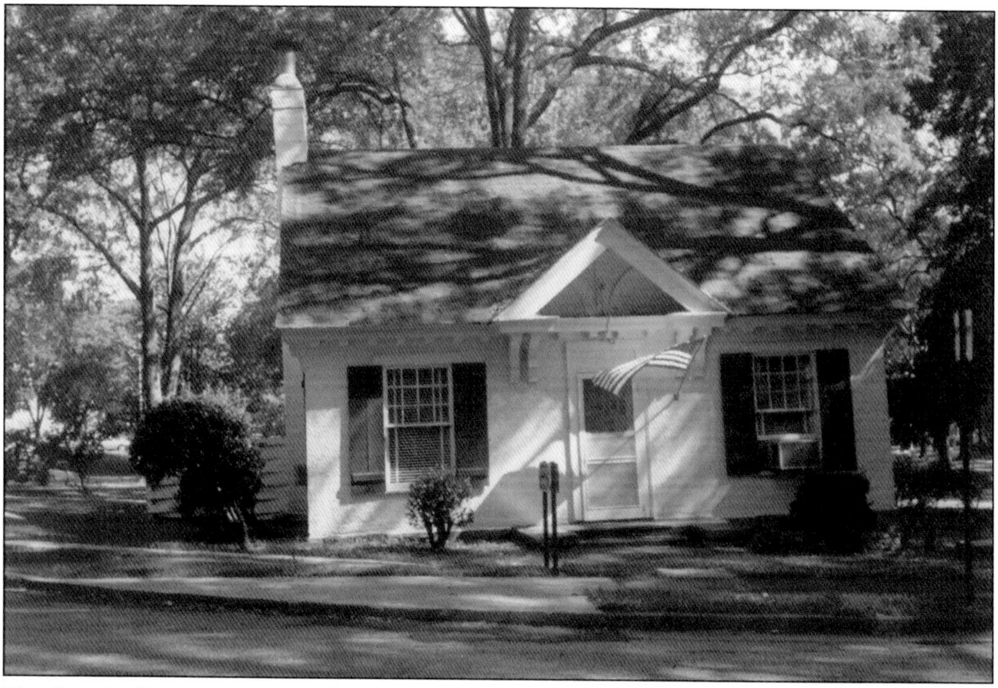

The Gate Lodge was constructed around 1919 to house the superintendant of the grounds and buildings. Providing at different times residential and office space, it now serves as the Campus Safety Office for the university.

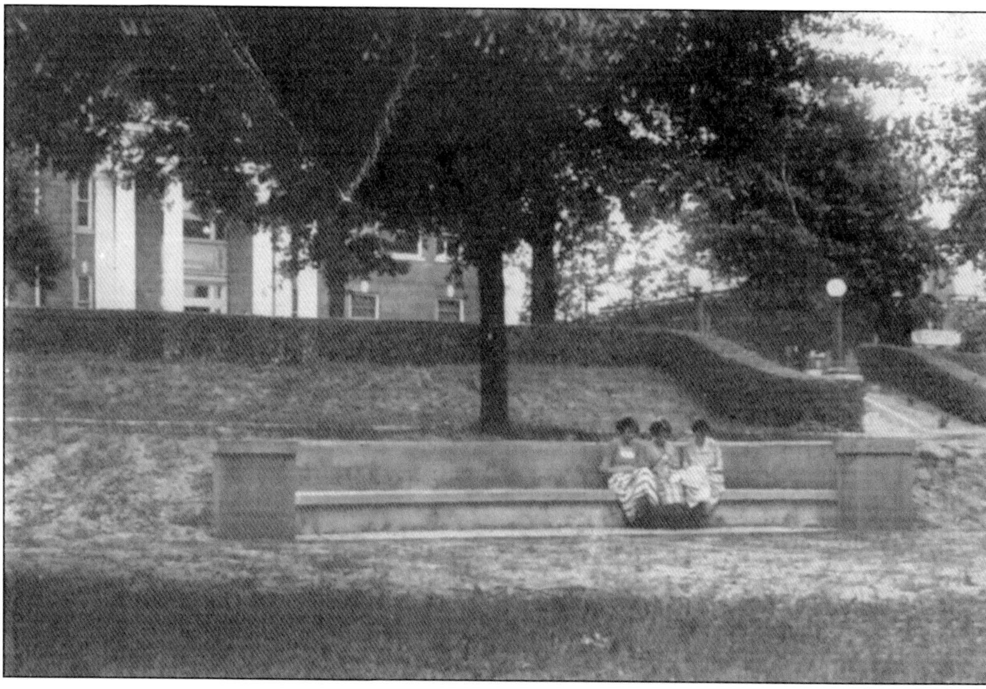

The front walk is featured in the earliest yearbooks of the front grounds. The front campus once had an open theater area for outdoor presentations. B. F. Moore planted all the oak trees and built the original walkway in front of the college.

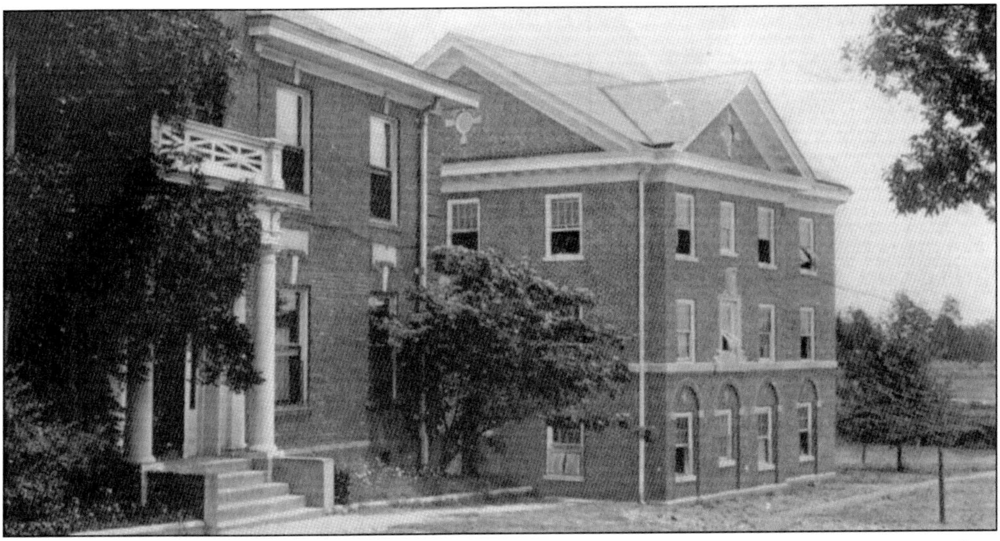

This photograph features the East Dormitory and a new building to house the growing number of students. The *Bulletin* described the following attractive features in this new residence: "it is attached by a corridor to the East Building, with [a] sun parlor between. Hot and cold running water, clothes closets, hospital beds, attractive oak furniture, perfect light and ventilation for every room in the dormitory." Notice the open windows and blowing curtains indicating the type of cooling available on warm days in that time. It was named the Whyte House after James P. Whyte, dean and professor of literature and sociology (1918–1921). A colonnade that enters the second story of the newer building connects both buildings.

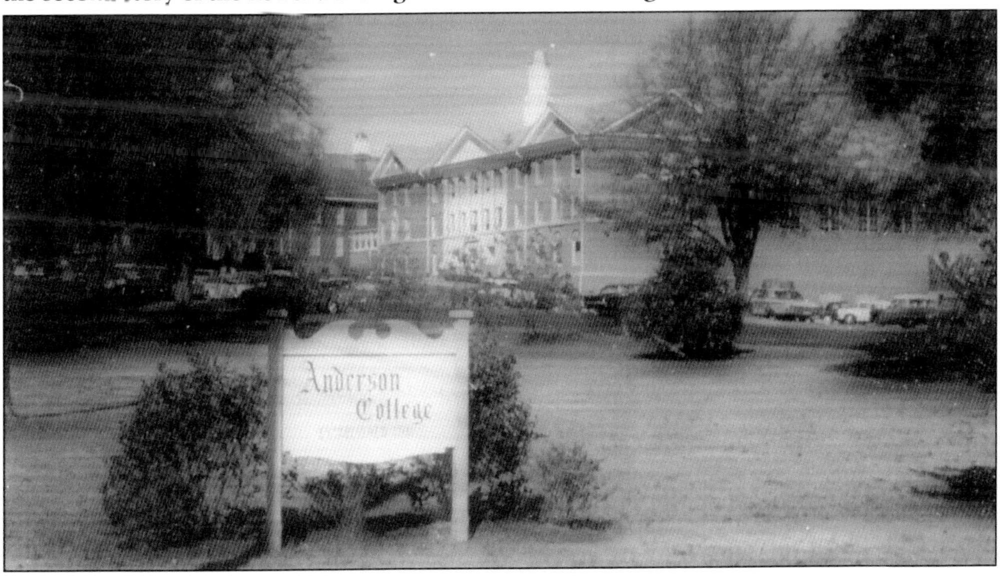

The gym and associated classroom space were added in 1960. Prior to 1960, the building also contained a canteen, the post office, the bookstore, music practice rooms, and classrooms. The gym continues to be known as the Whyte Gym, while the remainder of the building was renamed Vandiver Hall in 1995 in honor of David S. Vandiver Sr., his wife Eliza C. Vandiver, and their children. It now houses the College of Business. Before the addition in 1960, the studios for WAIM and WCAC-FM were located on the third floor; later they moved to a studio building next to the transmission tower. The lettering for the radio stations is still faintly visible on the front facade.

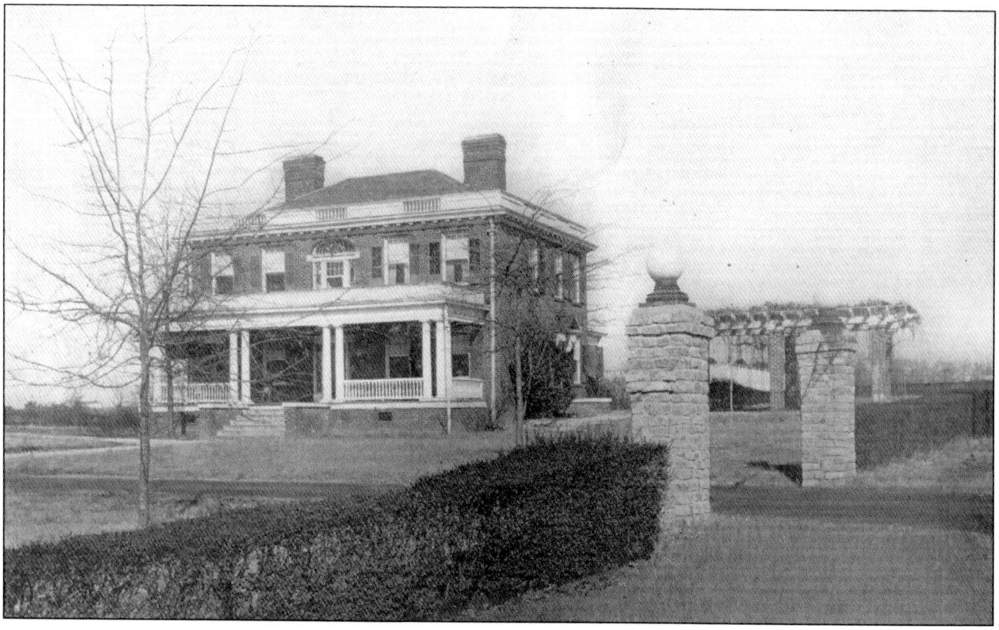

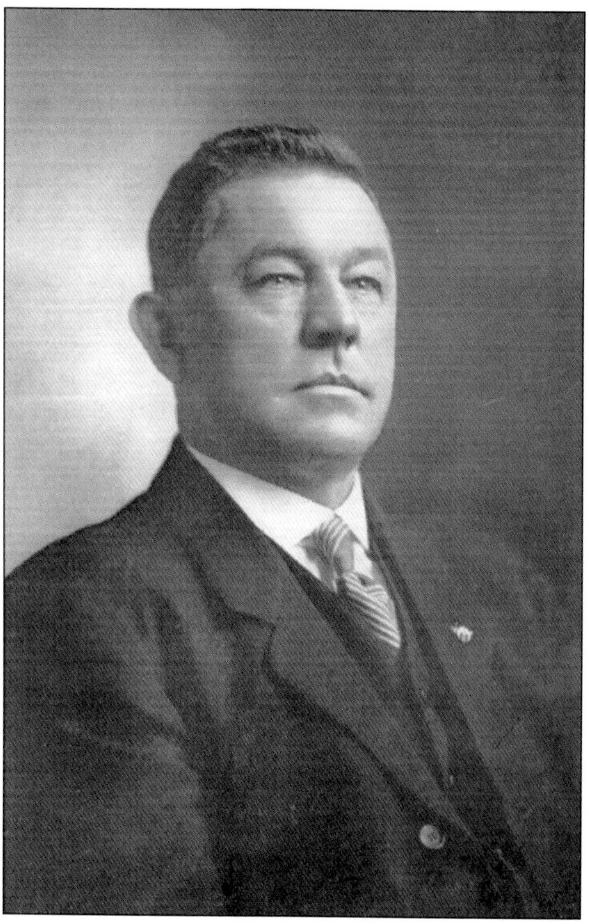

The Sullivan House, located at the east gate of the campus, was a 1916 gift from Anderson College founder and benefactor Charles S. Sullivan Sr., pictured on right. It was donated to become the president's home; however, since the majority of the first presidents were also pastors of the city's First Baptist Church and lived in the church parsonage and Dr. Denmark lived in a dormitory apartment, no president lived there until the 1950s. It served in that capacity until 1965, when it became the Sullivan Music Building. This building has been the site of much lore and speculation about the presence of a piano-playing ghost.

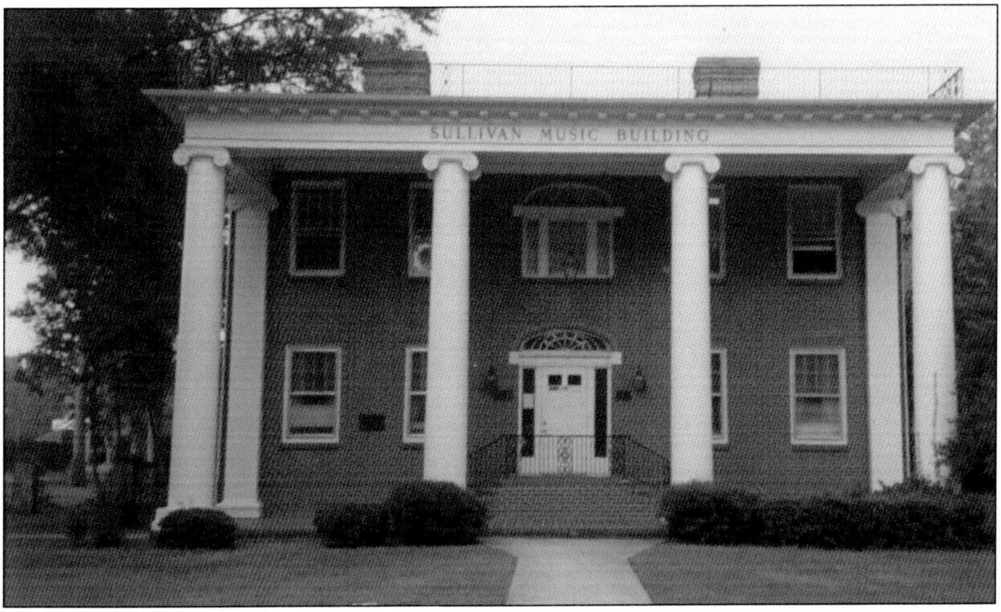

The Sullivan Building for a time housed the music department. The renovations that converted the building from home to academic use included adding four columns on the front that came from the women's college campus of Furman University, which was demolished after it was sold to the city of Greenville. A chapel was added in 1966 and named in 1998 in honor of LaVern Raines Hunt '41. Further renovations took place in 1977, and with the opening of the Rainey Fine Arts Center in 1982, the building saw new life as the Baptist Student Union.

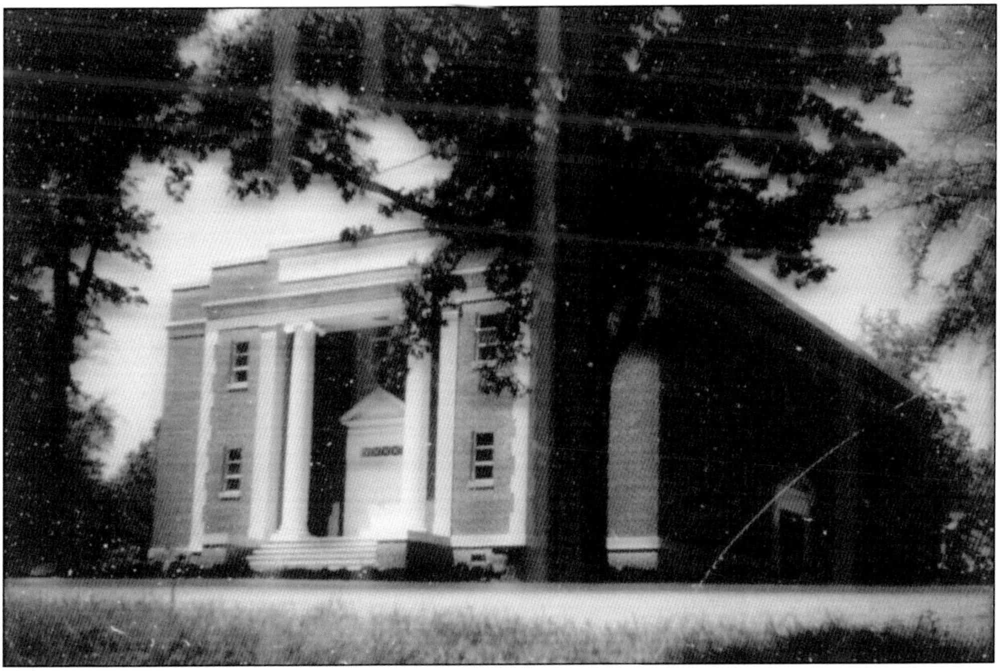

A new library was built in 1956 that was later named for Olin D. Johnston, honoring the distinguished former senator and governor of South Carolina. The donations to build the library were made by the Johnston family.

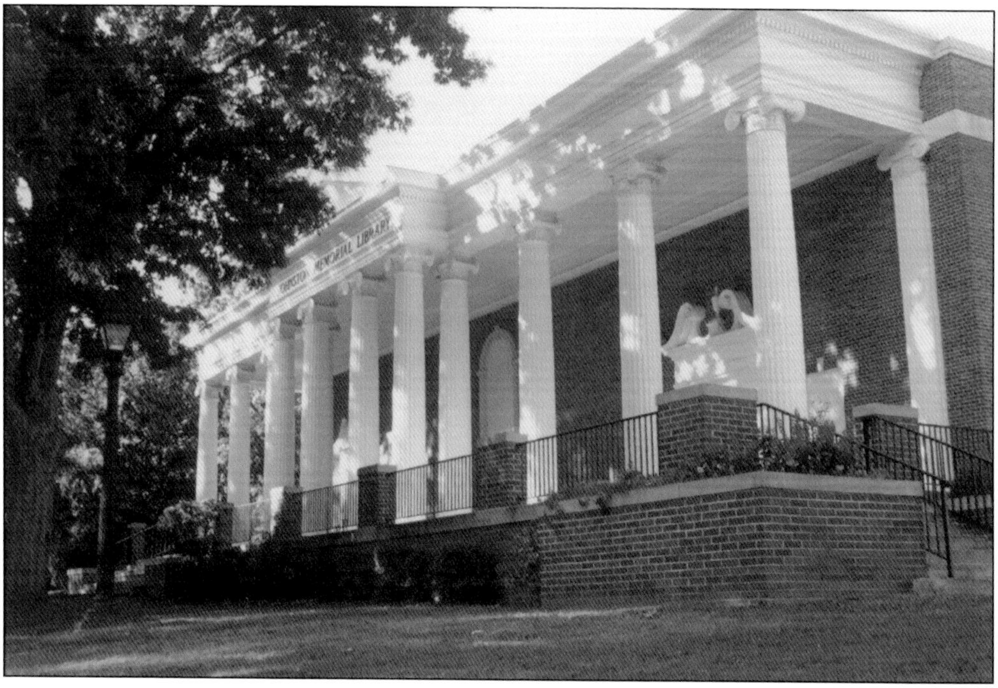

An addition was dedicated in 1975 that expanded the library's services. In 2006, with the completion of the Thrift Library, the Johnston Building was renovated to become the home to the College of Education and the School of Interior Design.

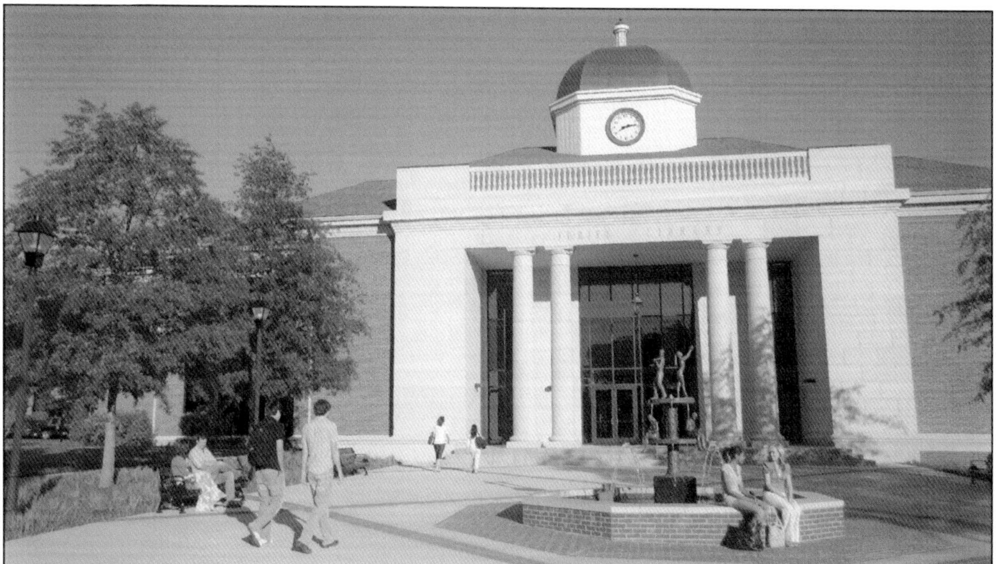

The Thrift Library opened in January 2007 and is aptly described as a "learning commons." This modern 50,000-square-foot facility houses not only the library of Anderson University but also multiple study rooms, a music lab, a high-tech multimedia hall, and an art gallery on the main floor and a coffee shop, restaurant, student computer lab, and the university's central computing systems on the ground level. The library is named in honor of twin brothers Sam and Tom Thrift and their wives, Joellen and Patsy.

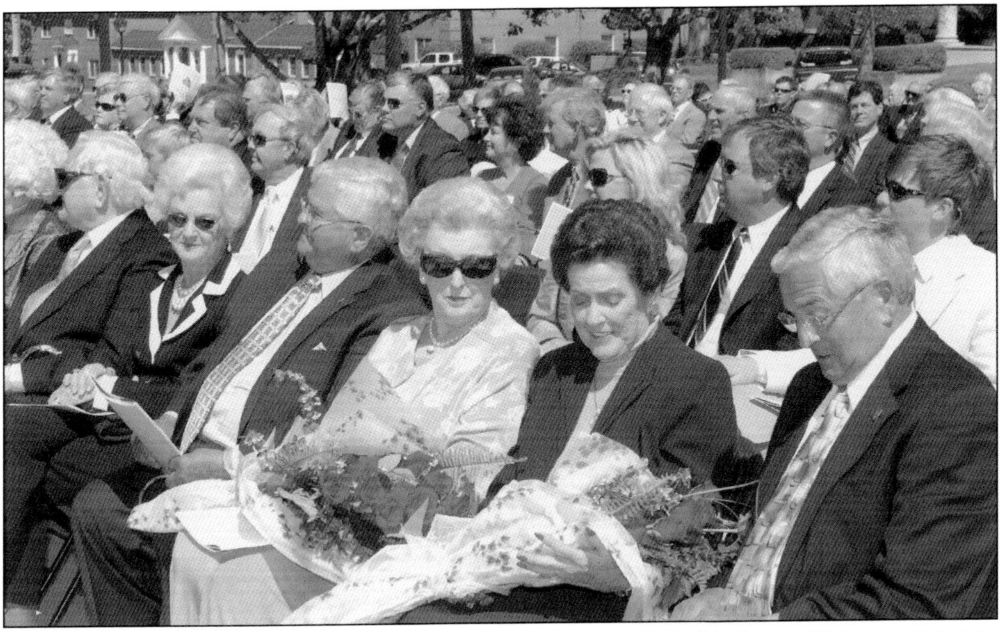

This building has become the heart of the campus and the symbol of Anderson University's bright future in the 21st century. Pictured at the dedication ceremony on April 12, 2007, are, from left to right, Judge G. Ross Anderson Jr. and his wife Dot, Samuel F. Thrift and Joellen Thrift, and Patsy and Thomas E. Thrift. Further down the second row, located directly behind Judge Anderson, is Dicky McClellion, for whom the library's downstairs café is named.

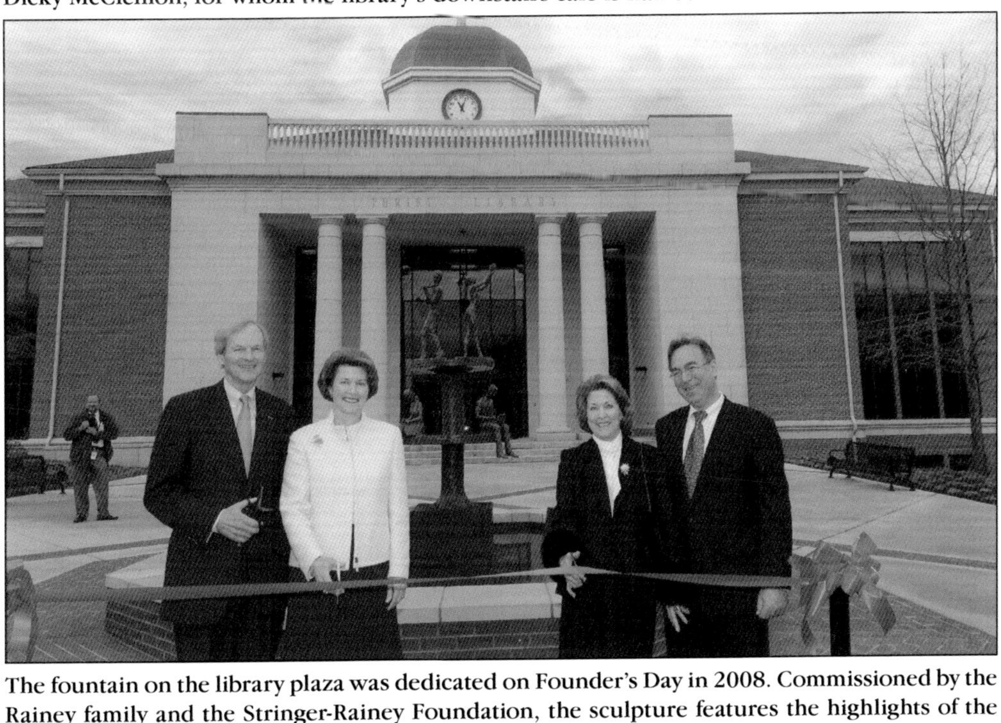

The fountain on the library plaza was dedicated on Founder's Day in 2008. Commissioned by the Rainey family and the Stringer-Rainey Foundation, the sculpture features the highlights of the variety of avenues open to students on the campus. Pictured are, from left to right, John Rainey, Mary Rainey Belser, Nancy Rainey Crowley, and sculptor Marc Mellon.

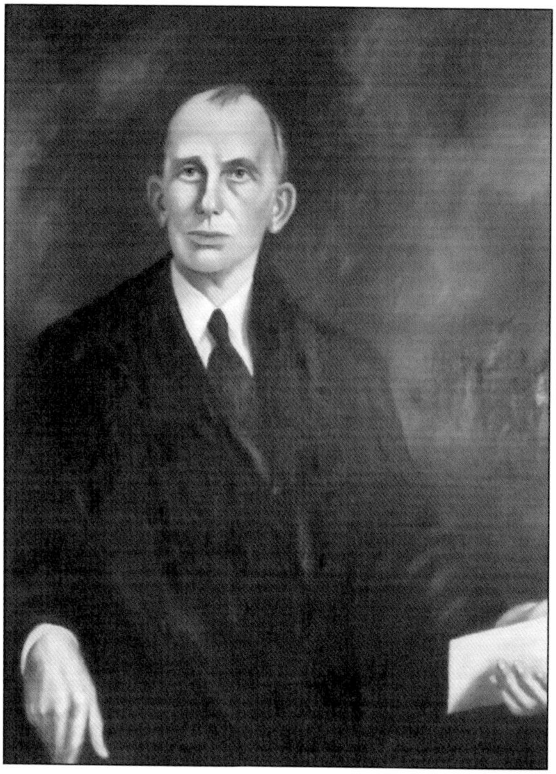

Watkins Teaching Center was built in 1967, during the administration of Pres. J. E. Rouse. It is named in honor of Judge Henry Hitt Watkins (left) and his wife, Maude Wakefield Watkins (below), whose estate bequest provided a substantial gift for its construction. Watkins was a distinguished lawyer and federal judge, an original contributor to the fund to build Anderson College, one of the first trustees, and chairman of the board from 1911 to 1927. The limestone front columns at the entrance of Watkins Teaching Center were once at the entrance of the Ramsey Fine Arts Building on the Limestone College campus.

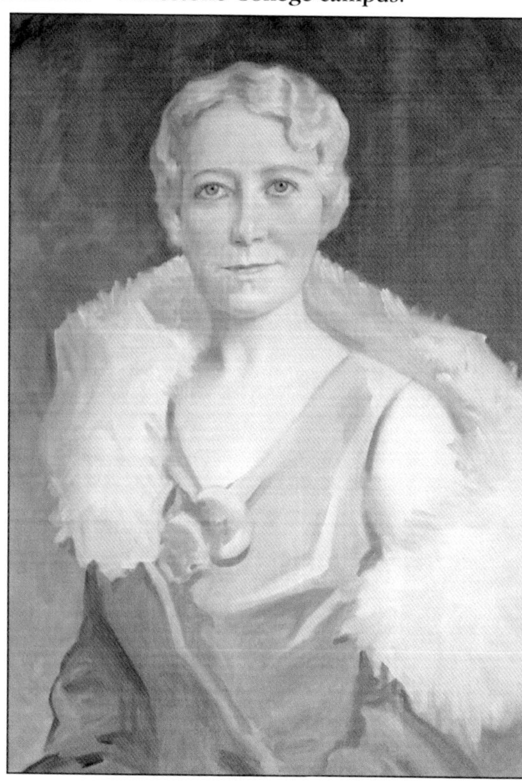

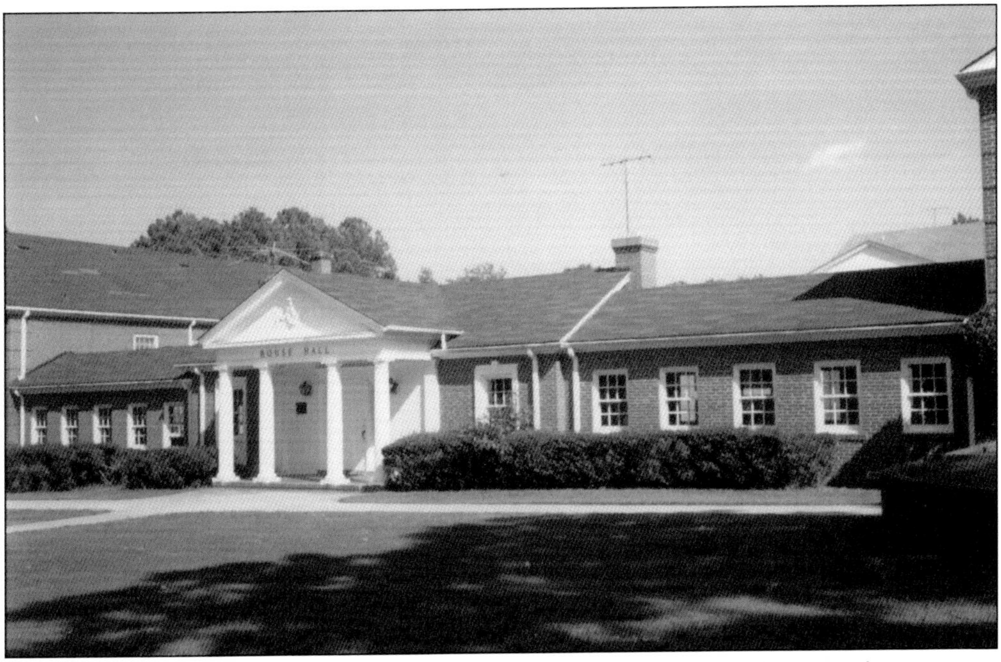

The first residence halls for men were built in two phases, between 1962 and 1963. Men were commuting students until the completion of these buildings. The first was named for Rev. J. K. Lawton, who was a member of the board of trustees in 1964 and vice president of Anderson College in 1966. The second was named for former president J. E. Rouse.

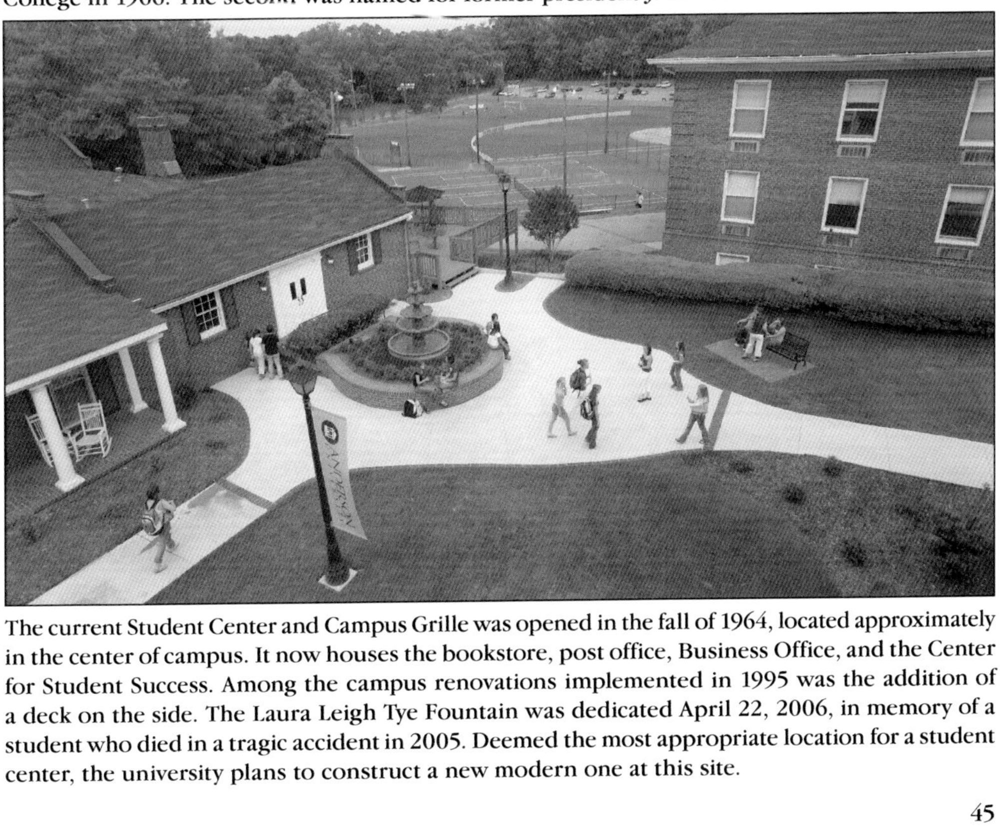

The current Student Center and Campus Grille was opened in the fall of 1964, located approximately in the center of campus. It now houses the bookstore, post office, Business Office, and the Center for Student Success. Among the campus renovations implemented in 1995 was the addition of a deck on the side. The Laura Leigh Tye Fountain was dedicated April 22, 2006, in memory of a student who died in a tragic accident in 2005. Deemed the most appropriate location for a student center, the university plans to construct a new modern one at this site.

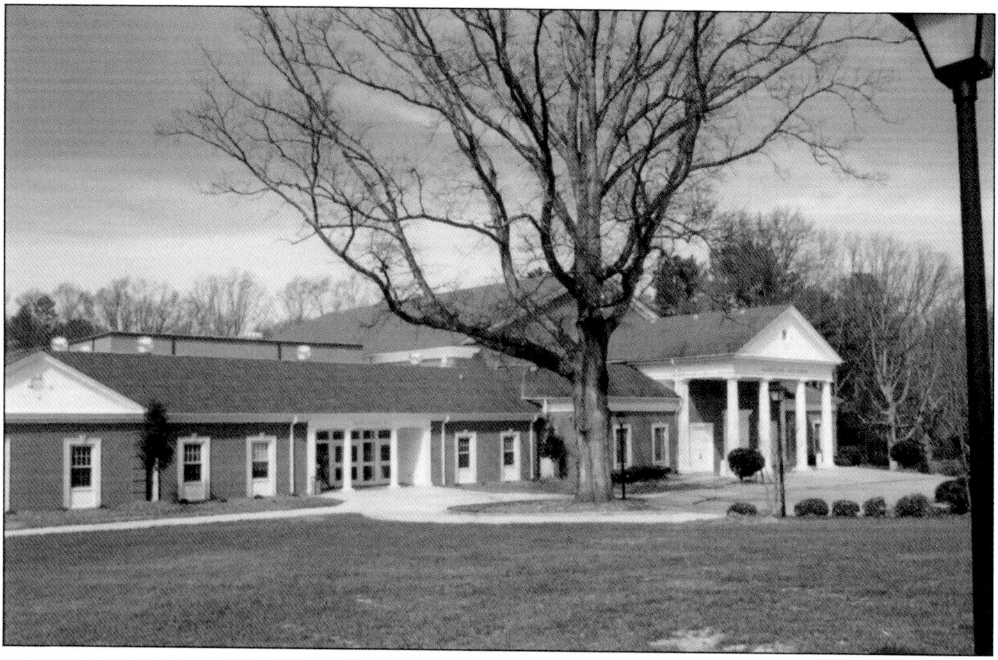

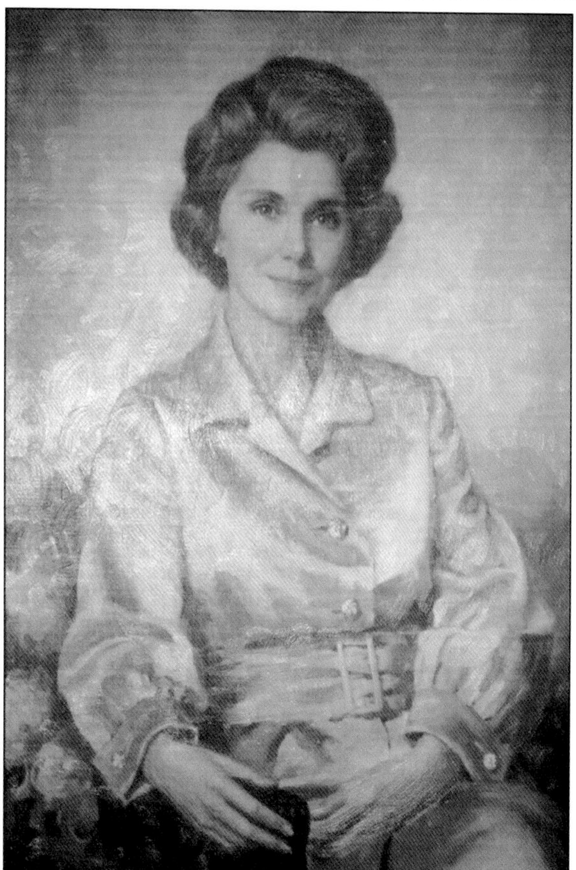

The Callie Stringer Rainey Fine Arts Center was built in two phases. The first opened in 1983, and the second was completed in 1995, which was when it also was named in memory of Callie Stringer Rainey, a member of a family that has been distinguished as friends and benefactors of Anderson University. This complex contains Henderson Auditorium, the Belk Theater, Daniel Recital Hall, an art gallery and studio space, music practice space, offices, and classrooms.

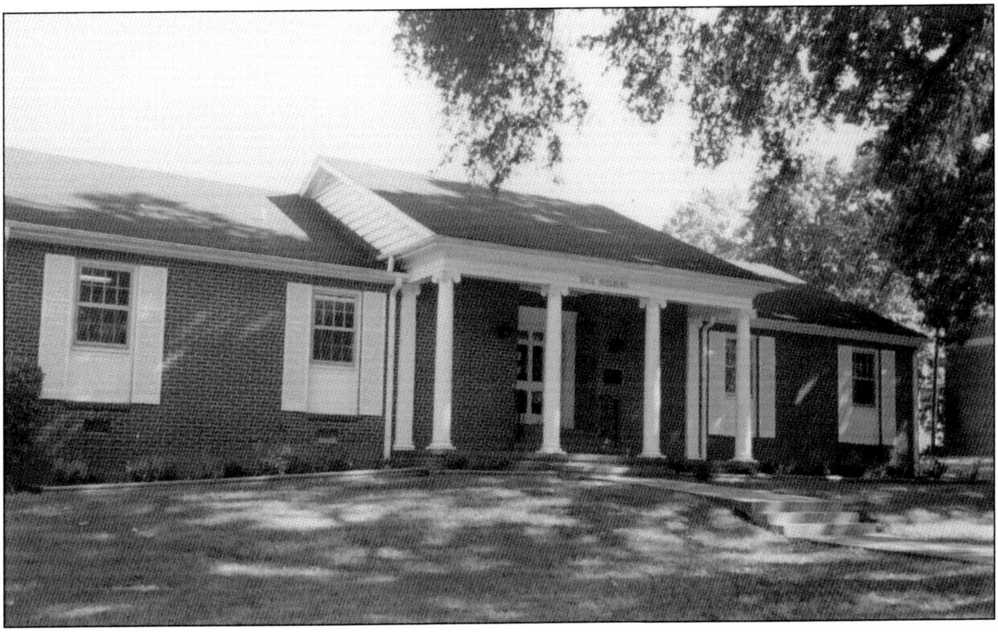

The Rice Building, formerly known as the Rice Infirmary, now houses the Financial Aid Planning Office and is the home of Anderson Central, which provides centralized services for students. It was originally built in 1960 as the infirmary and later served as the Admissions Office. Naming funds were given by the family of Max Rice, whose wife, Janie Haynie Rice, was a 1923 graduate. The couple received the Annie Dove Denmark Award in 1961.

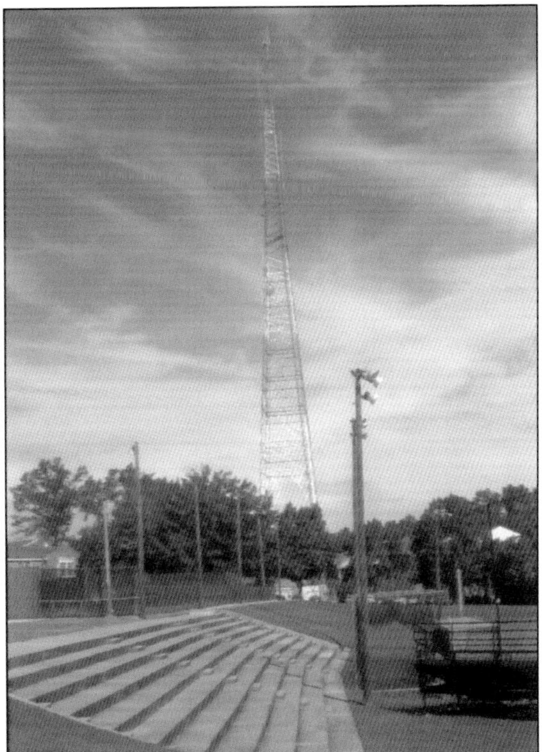

The transmission tower, built around 1947, replaced earlier structures and remains a distinguishing feature of the campus. WAIM built a studio at the base. Once the radio station moved away from the campus, the building was used for a variety of academic areas, among them the art and journalism departments. Following the construction of the Fine Arts Center in the early 1980s, the building was removed. The softball field at right was named Smethers Field in 1966 after Dr. A. L. Smethers, who had served as a member of the board of trustees from 1925 until 1954.

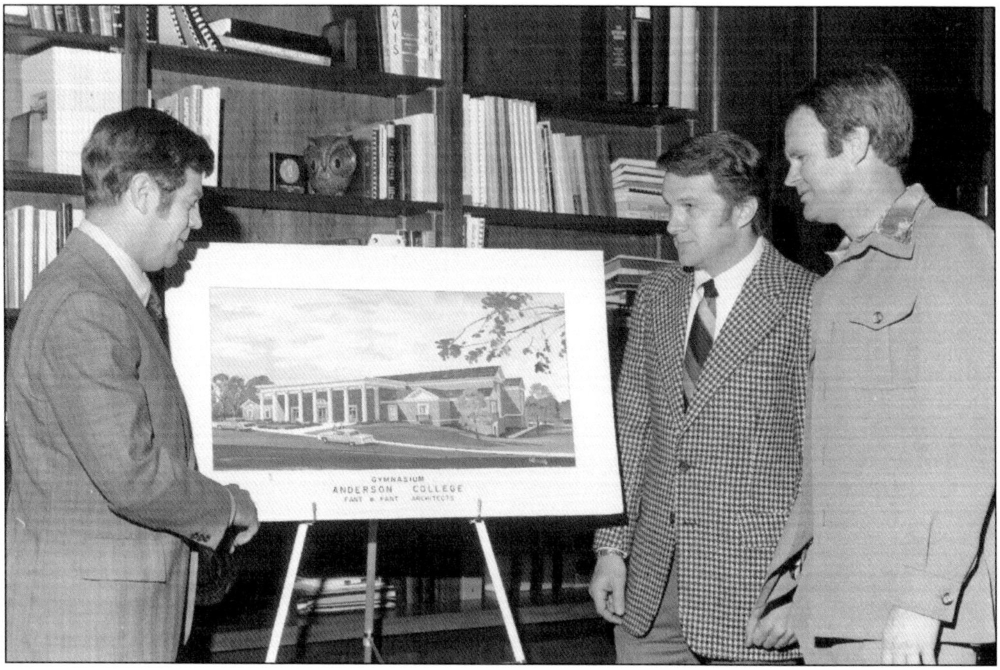

Abney Athletic Center was completed and dedicated November 16, 1979. Thanks to the generosity of the Abney Foundation and John R. Fulp Jr., this complex gave the campus a much needed gymnasium for its nationally recognized basketball team. The gymnasium also contains a weight room, a concession stand, locker rooms, a wrestler's practice room, space for the trophy case in the foyer and reception areas, and office space for the athletic director and the coaches. Pictured are, from left to right, Pres. Cordell Maddox, John Fulp Jr., and basketball coach Jim Wiles.

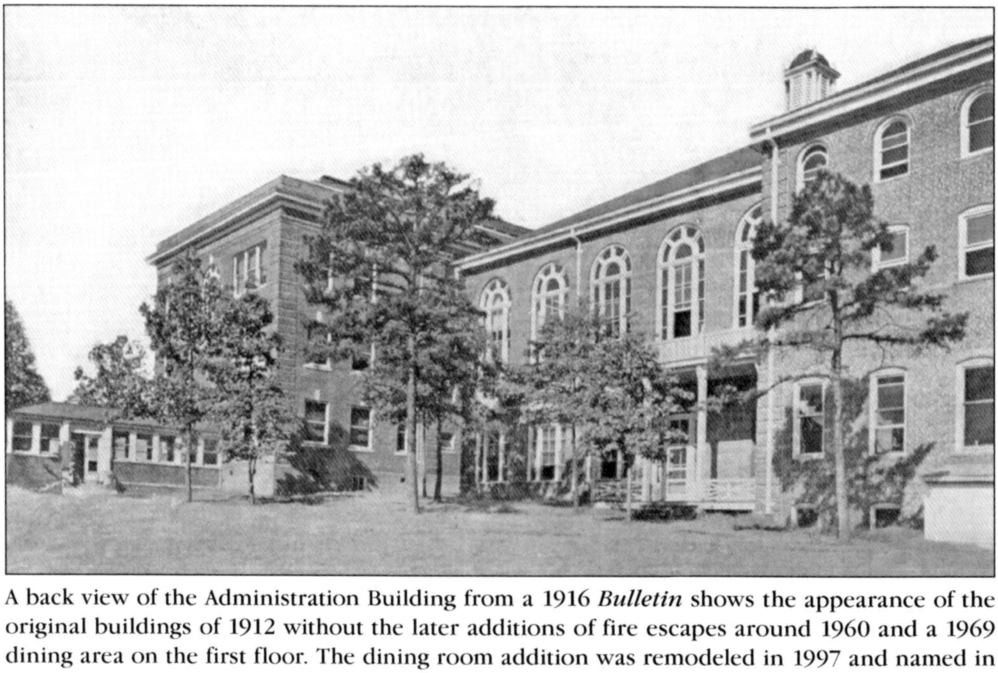

A back view of the Administration Building from a 1916 *Bulletin* shows the appearance of the original buildings of 1912 without the later additions of fire escapes around 1960 and a 1969 dining area on the first floor. The dining room addition was remodeled in 1997 and named in memory of E. Hugh Agnew, his wife, Izetta Pruitt Agnew '16, and Judge Harry Agnew.

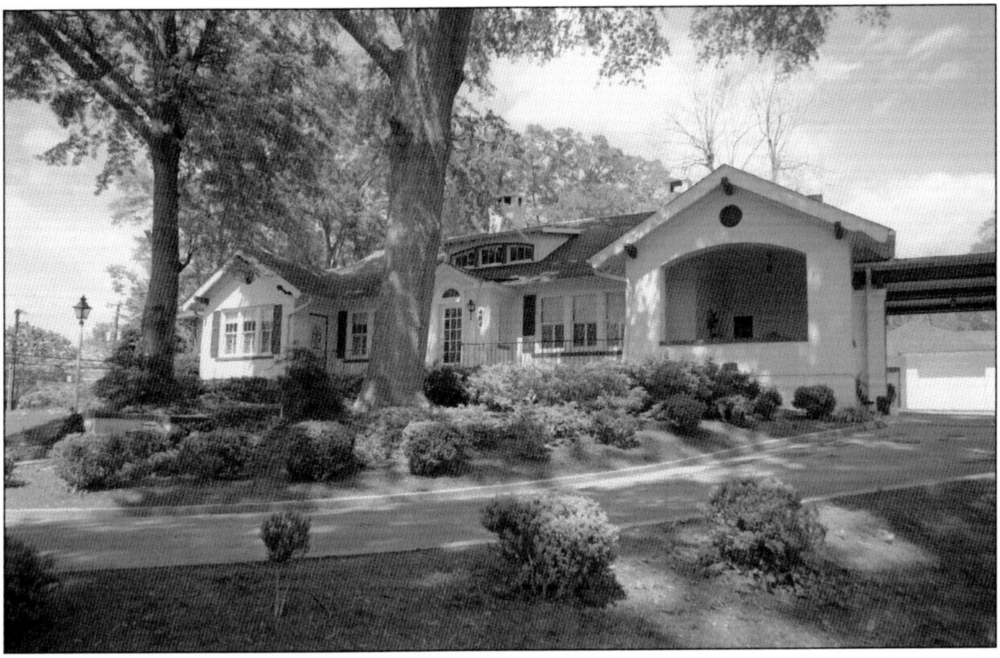

The current Office of Admissions moved from the former Rice Infirmary to the former Keller Home on the corner of Calhoun Street and Boulevard in 2005. This was a residence from the 1930s until the owner's death. It was then operated as a bed-and-breakfast prior to its purchase by the university.

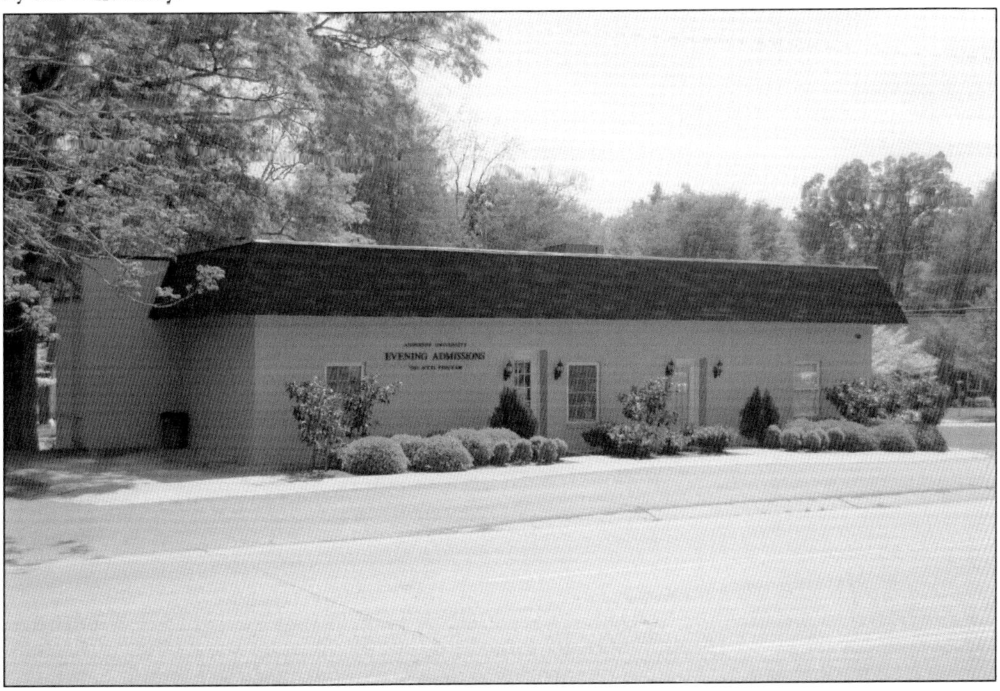

The Office of Graduate and Evening Admissions once was a gas service station. Before its purchase and renovation as office space for the night adult program in 2007, it served as an apartment for a time.

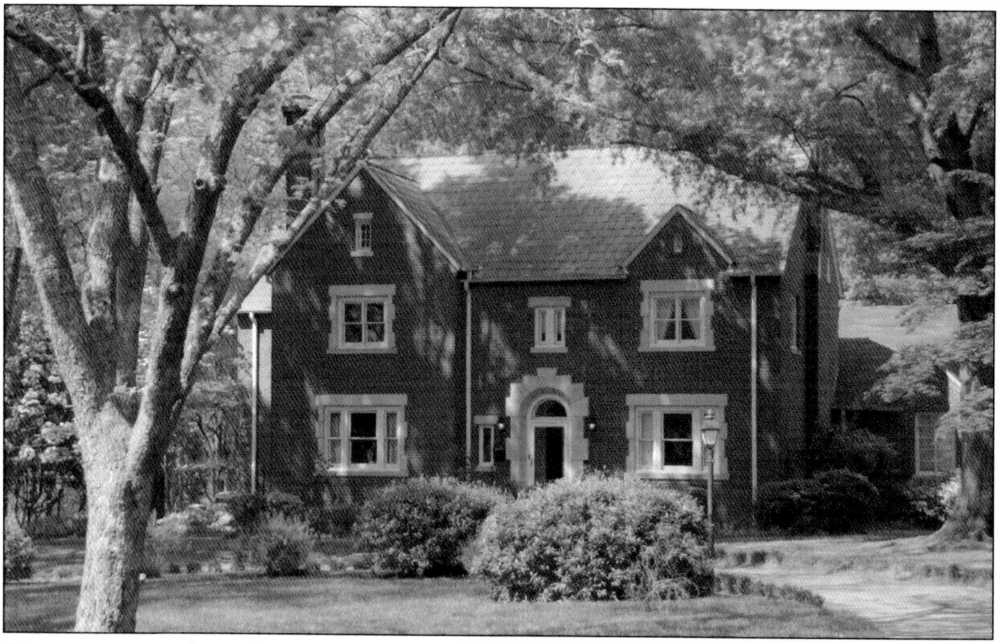

The current president's home, purchased in 1969 from the Sullivan family, was built in 1938 for Pat Sullivan of Sullivan's Hardware, which was a well-known store in Anderson's downtown. In 1973, it was renovated and enlarged for the residency of the first president to live there, Dr. Cordell Maddox.

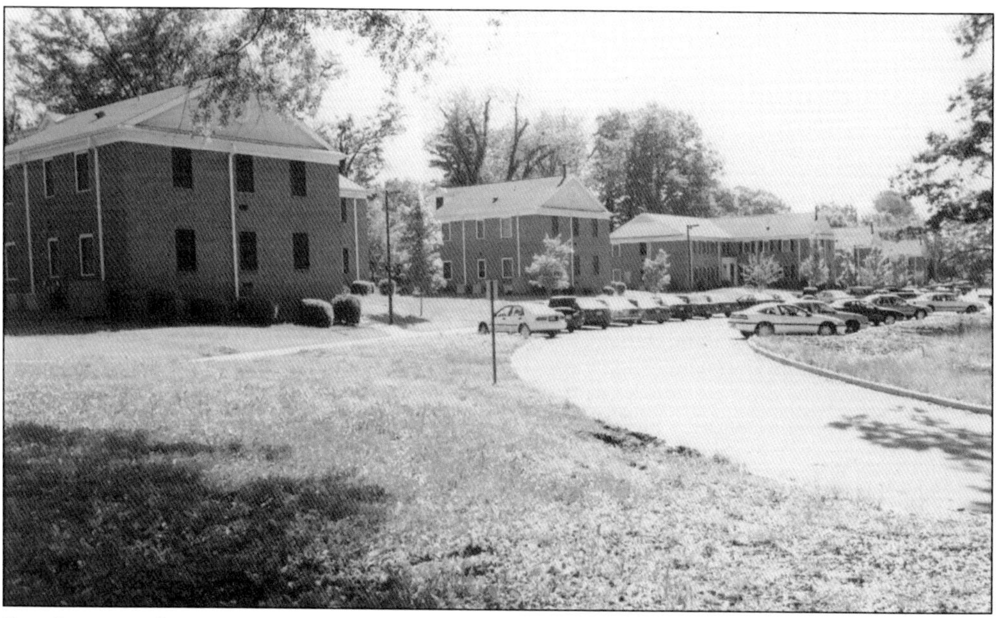

East Commons became Stringer Commons on February 5, 1998. Built in 1990, these five buildings provided additional housing for students adjacent to the campus. The name was changed with an endowment gift for facility maintenance, which was made by the Stringer Foundation with the help of the John and Callie Rainey Foundation. The suites provided a flexible housing arrangements for students. Each of the five buildings has four apartments, and each apartment has two baths, a common kitchen/living area, and accommodations for eight students.

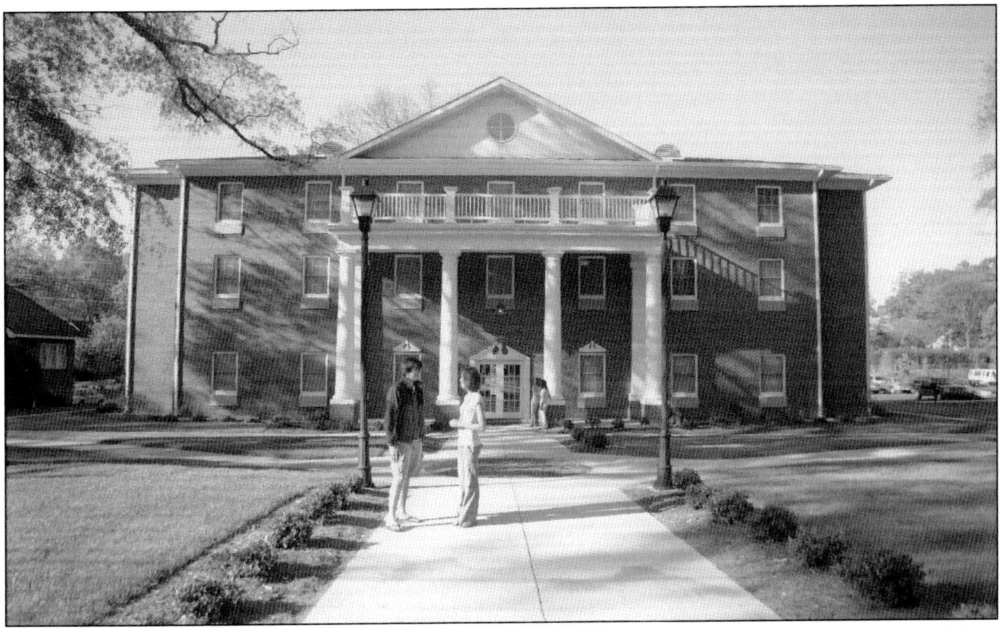

Boulevard Residence Hall was built directly across the street from Merritt Administration Building in 2007. This three-story building has a lounge, kitchen, and laundry room on the first floor and suites of rooms on the upper floors. A new residence hall was constructed on either side in 2010 for the opening of fall classes. Ultimately, six residence halls are planned for that section of Boulevard.

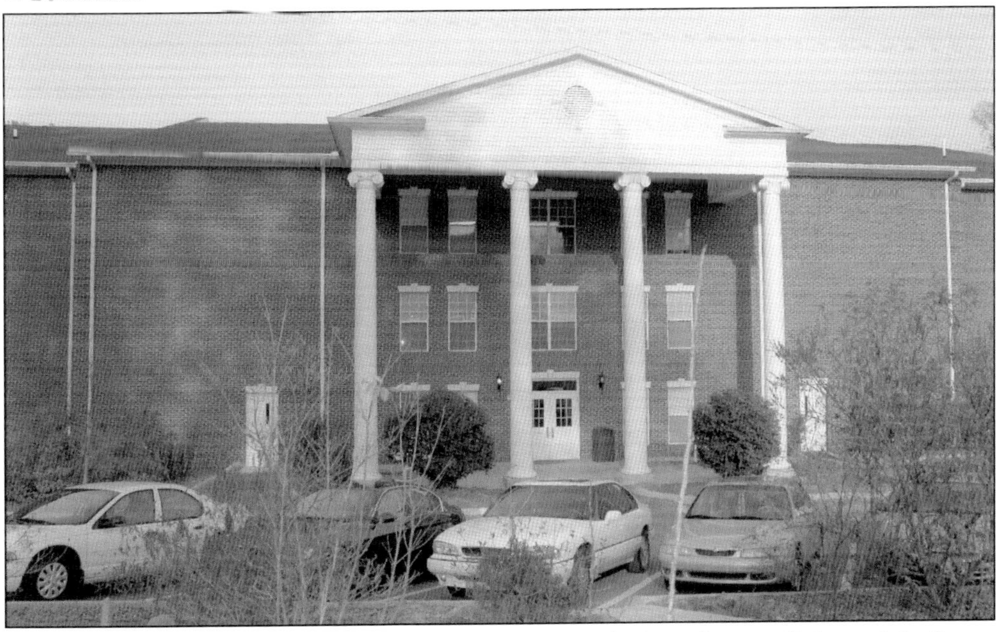

The Village, constructed in 2002, has individual rooms with baths and originally housed the Career Office, the health center, and the Physical Plant Office. In 2010, the ground floor of the Village was converted to create additional student residential space, while the Physical Plant Office was moved to the Athletic Campus. Beside the Village is Kingsley Hall, which was built in 1983 and named in 2000. The health center was located there until it moved to the Village.

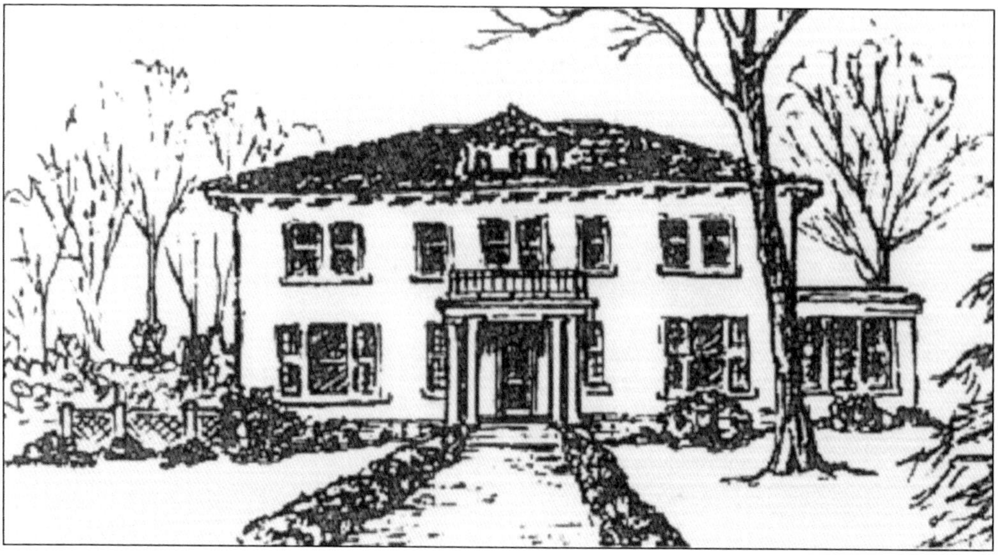

The Watkins Home at 600 Boulevard, built in 1919, was the residence of Judge H. H. Watkins, who served for many years as a trustee. The home was given to the university in the 1960s and was the home of Pres. John E. Rouse, who continued to live there following his retirement in 1972. He died in 1981, and the university later sold the property. Fant and Fant Architects also designed it. Gifted artist Ruth A. Hopkins, wife of Pres. Mark Hopkins, did this sketch of the house. Her many contributions to the college included drawings of all the campus buildings. (Courtesy of Ruth A. Hopkins.)

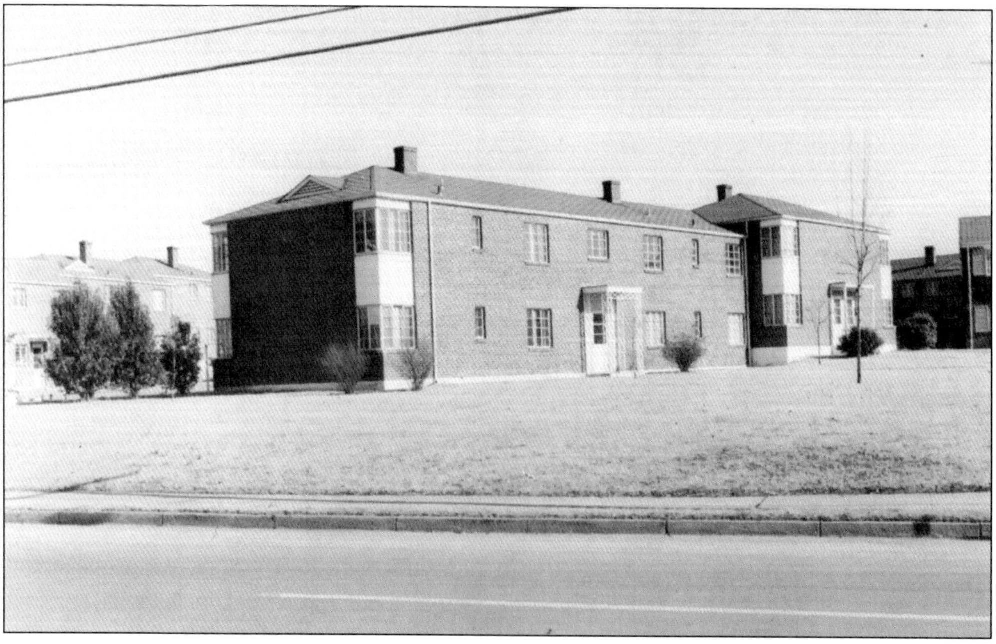

An apartment complex known as Bailey Court, located about 2 miles from the campus, was owned by the institution from 1959 to the 1970s. It provided inexpensive housing for faculty, staff, and married students, as well as for the general public. Located at the intersection of Concord Avenue and Main Street, it was within walking distance of the college as well as various churches and retail establishments, allowing a person to get along without owning a car.

Four

Academics and Cultural Life

"When you graduate from college your name ought to have some content and meaning. The alumni directory is full of the names of those who have lived gloriously. You are feeling, stirring within yourselves, the longing to be better than anything you have ever been before. Nobody needs to stay as [s]he is today. Unless a student is flexible and knows how to change, she might as well pack her trunk and go home."

This statement, attributed to Dr. Annie Dove Denmark by a former member of the board of trustees, Ruth Hill, lays out the challenge provided by the academic and cultural program at Anderson University since its inception. As the academic program expanded, the college maintained a high standard of quality and excellence, achieving its Southern Association of Colleges and Schools accreditation in 1959. It continued to maintain its edge with the technological developments of the day, offering radio and then television broadcasting opportunities from the 1930s to the first Educational TV course from Columbia and a math class in the fall of 1962. In 2010, an extensive listing of classes from across the curriculum is provided online. The student population increased through the offering of night classes for adults, which began in 1958 with five courses. By the next year, enrollment had doubled, and 12 courses were being offered, meeting four nights a week. The program has grown over the years and now operates as ACCEL. With the addition of graduate classes, the university has a breadth of influence undreamed in its early years. Online education grows rapidly and expands the student population beyond those in commuting distance. December 2009 had the first graduate to receive a degree who never had to set foot on the campus.

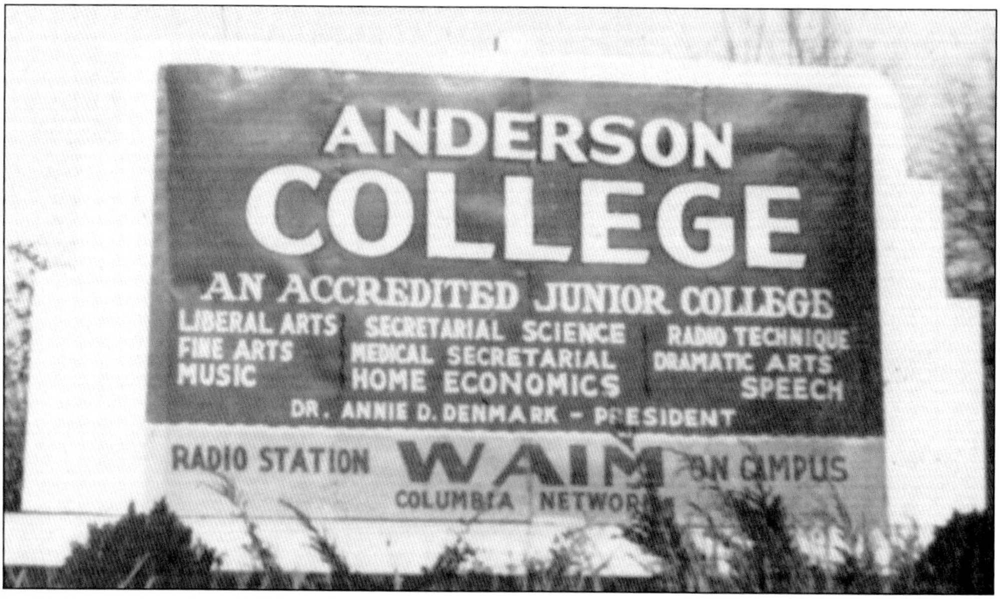

In 1943, an advertising billboard gave the passing motorist a good overview of the programs and offerings of the college.

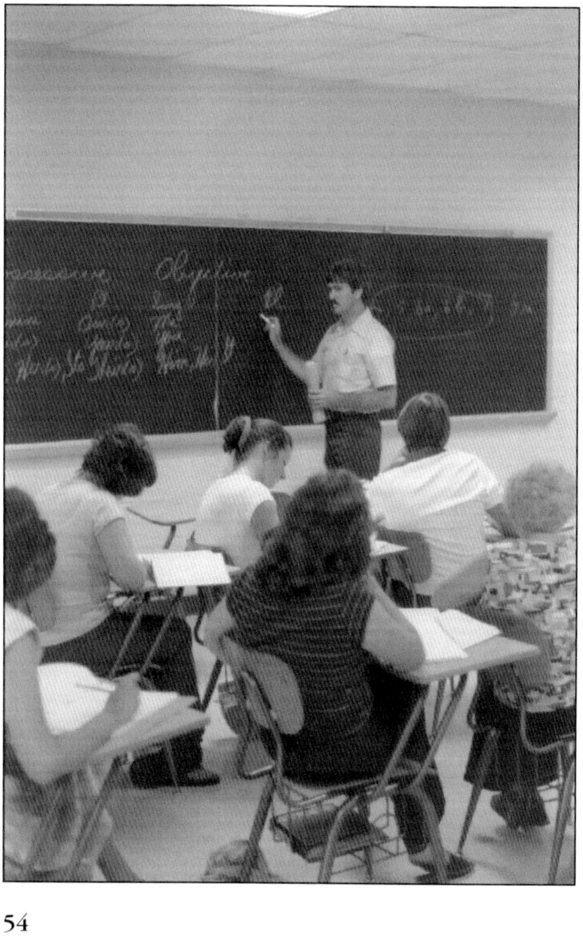

At the heart and core, college memories include classes. Prof. Dennis James teaches an English class in the newly constructed Watkins Teaching Center. The written word through literature and writing in many different forms has been part of the curriculum and life of the university from the very beginning.

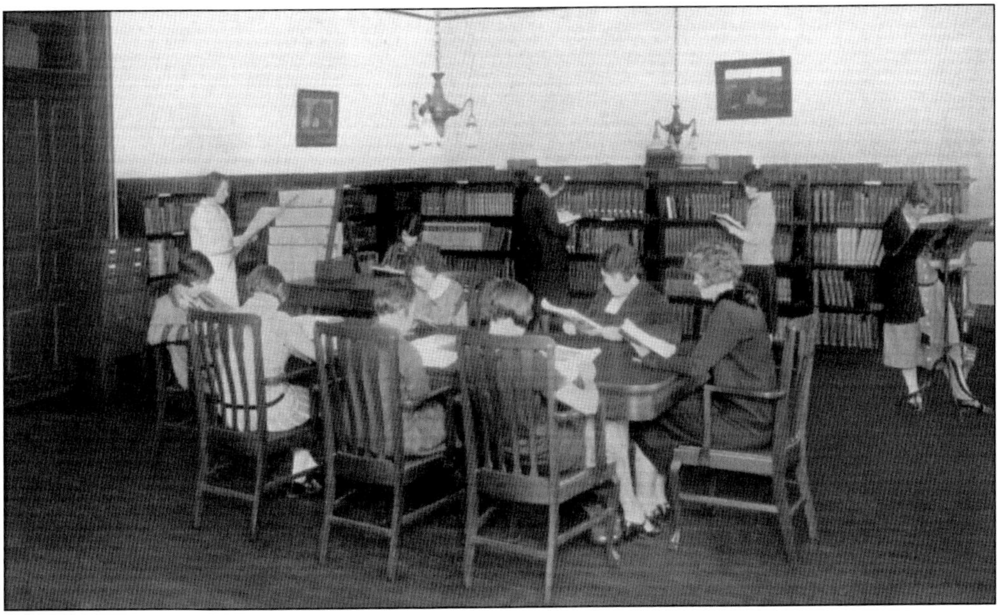

The original library was located on the second floor of the Administration Building. After the construction of the Johnston Library in 1956, the room was used as an art studio before being remodeled for its current use as the Trustee Room. This view from the 1927 Anderson College *Viewbook* shows the resources available for students at that time.

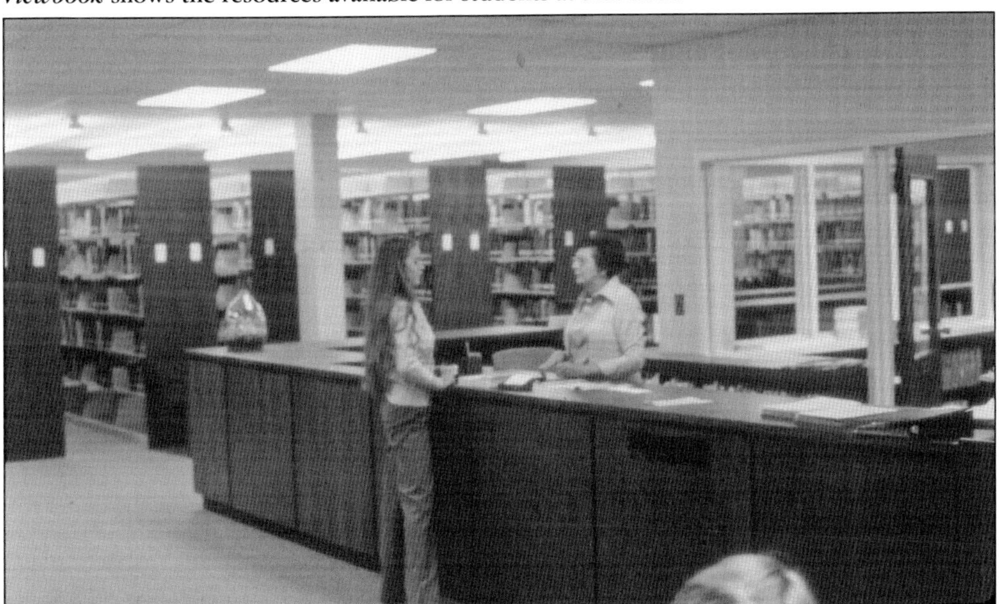

Seen here in her role as an assistant librarian at the circulation desk in the Johnston Memorial Library is Dora Hancock, a woman of many skills. She represents a success story repeated many times during the years of Dr. Denmark's presidency, which is characterized with opening doors and providing opportunities for individuals whose circumstances made an education seem out of reach. Hancock also taught in the business department, was the president's secretary in the 1950s, was the Baptist Student Union director, and was also the sponsor for other denominational organizations on campus.

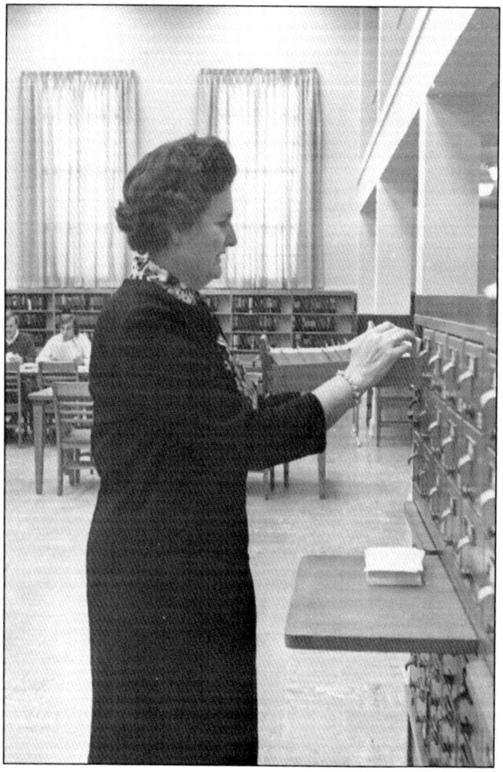

Head Librarian Annie Frances Blackman uses the card catalogue, which was the heart of the library before computers were introduced.

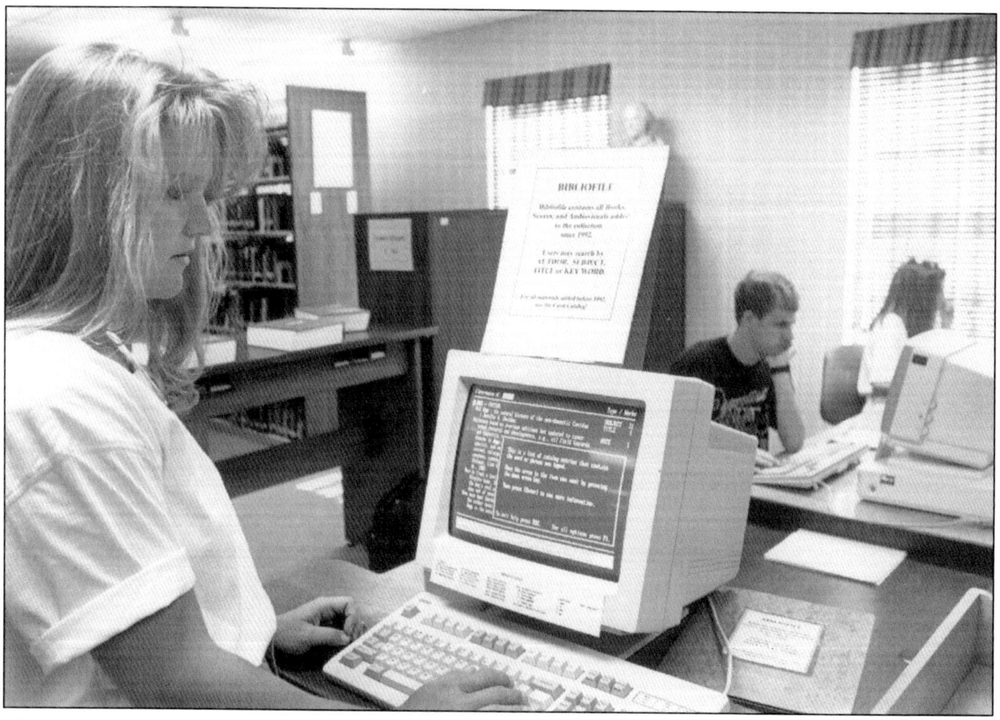

The card catalogue was replaced by an electronic catalog system in 1994. Student Anissa Jones uses the new interface to do research.

Frances Mims, an English professor, helps a student register for classes before computers transformed the process. Today students register and transact most business with the university online. Dr. Mims taught at Anderson from 1956 to 1967 and again from 1974 to 1992.

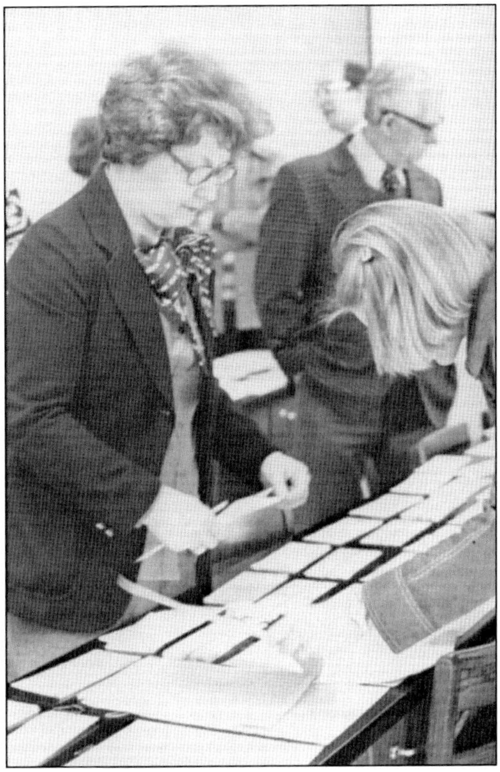

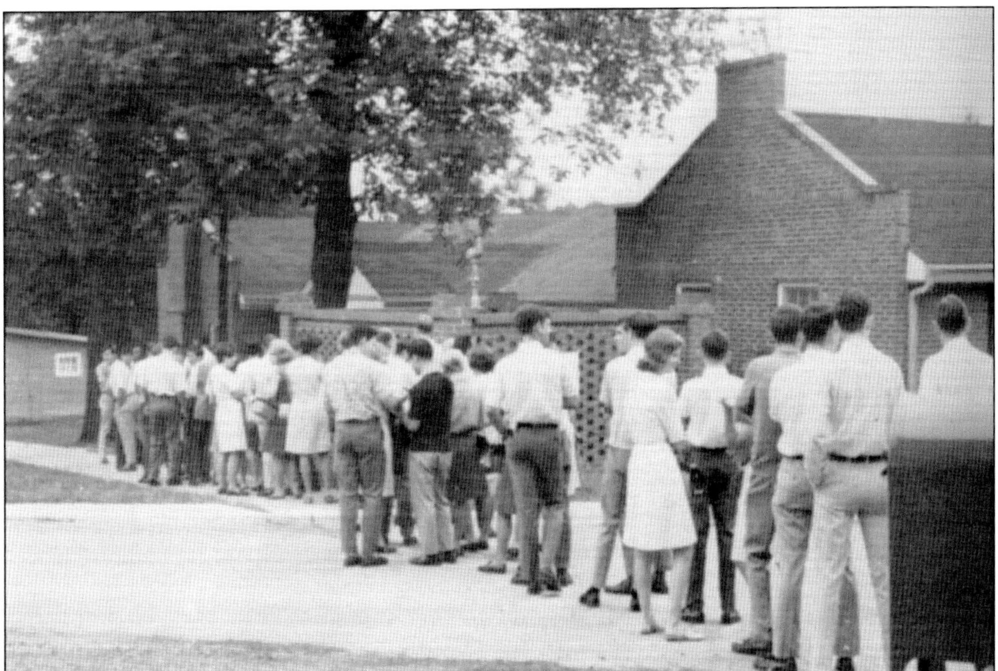

For many years, one of the rituals for the beginning of classes was standing in long lines to get schedules changed and to buy textbooks and supplies. This line in the photograph formed for the Registrar's Office in 1968.

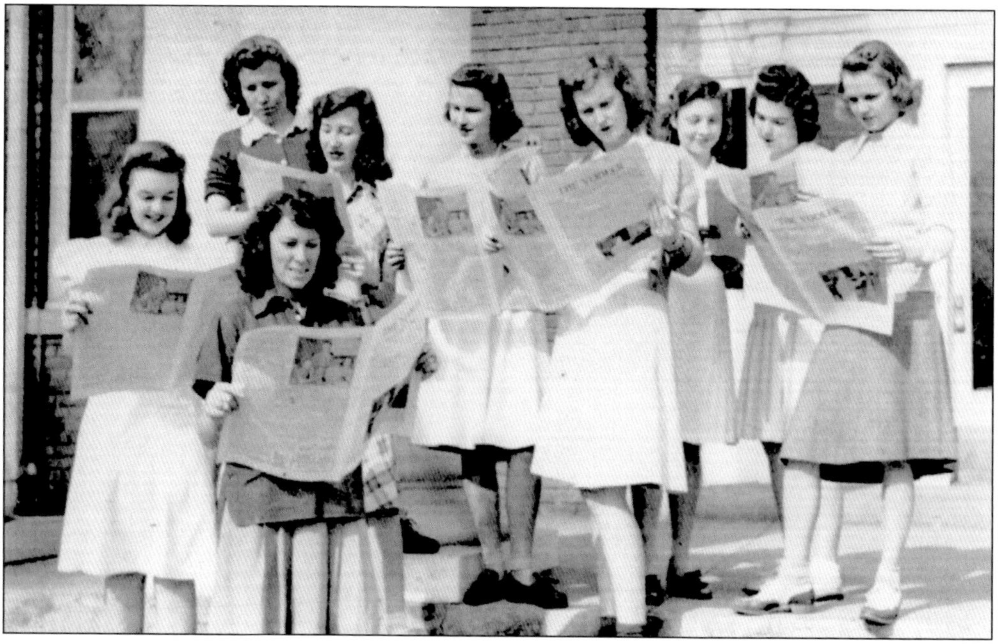

Journalism has been an important part of the Anderson University curriculum experience from the very beginning. Students in 1943 enjoy the freshly printed copies of the *Yodler*. In January 1974, the newspaper changed its name to *AC Echoes*. A weekly newsletter that was printed on yellow paper disseminated campus news, and by the end of the century, an online feature called *411* replaced the yellow newsletter.

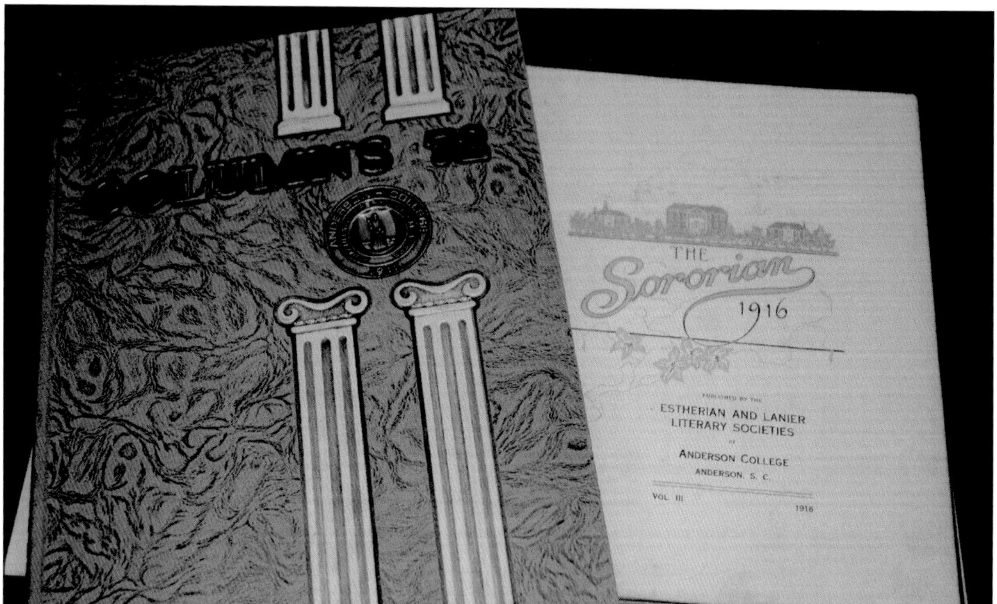

Another important campus publication for many years was the yearbook. The first yearbook, called the *Sororian*, was published from 1914 to 1930; no yearbook was published during the difficult days of the Depression. The tradition was revived in 1942, and the title changed to the *Columns*. The last yearbook was published in 1996. A centennial yearbook is being published in 2011.

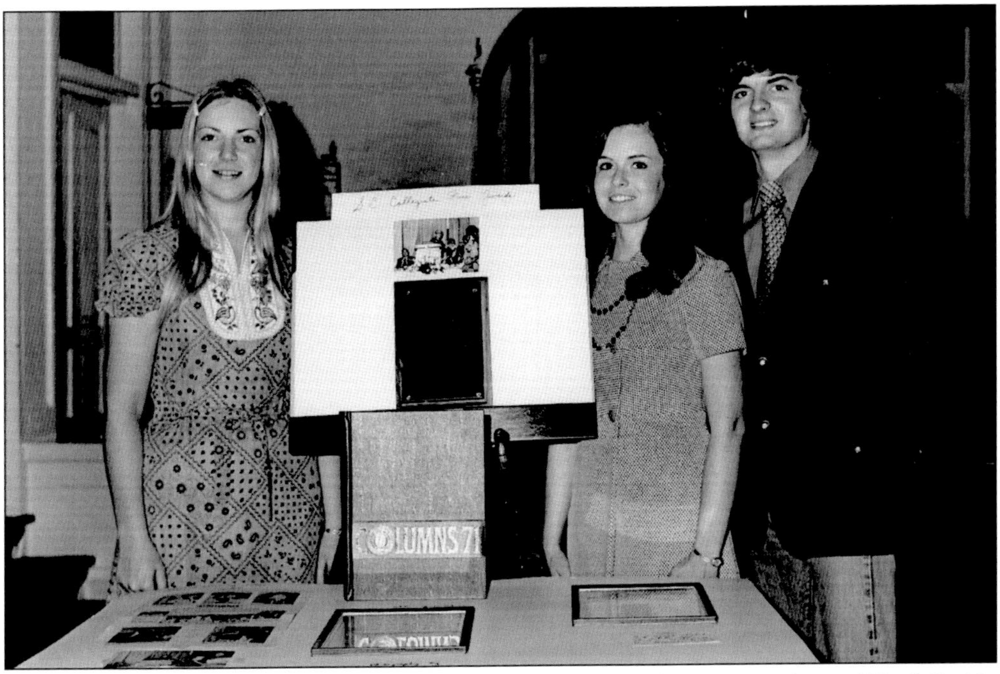

Those pictured are, from left to right, editor Julie Osborne, Shirley Ann Hamby, and Hugh Smith. They are celebrating the "SC Collegiate Press Award" for the 1971 edition of the *Columns*.

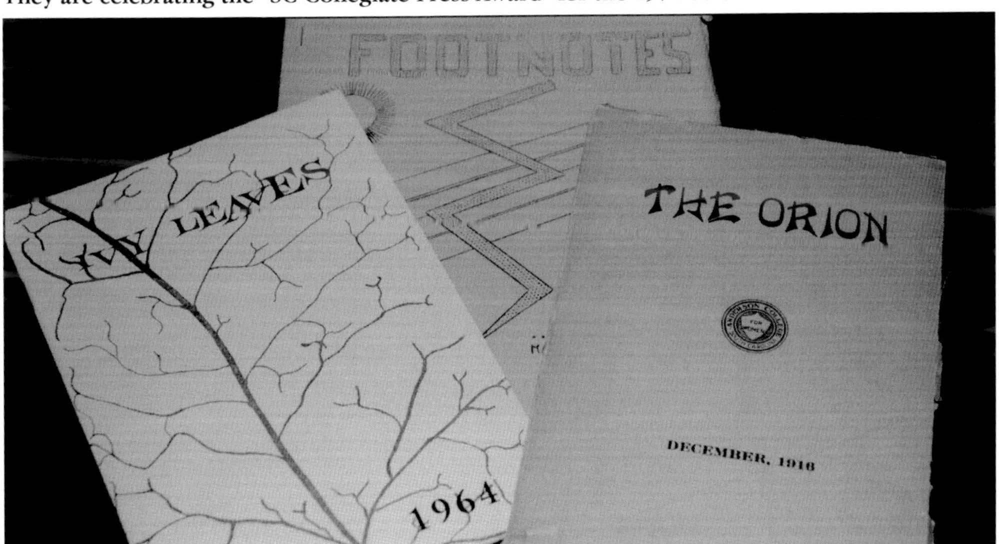

The first literary magazine, the *Orion*, was printed in October 1916. It selected works that were submitted by the Lanier and the Estherian Literary Societies, which provided the editor and staff of the *Orion*. In addition to literary pieces such as poetry, short stories, and criticism, the publication also included news, activities, exchanges, and alumnae notes. It was published five times a year and financed by local advertisements. Another brief publication in 1950 was called *Footnotes*, which also followed a literary format. The *Yodler* replaced the *Orion* in 1925 and began publication on January 15, 1926. Student literary accomplishments were included as a supplement in the May edition of the *Yodler* in the 1960s. A separate publication, called *Ivy Leaves*, began in May 1964 and continues to showcase student achievement in both the literary and visual arts.

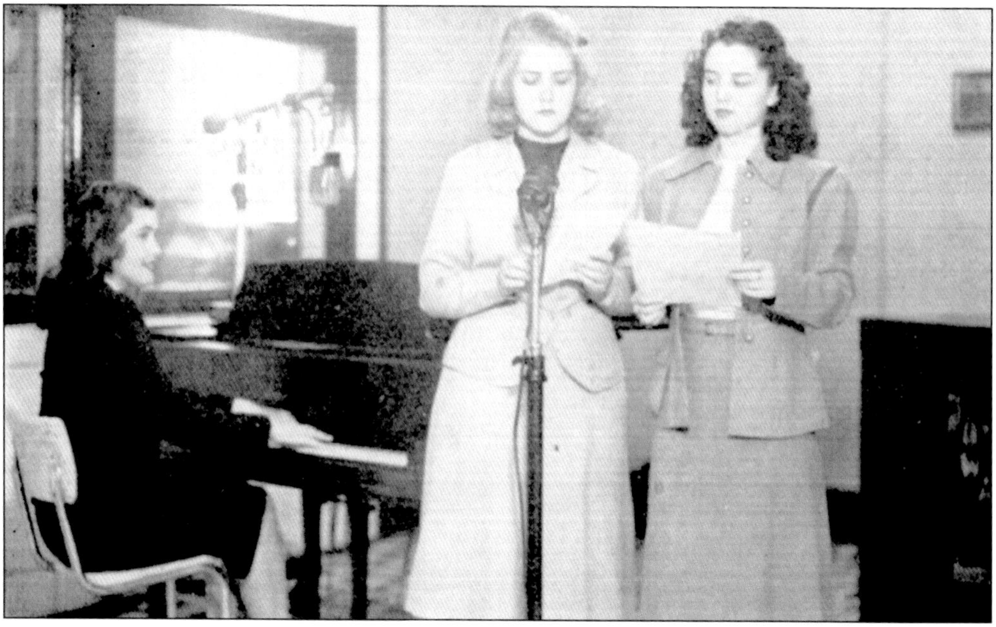

In the 1940s, one of the forward-thinking technological opportunities available to students was the study of and participation in radio programs that were broadcast from campus. Anderson's first radio station, WAIM, was founded by Wilton E. Hall and began broadcasting in 1935 in space leased on the second floor of Whyte Building, now Vandiver Hall, for $12.50 a month, including steam heat when available. WANS-FM in the 1960s aired programs in which journalism students participated. Later the facilities included a television station, which was also located on the campus until the 1970s. The transmission tower remains as part of the local landscape to this day.

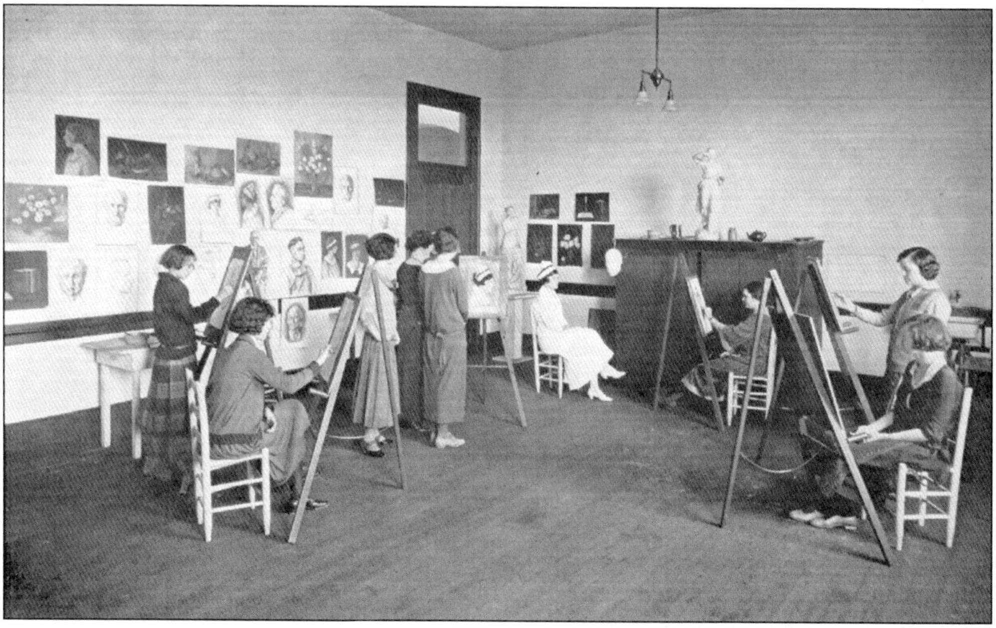

Art was one of the earliest subjects of study at Anderson University. As seen here in the 1927 *Viewbook*, one classroom on the top floor of the Administration Building was devoted to the study of drawing, painting, and sculpting.

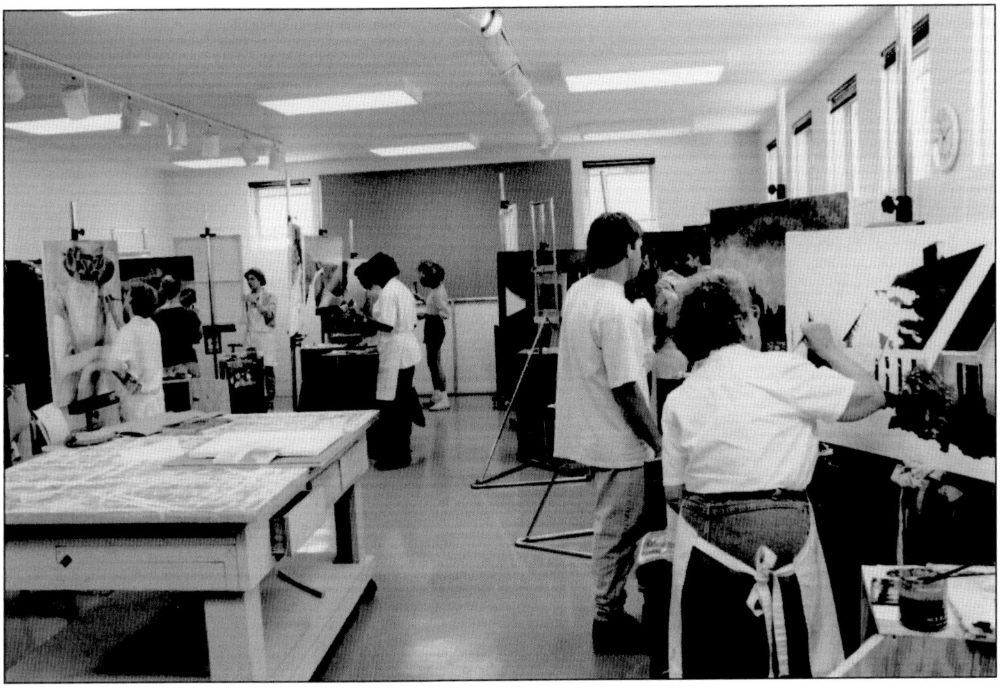

The arts continue a century later in a much expanded facility of the Rainey Fine Arts Center and with more faculty. Here a painting class works in the art studio.

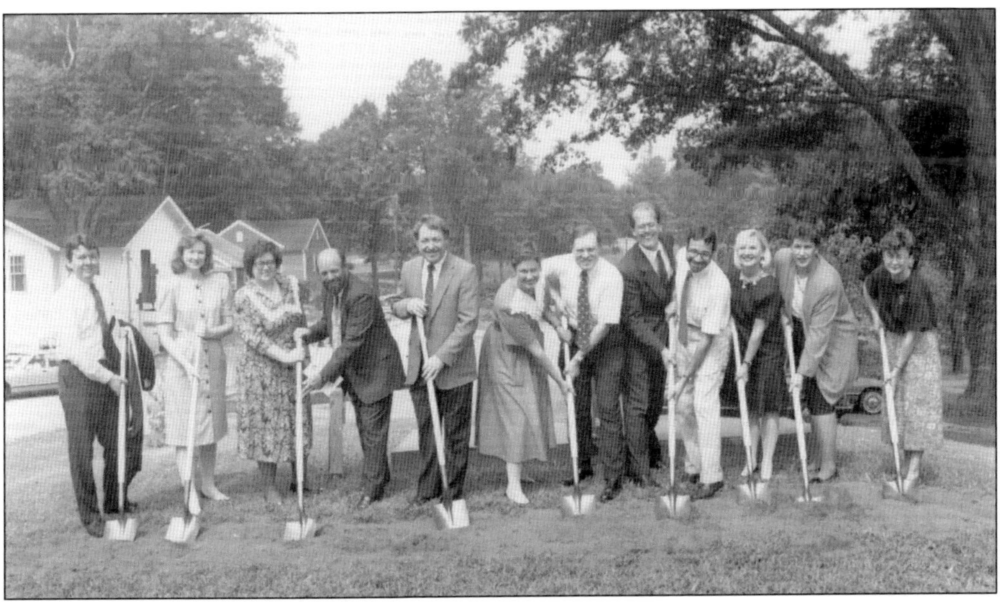

The ground-breaking ceremony for the Fine Arts Center included many members of the arts faculty. They include, from left to right, music instructors Lyman Golden, Susan Blair Green, Janet Roberts, Bob Heritage, and James Clark; art instructor Susan Wooten; music instructor Perry Carroll; department head and later dean Dave Larson; art instructor Peter Kaniaris; Anne Martin, interior design; Denise Stevenson-Oxford, theater and speech; and art instructor Jo-Carol Mitchell-Rogers.

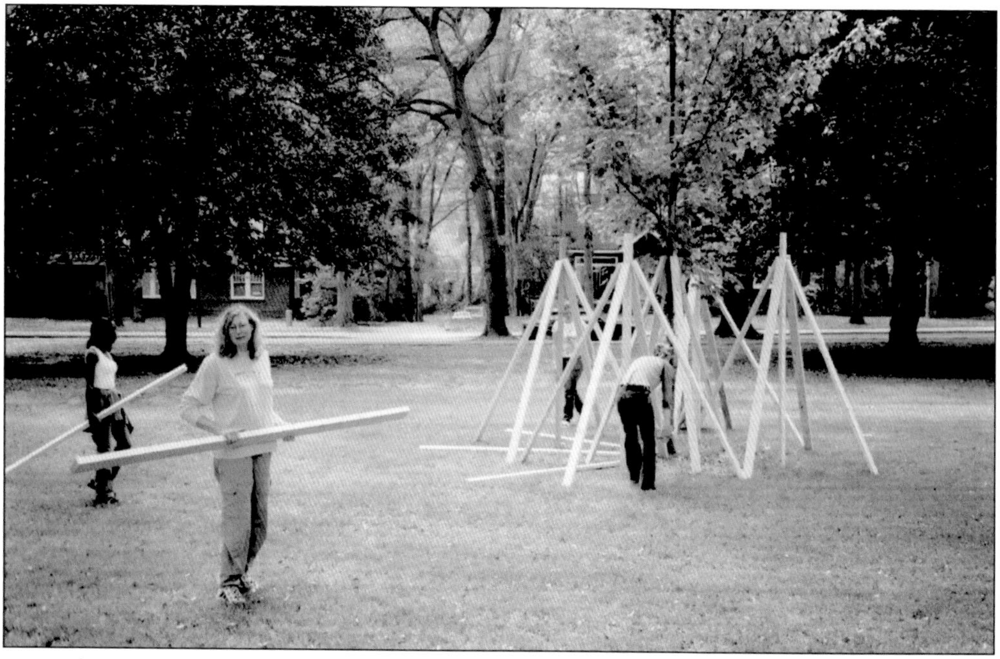

Rites of spring in the art department included "flowers" that were created by students, which were placed throughout the campus for several days.

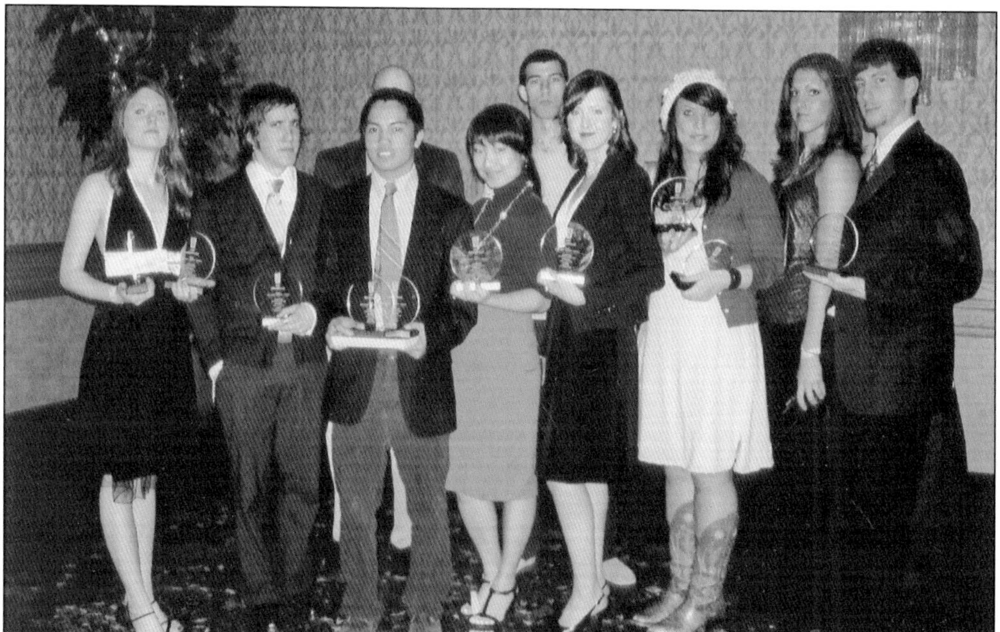

The arts program at Anderson University has been garnering increasingly prestigious awards. In 2008, graphic design students won 16 out of 26 ADDY awards and were recognized again for outstanding achievement in 2009 and 2010 at local, regional, and national levels of competition. Pictured here are, from left to right, left to right, Amber Isbell, Josh Rigsby, Luan Jenkins, Kim Bolton, Maggie Irwin, Christina Heaston, Kelley Shaw, and Brandon Chandler; in the back center is Wellington Payne. (Courtesy of Jo-Carol Mitchell-Rogers.)

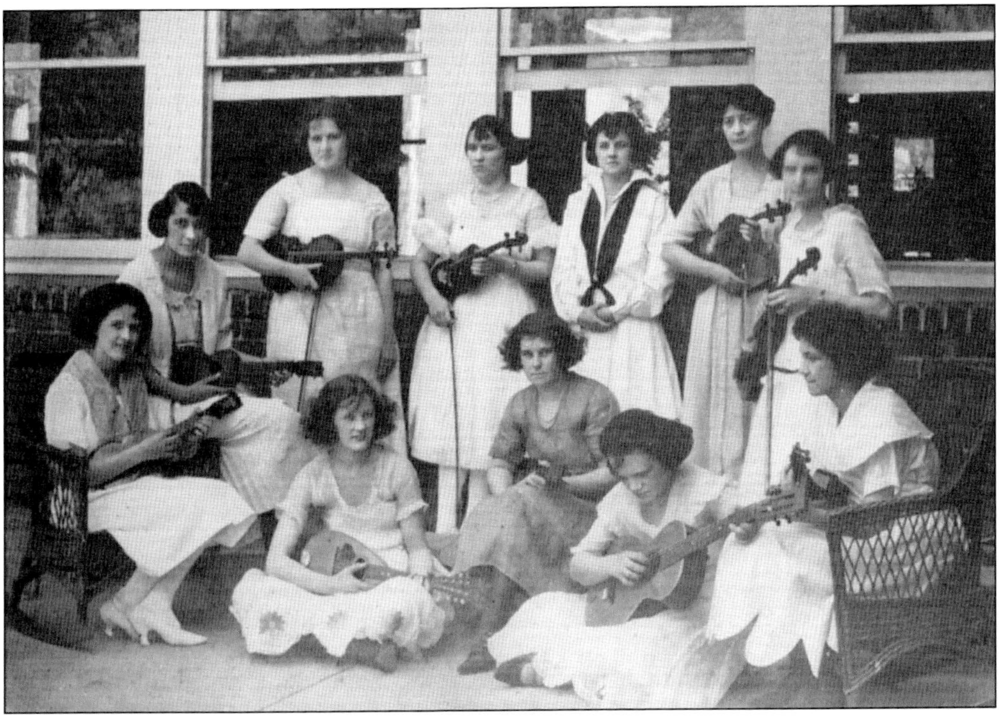

Music has been another important area of study for students throughout the history of Anderson University. This orchestra is featured in the *Bulletin*, published around 1920.

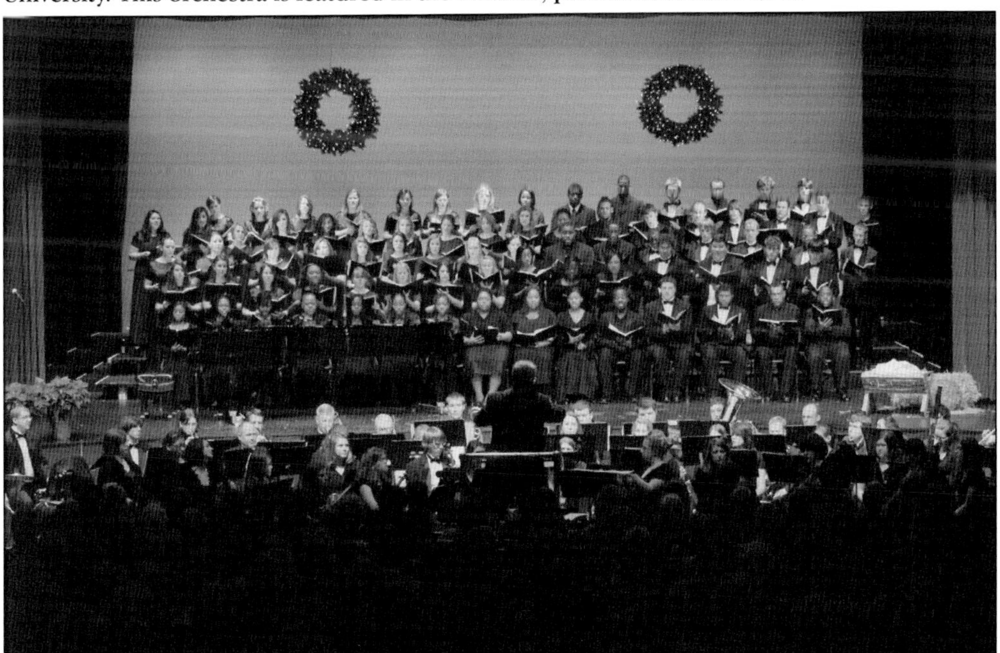

Ensemble singing and performance has also been an enduring part of the curriculum. This photograph showcases the combined vocal and instrumental talents of the music program at Christmas First Night, December 3, 2009, conducted by Dr. Richard Williamson.

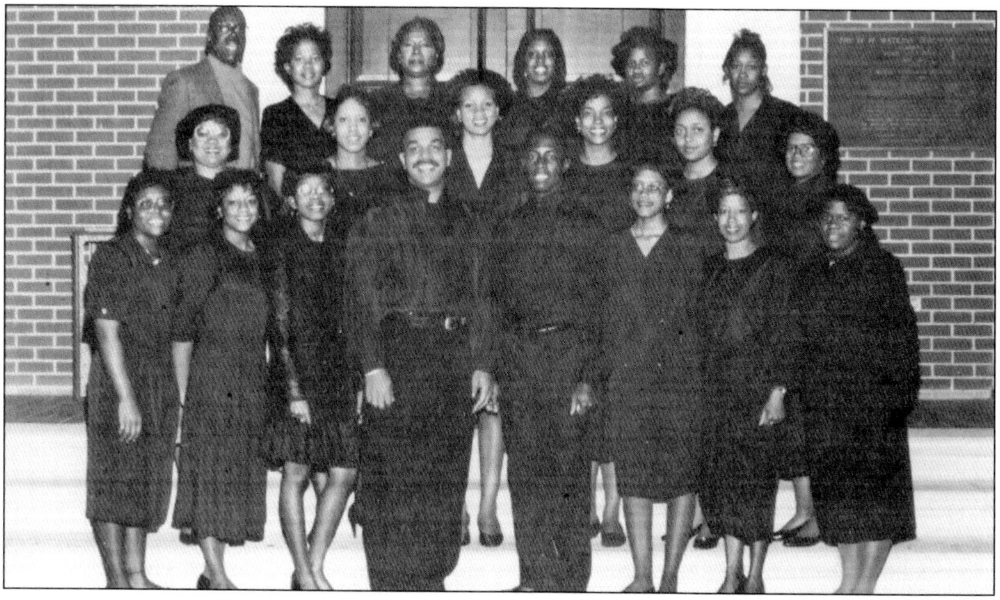

The AC Ensemble began in 1984 as the Inspirational Choir. Pictured here in 1992 are, from left to right, (first row) Denise Carter, Nicole Cohen, Trina Brown, Clark Nesbit, Carlton Willis, Catina Posley, Malinda Ward, and Shalisa Lee; (second row) Gerlinda Witcher, Angela Walker, Robin Salley, Carla Waddell, Shenea Perry, and Kathy Borders; (third row) director Leonard Johnson, Deborah Pickins, Jean Thomas, Kim Stewart, Zolanda Arter, and Shereeta Lee. Today the group continues under the name AU Ensemble.

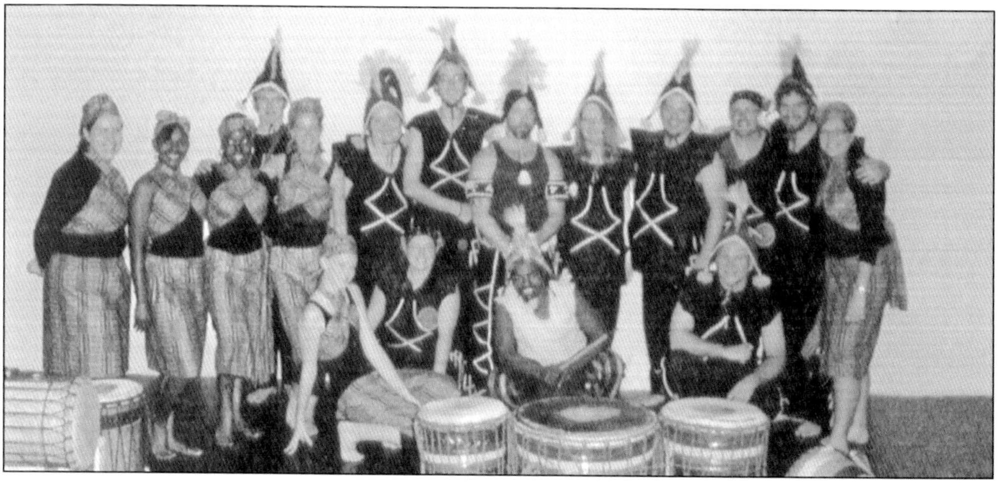

An interest in world musical traditions led to the creation of the AU West African Ensemble by music professor Dr. David L. Perry in 2007 with Darren "Bibi" Gilley as guest artistic director and guest artists from Conakry, Guinea. The Anderson University West African Ensemble is a student organization dedicated to performing music and dance practices of the Malinke and other West African cultures and has performed for over 16,000 people at concerts, festivals, schools, conferences, and community venues. The performers for the November 22, 2008, concert were, from left to right, (first row) Laura Fontana, Deanne Terry, Amara Camara (guest artist), and Dr. David L. Perry (director); (second row) Kristin Blackwell, Jasmekas Daniels, Hope Campbell, Payden Nichols, Kate Faires, Laura Arrasmith, Sean Kerr, Darren "Bibi" Gilley (guest artistic director), Andi Swarner, Andy Daniels, Ryan Whetstine, John Miller, and Gleynnda Craig.

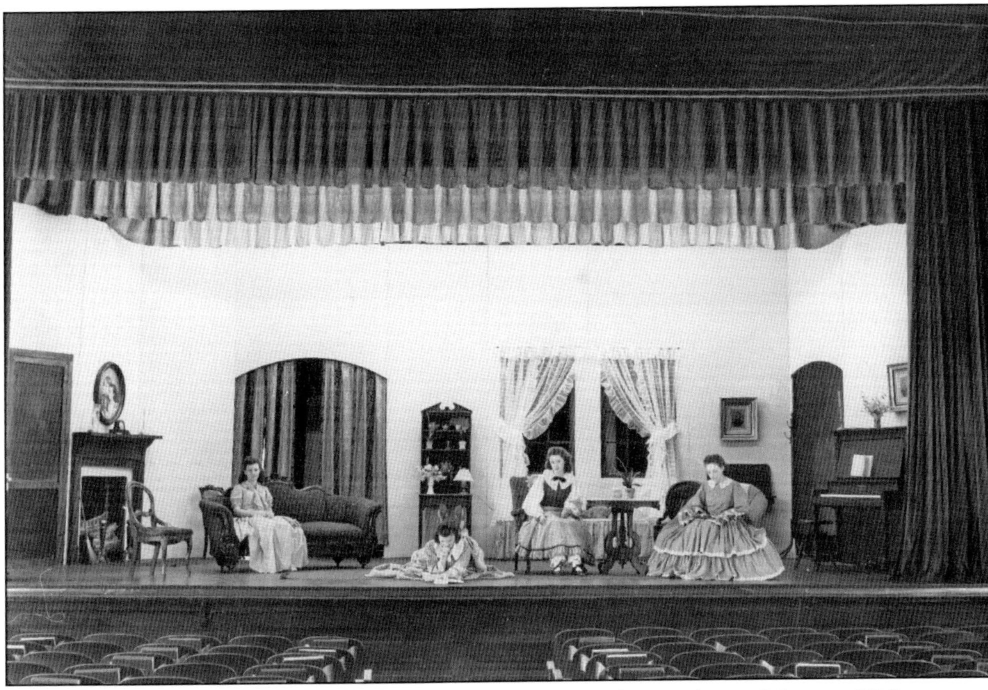

Another enduring feature of the Anderson experience has been a love of theater. With so many fine productions to choose from, it is fitting to select *Little Women*. It was performed in 1942 as a stage play and again in 2008 as a lavish musical, which was under the direction of Dr. Deborah McEniry. The part of Marmee, the mother, was played by the wife of the president, Diane Whitaker (center). The students playing the four sisters are, from left to right, Meghan Mathis, Maggie Hill, Phyllis Goins, and Anna Franklin.

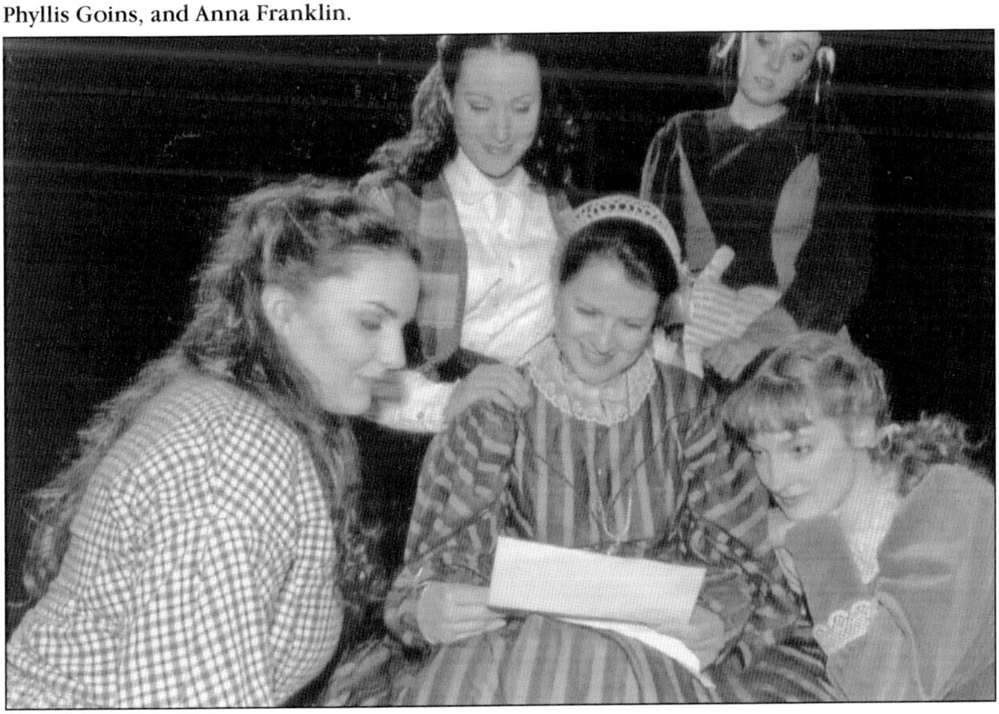

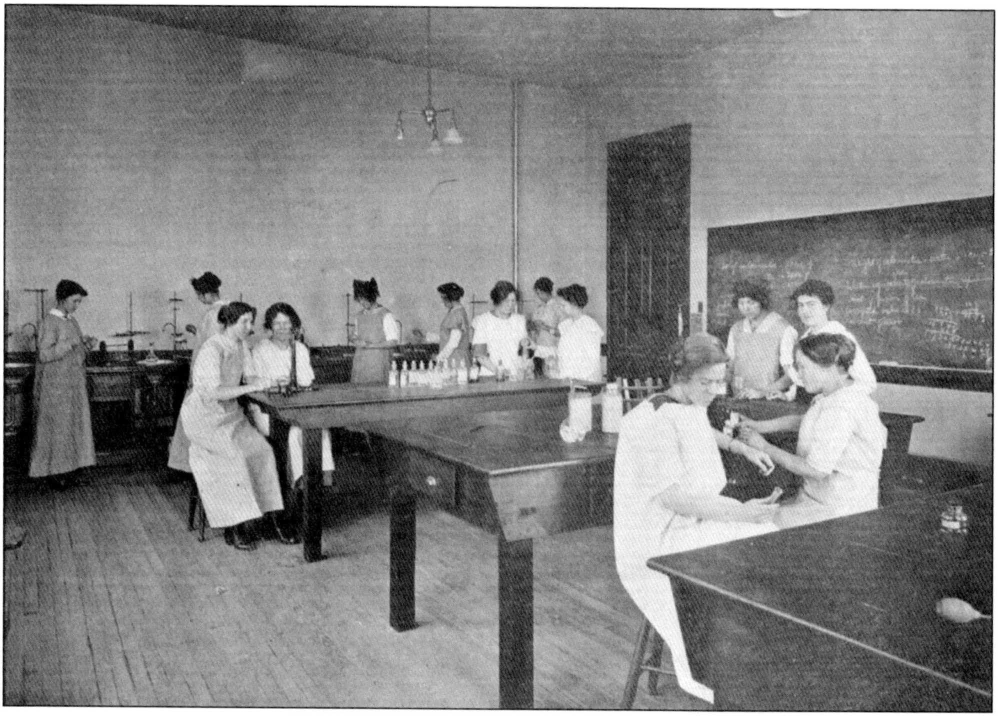

The chemistry laboratory in 1914 shows the well-rounded education expected of an Anderson College graduate.

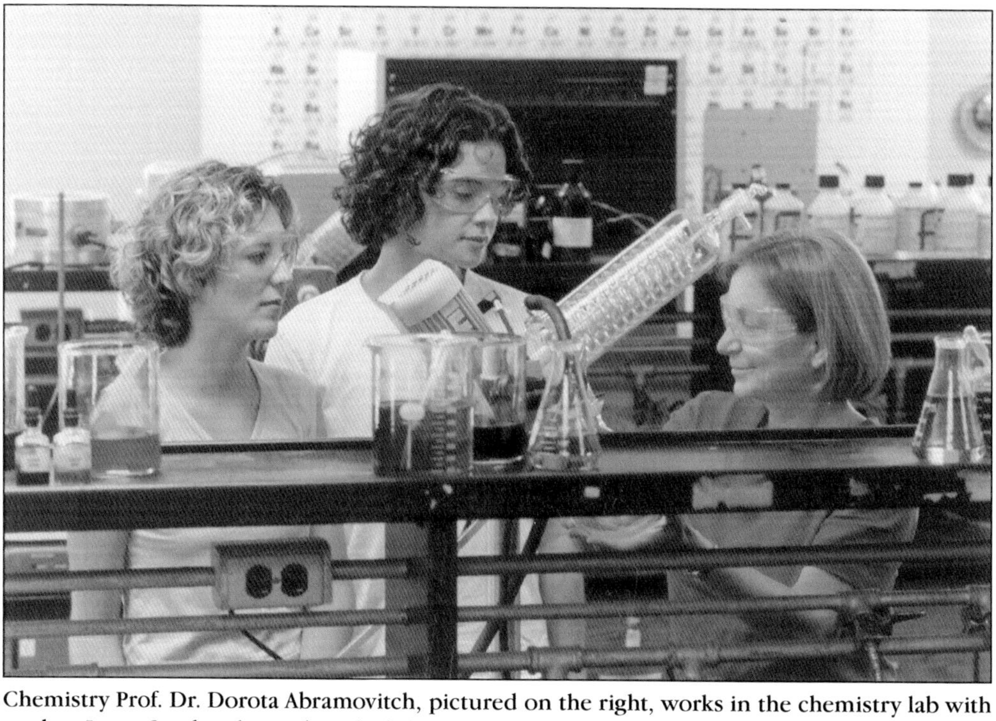

Chemistry Prof. Dr. Dorota Abramovitch, pictured on the right, works in the chemistry lab with student Jenny Stoeber, located on the left. Dr. Abramovitch has won the Michael Boles Excellence in Teaching Award and garnered numerous grants for student research.

Laboratory learning opportunities continued to develop. Here is a biology lab class from 1963.

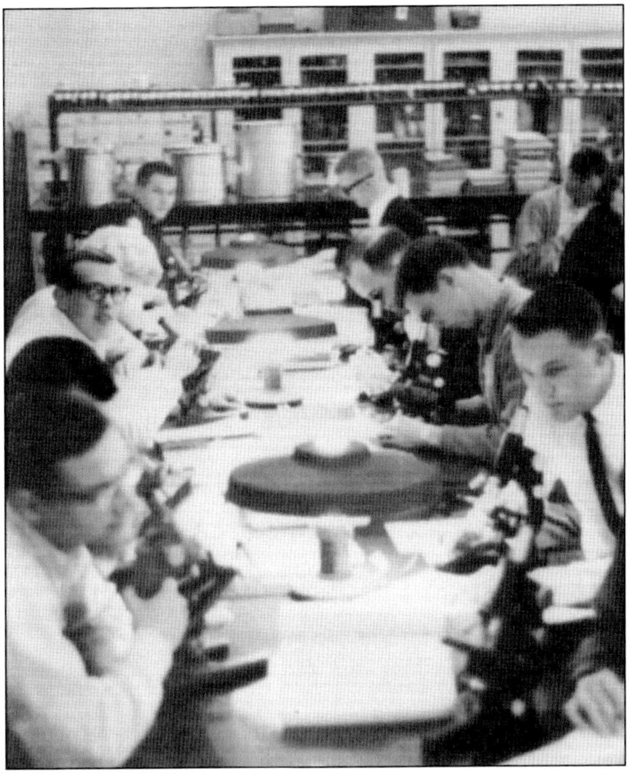

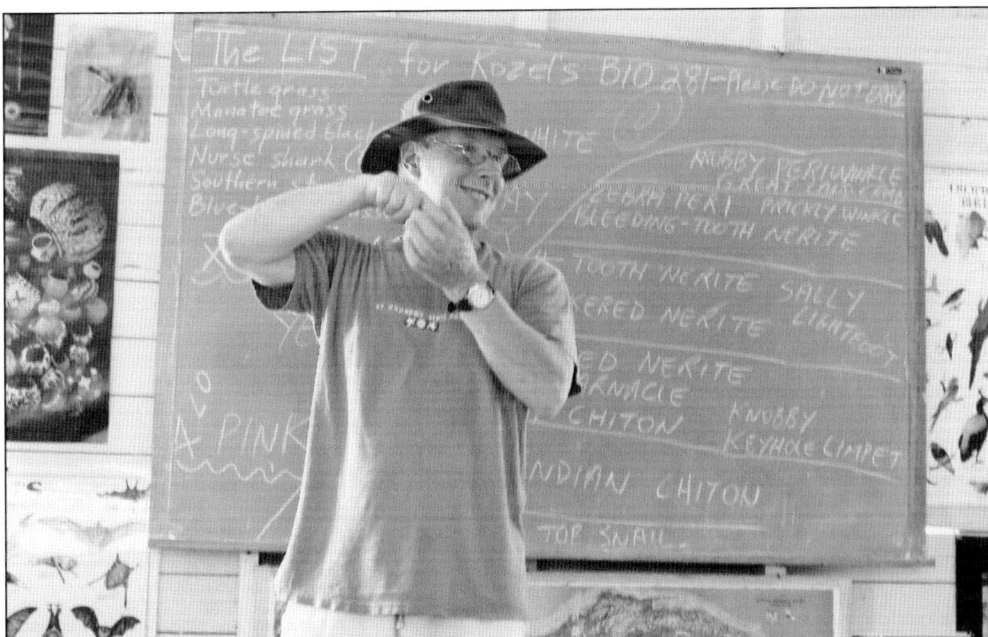

Biological study is no longer confined to the classroom laboratory. Classes travel to nearby Cox Creek, the Amazon, and the Galapagos Islands in order to do research. Here Dr. Tom Kozel conducts a biology class at the Institute for Tropical Ecology and Conservation field station at Boca del Drago, Isla Colon, Panama.

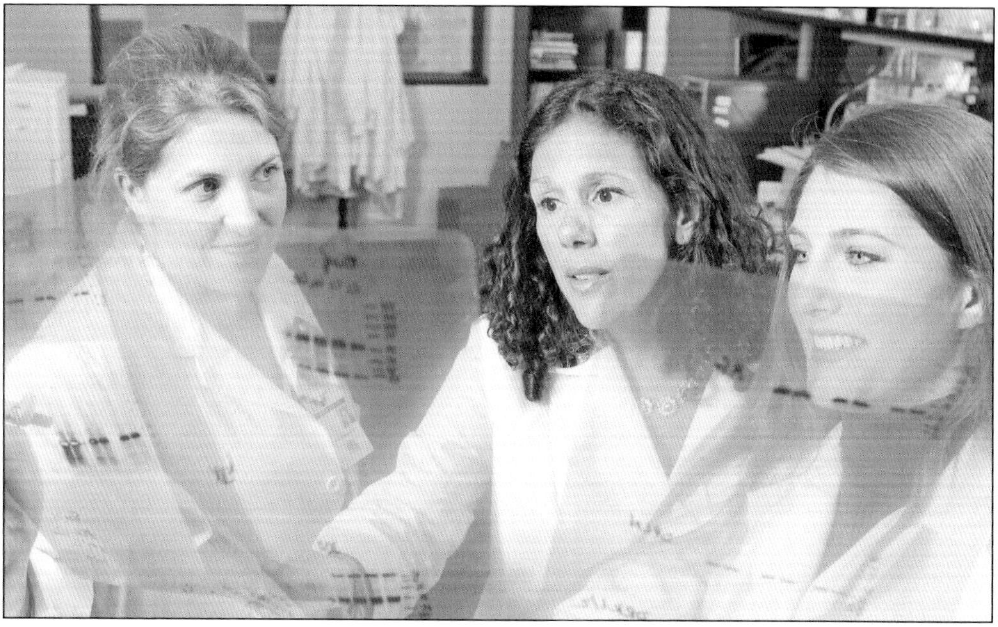

Biology professor and cancer survivor Dr. Diana Ivankovic is at the center of this photograph, flanked by student Victoria Herold on the right and biology adjunct professor Dr. Allison Springs on the left. Dr. Ivankovic, the Dr. James Henderson Director of Anderson University's Undergraduate Cancer Research Center, states that "[T]he Center's mission will be accomplished through the preparation of students who will join new generations of physicians, researchers and health educators dedicating their lives to seeking the causes and the cures of cancer, and to educating the public in regard to cancer awareness, diagnosis, treatment, and living the life of a cancer survivor." Dr. Ivankovic has won numerous awards for her teaching and research, including the prestigious Michael Boles Excellence in Teaching Award in May 2010.

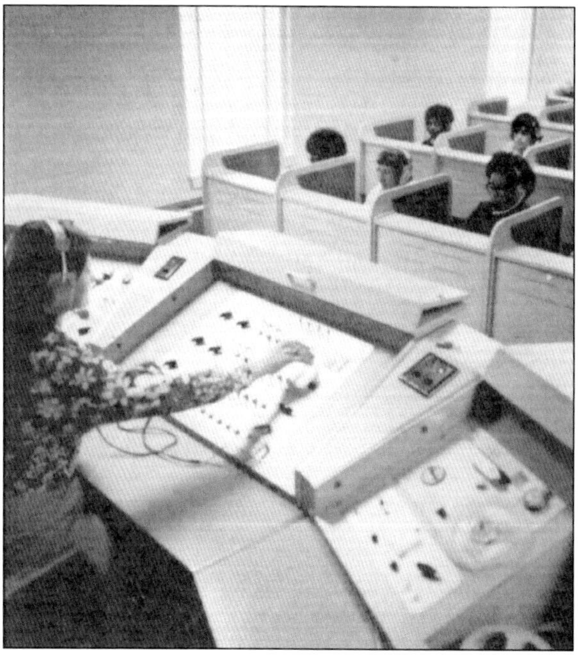

A technological innovation when the Watkins Teaching Center was built, the Language Lab once was a specialized location with headsets in Watkins 002. This aspect of language instruction is now done online.

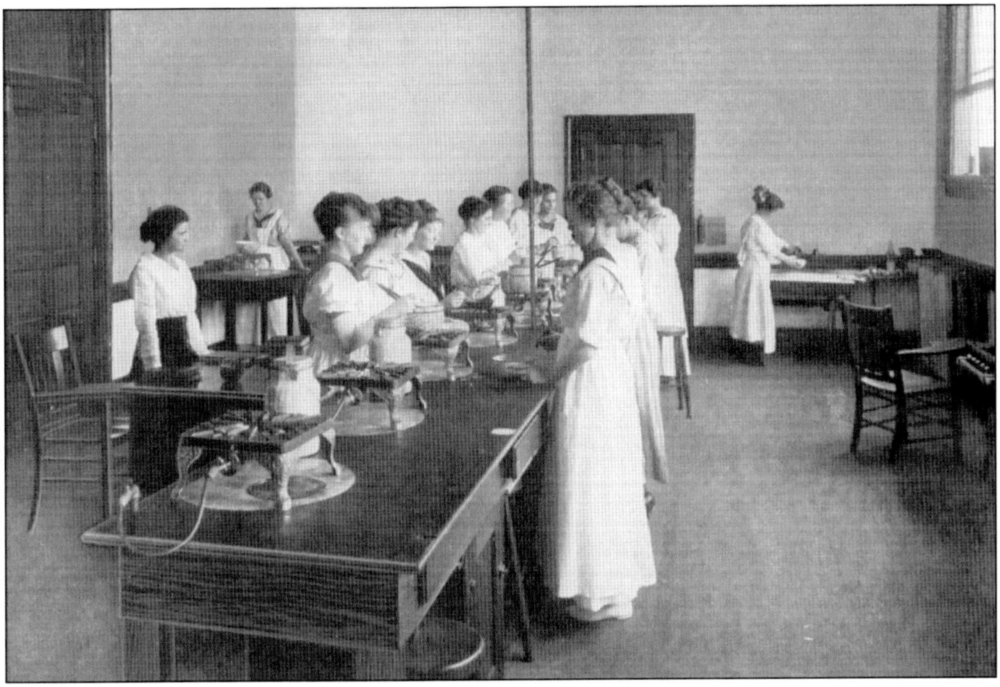

Among the courses of study available to the young women of Anderson College in the early years were the domestic arts, which included sewing and cooking. One such class from 1916 is featured in the *Bulletin* of that year.

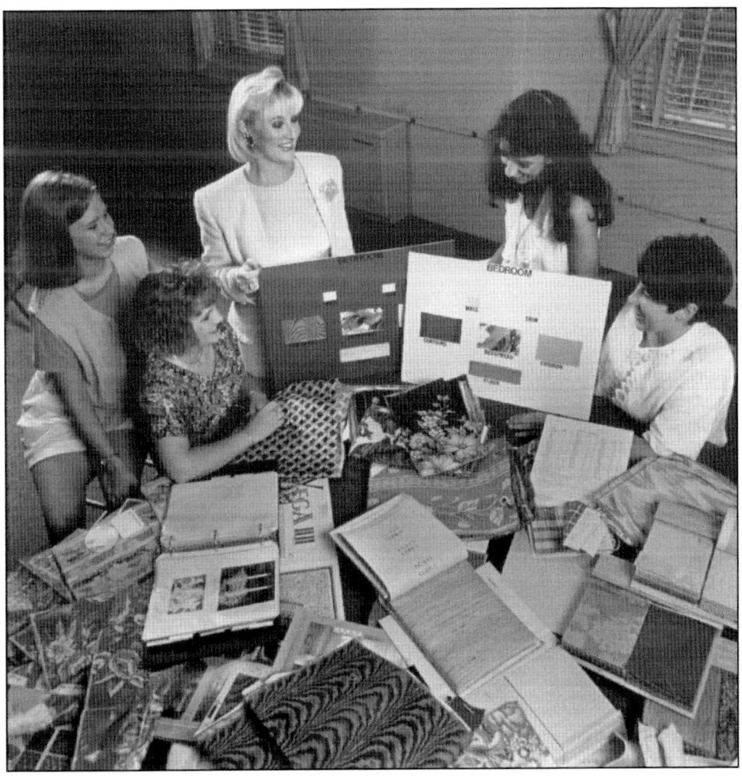

What started out as the domestic science program has changed with the times to become the College of Interior Design. Professor and Associate Dean Anne Martin, daughter of longtime professor Mary E. Martin, is seen here with several students. Students in the program have garnered national recognition.

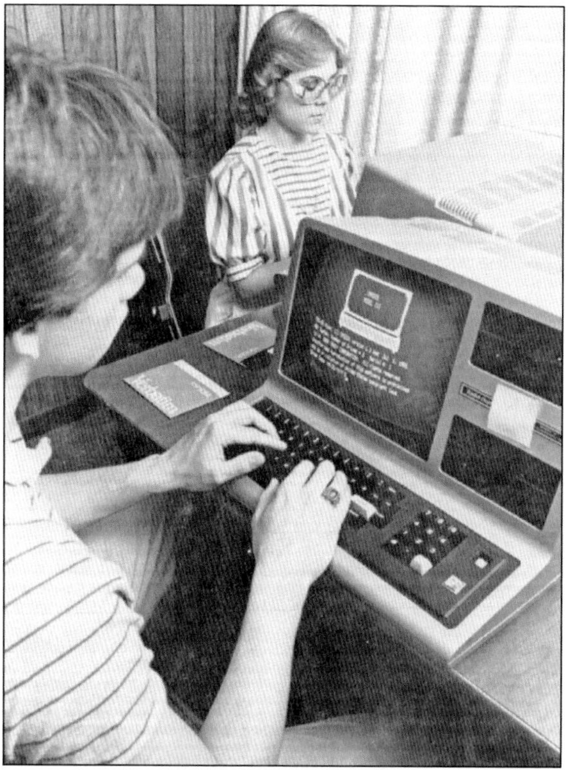

By the 1980s, the campus was being transformed by the arrival of the computer and the Internet. They became increasingly integral to all aspects of campus operations. To be sure all students had access to the new technology, computer labs were opened, the first of which was on the main floor of the Watkins Teaching Center.

Wanda Staggers, assistant professor of computer science from 1984 to 1994, was the first African American professor at Anderson. She introduced many students to computers on campus.

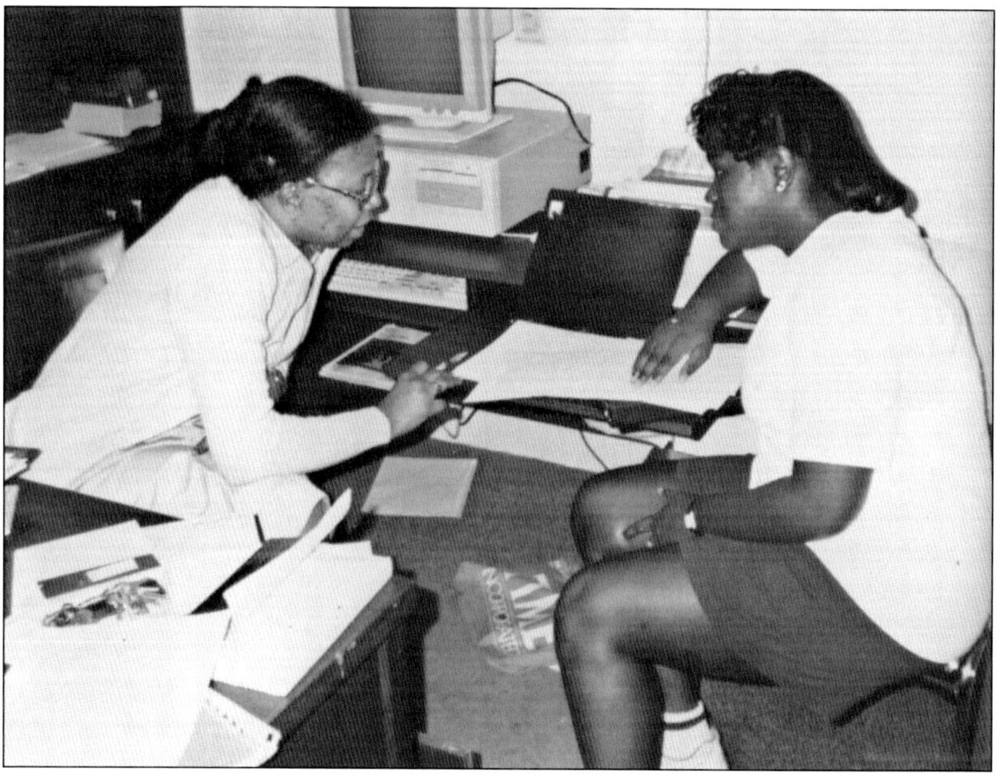

Mathematics was also a part of the well-rounded education for Anderson students from the beginning. A professor who did much to take away the fear of the dreaded math course, Glen Hughey (1964–1997) was honored by the first named award given at the Honors Day convocation in the spring. This award goes to the freshman who improved the most in his or her introductory mathematics class.

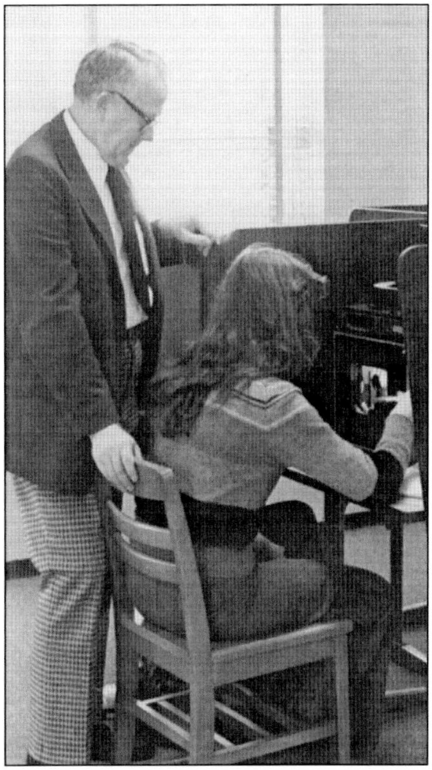

Good relationships between students and the administration have long been the hallmark of Anderson education, which is exhibited in this photograph that was published in the May 16, 1952, *Yodler*. Pres. Annie Dove Denmark is listening to the plans for the coming school year being presented by Vera Lee Mullikin, representative of Student Government Association, and Betty Allison, president of the freshman class and the Baptist Student Union. The conversation is taking place in Dr. Denmark's apartment in the residence hall that now bears her name.

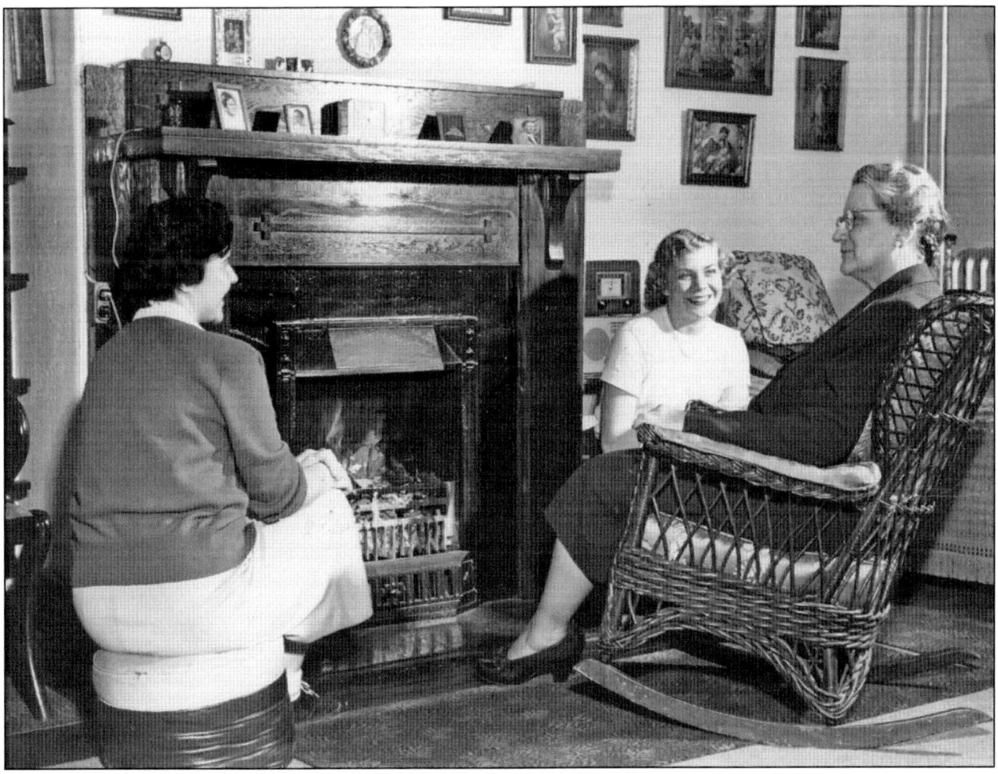

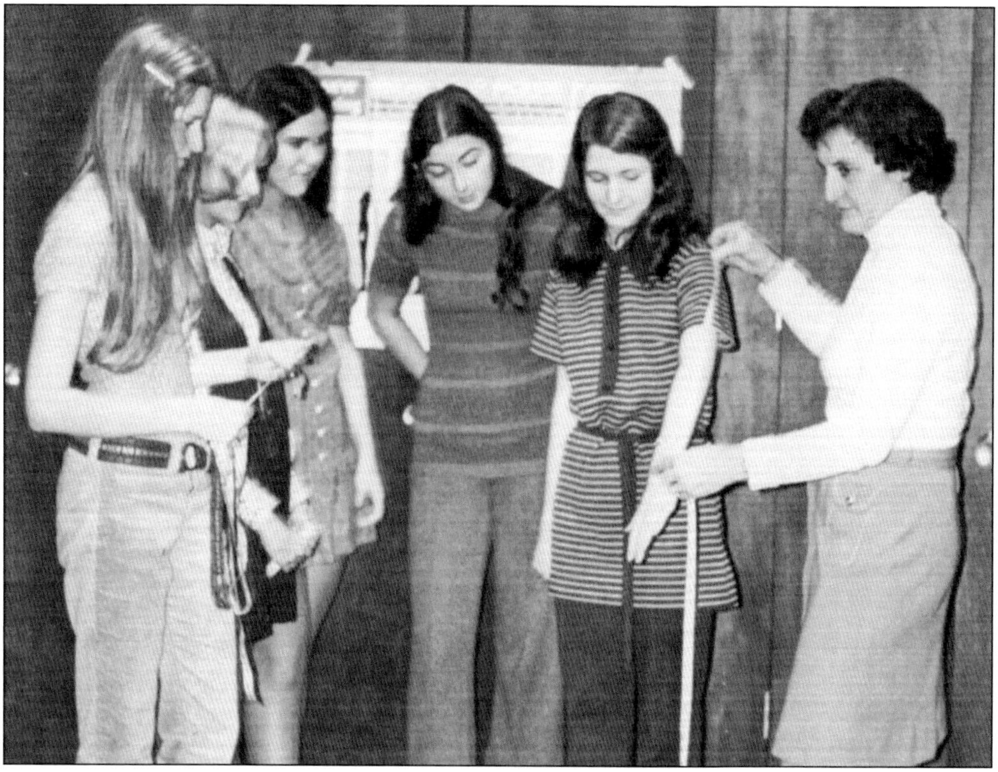

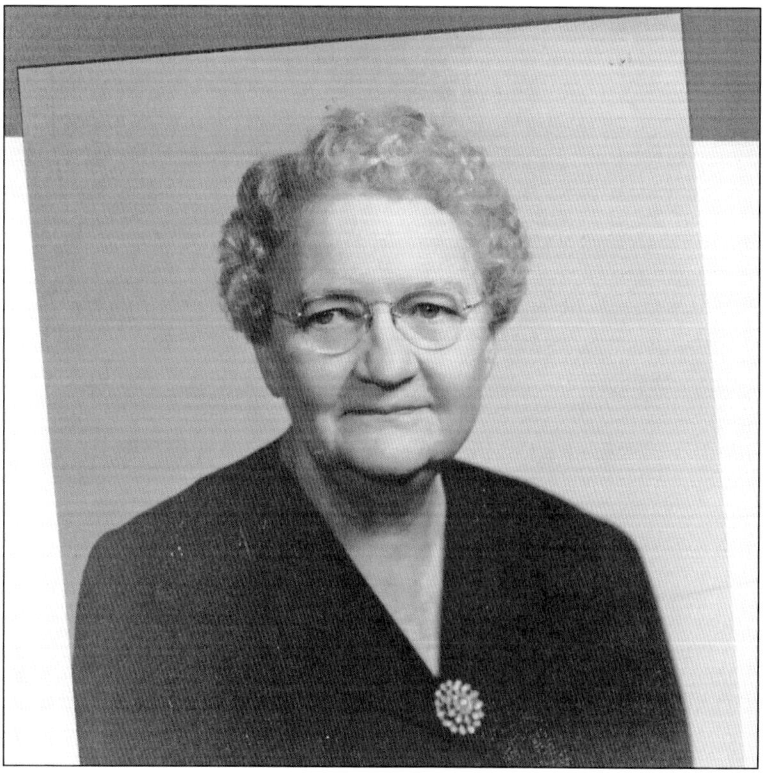

Legions of students fondly remember Lula McClure (1948–1949, 1951–1962), pictured on the left, for her interactive literature classes and Mary Martin, pictured above, for her helpful classes in home economics, political science, fashion and retail merchandising, and the hospitality industry. Martin's career at Anderson spanned 40 years, from 1958 to 1998.

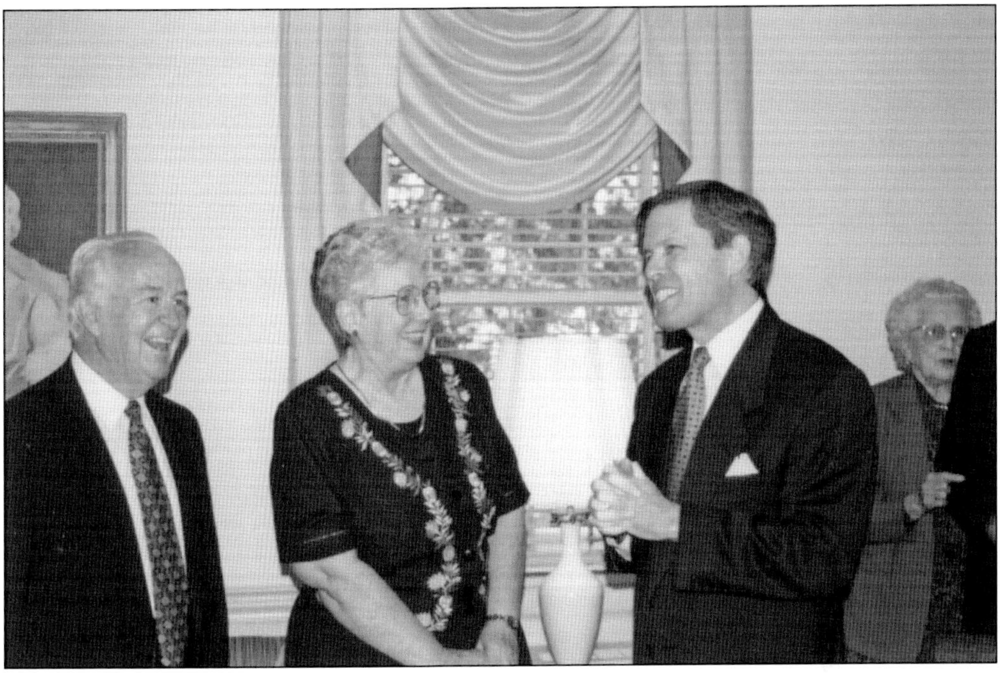

The married couple Dr. Nelson Eugene Mandrell (1964–1992) and Marion D. Mandrell (1965–1991) is a great example of the combination of dedication and service that is an important contribution to this university. They have taught for years at Anderson University in the field of psychology. Upon their retirement, a suite of offices and a classroom were renovated as the Mandrell Psychology Laboratory in the Watkins Teaching Center. Here they are photographed with Pres. Lee Royce in the Maude Watkins Parlor at the dedication reception. (Courtesy of Marion Mandrell.)

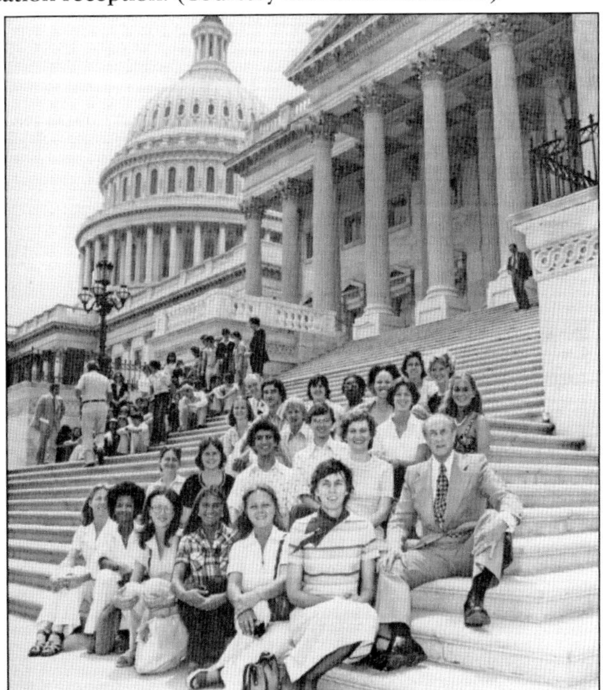

Sen. Strom Thurmond is pictured with an AC tour group led by professor of history and political science Pat Mulligan around 1978. The first academic study tours started in the 1970s. Initially, the tours were domestic.

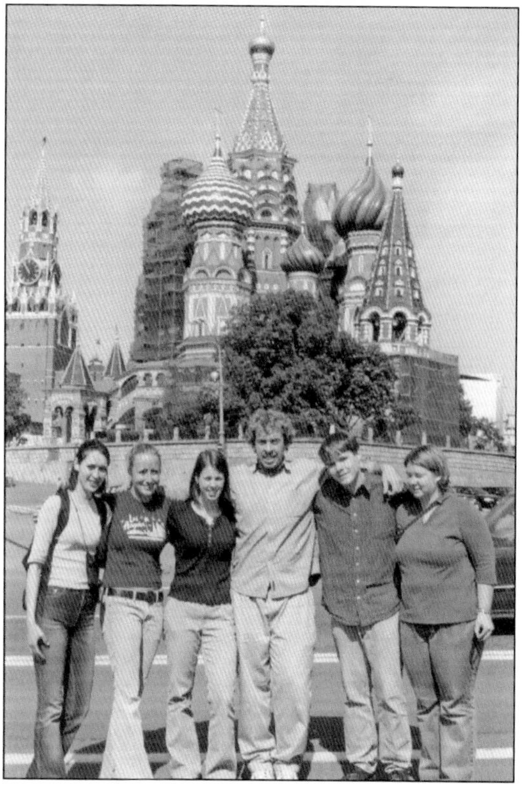

The Anderson University experience increasingly utilizes the globe as a classroom. One of the early opportunities to study in Russia after the fall of the communist government was enjoyed by this group. Standing in front of St. Basil's cathedral in Red Square in Moscow are, from left to right, the unidentified translator, Janie Whichert, Angie Boyd, Jeff Gilden, Brandon Smith, and Trish Tyndall, accompanied by business professor, Dr. Danny Rhodes, not pictured.

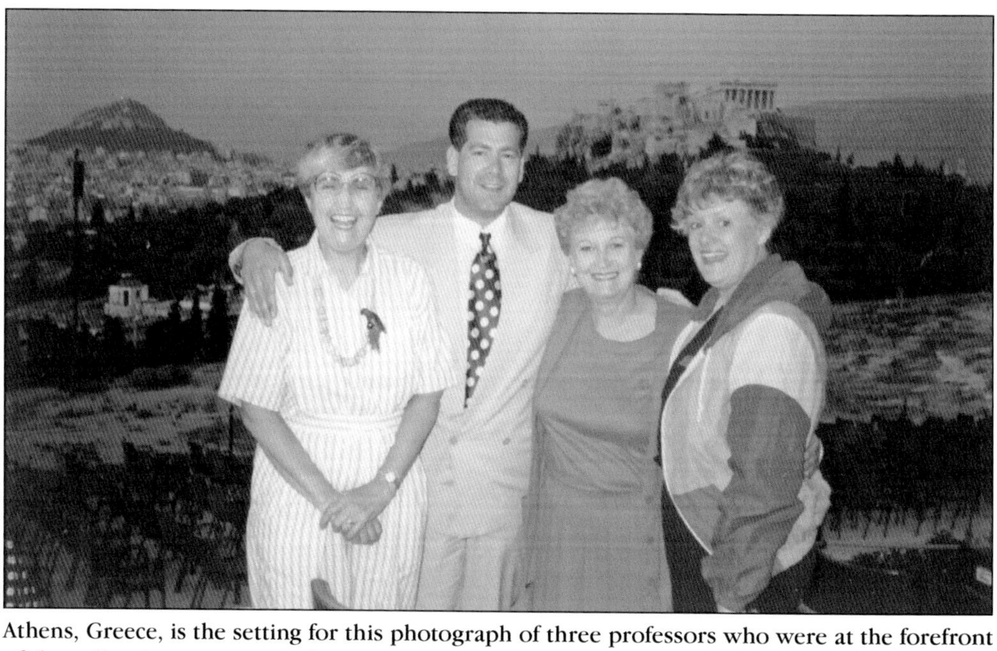

Athens, Greece, is the setting for this photograph of three professors who were at the forefront of the college's overseas travel programs, launching tour and study opportunities for students, alumni, and community members alike. Those pictured are, from left to right, Dr. Shirley Jacks, professor of foreign languages; the unidentified Greek host; Pat Mulligan, professor of history and political science; and Dr. Brena Walker, professor of English. (Courtesy of Brena Walker.)

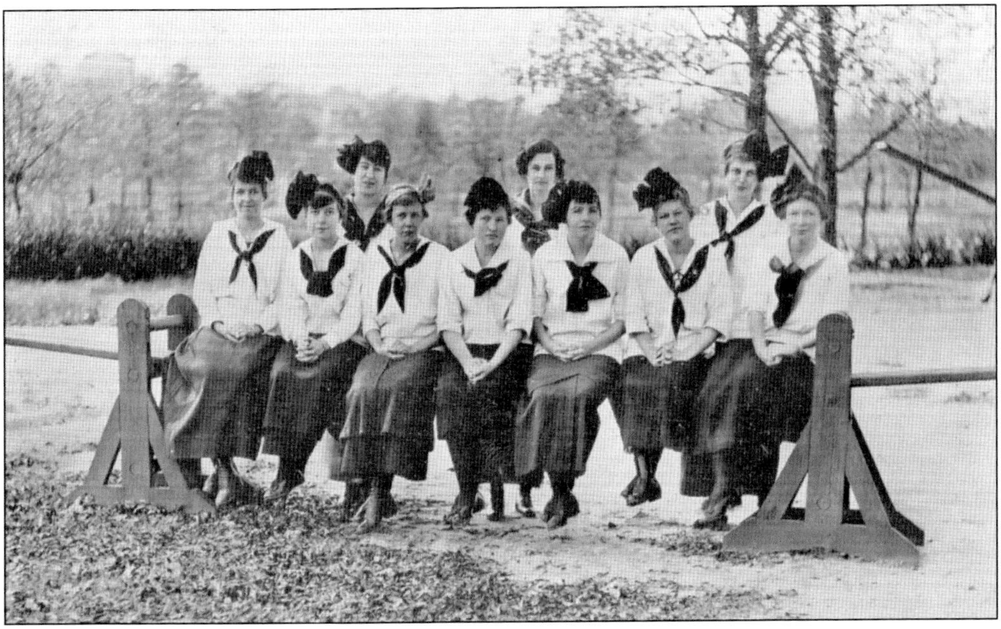

Over the century, transitions took place in the programs offered, as some disappeared and others were added. One program that is no longer available is shown in this 1915 photograph, which is of the members of the Preparatory Academy. They are seated on the joggling board on front campus. From its earliest years until 1956, Anderson College also had a Preparatory Academy on the campus to enable students to complete their high school credits.

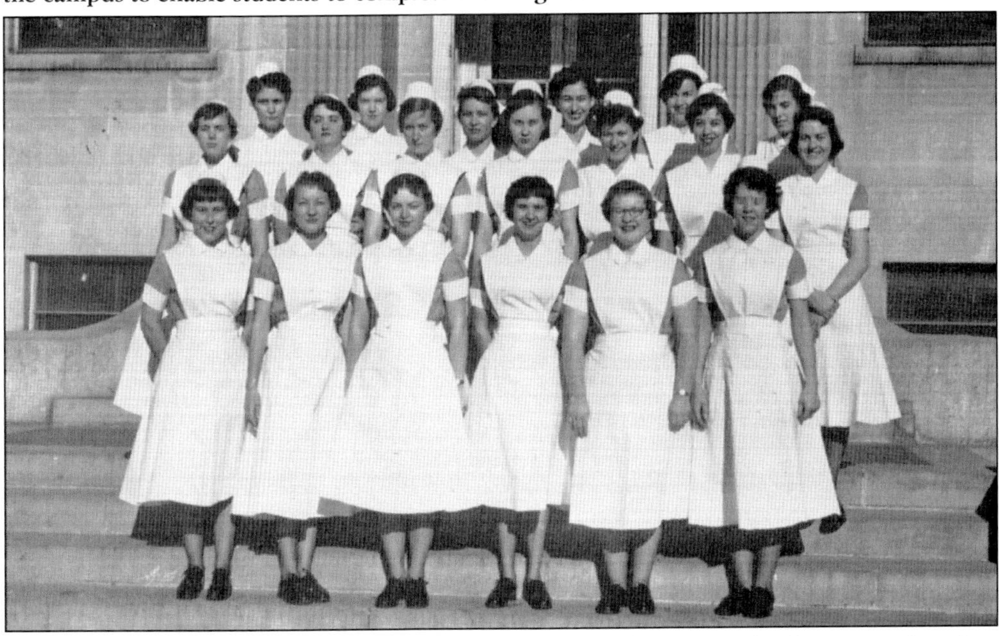

Another program that has disappeared is seen in this 1956 photograph of a group of student nurses who were part of the nursing program. The program partnered with Anderson Memorial Hospital from 1956 to 1959. The student nurses lived and took some classes on campus as well as participating in social functions such as the May Day Celebration. It has long been a dream to revive the nursing program.

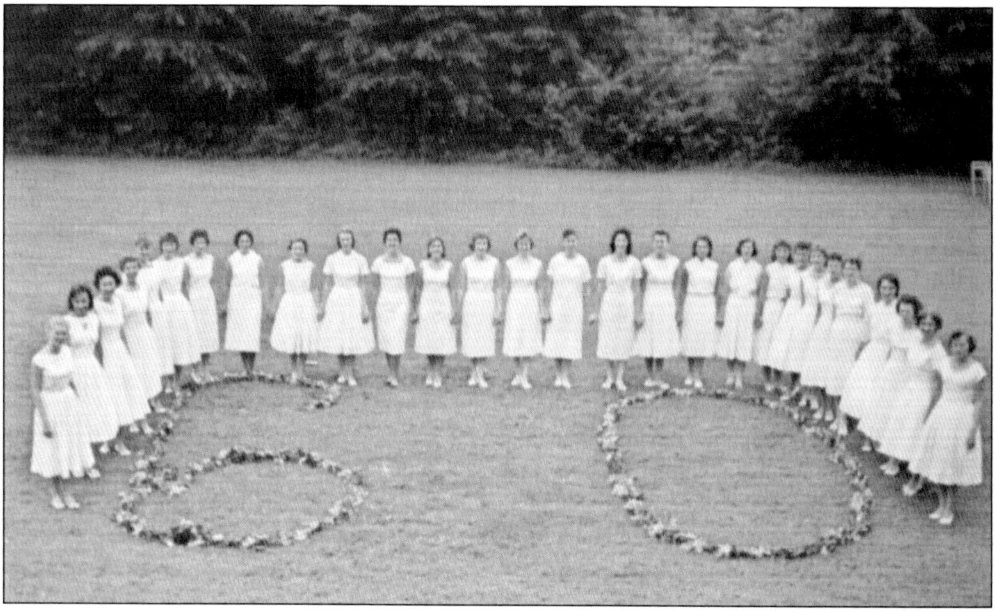

Class Day Exercises Spring 1960 was a day in which freshmen honored sophomores with a daisy chain. For many years, the freshmen would pick daisies and weave them into a chain. When graduation ceremonies were held outside, the freshman would form two lines and lay the ropes of daisies in front of the graduating class as they marched to the ceremony. The second photograph is a 1920s commencement ceremony that used the daisy chains.

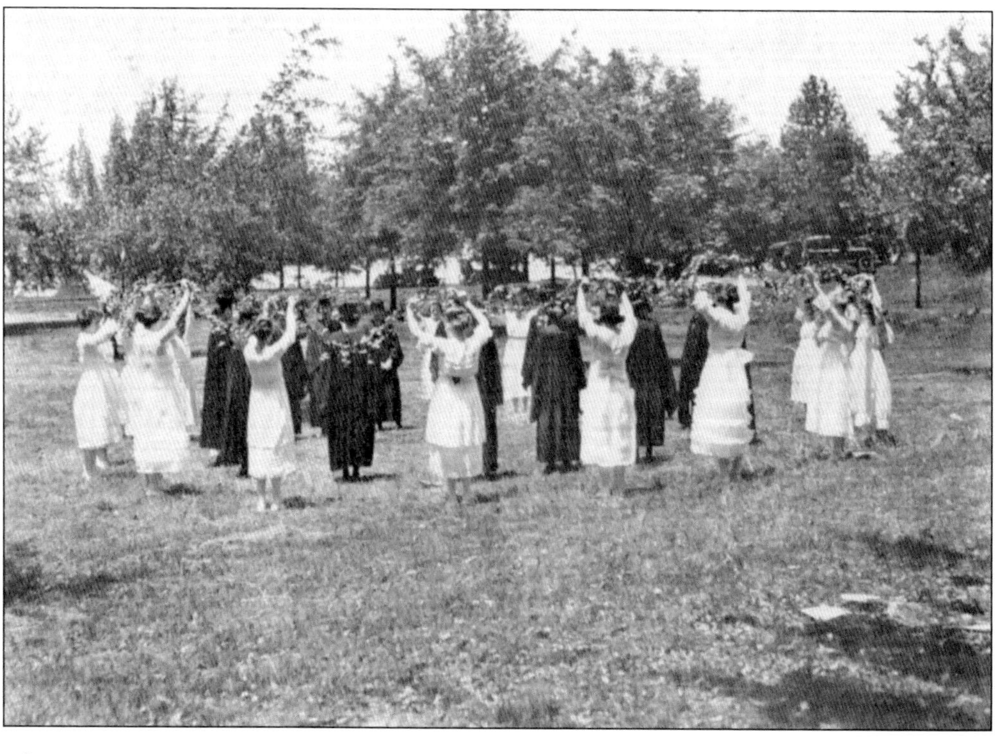

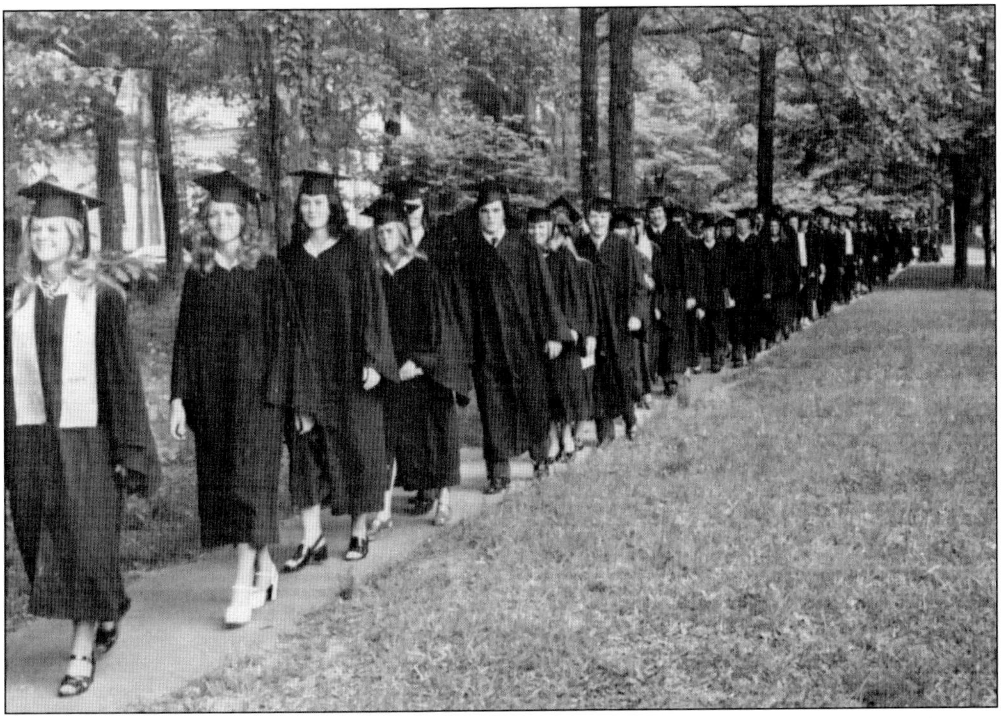

Here the graduates walk along Boulevard to get to Boulevard Baptist Church. Today the graduating seniors walk from the front of Thrift Library to the front campus.

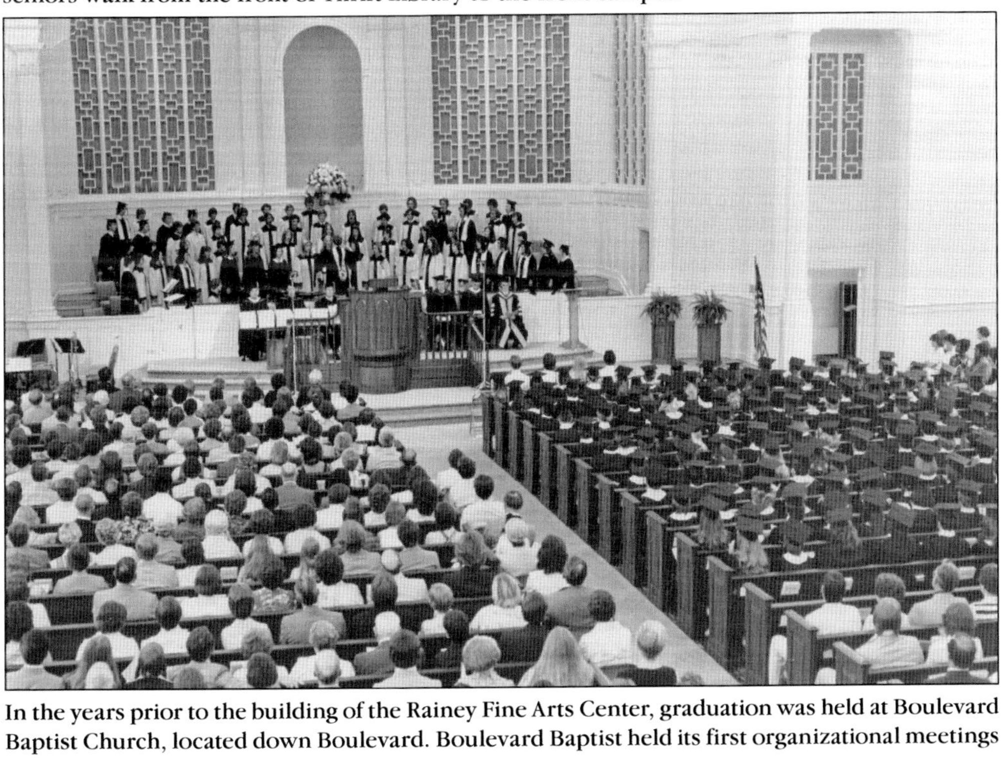

In the years prior to the building of the Rainey Fine Arts Center, graduation was held at Boulevard Baptist Church, located down Boulevard. Boulevard Baptist held its first organizational meetings on the campus.

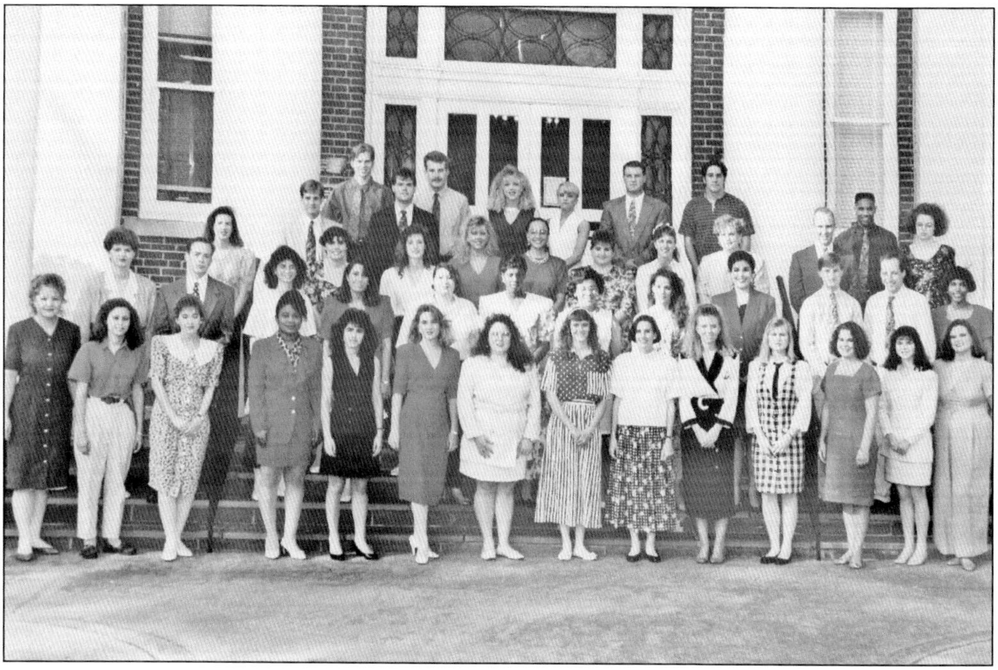

The 1993 portrait of the first baccalaureate graduating class since 1930 now hangs in the Sullivan Conference Room in the Rainey Fine Arts Center.

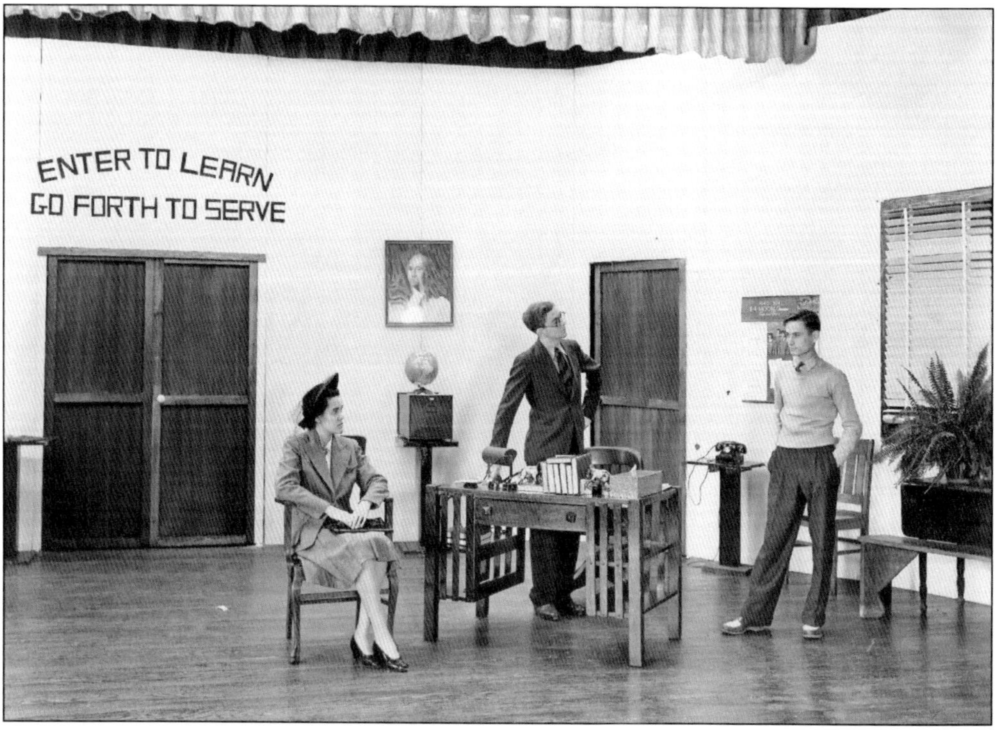

A play in the 1940s entitled *What a Life* utilized the mission-style furniture found on campus. The slogan on the wall epitomizes the core values of the college, reminding each student to "enter to learn, go forth to serve."

Five

STUDENT LIFE

Academic endeavors are at the heart of the college experience. However, the environment in which these studies take place plays an equally important role in the students' all-around development and memories. The students are shaped by their studies and their interactions with others. The goal is not only to gain a degree but also to grow spiritually as well as academically.

Historically, an enormous variety of activities are offered to students. These include campus ministries events such as a women's ministry, Fellowship of Christian Athletes (FCA), Baptist Collegiate Ministries (BCM), Reformed University Fellowship (RUF), Campus Crusade for Christ (CRU), and local, national, and global missions opportunities. With over 30 clubs and organizations, members of these groups are not only committed to improving life on campus but also to helping the lives of those in the community. The Anderson Student Government Association is one such group. Intramural sports, residence-life events, and specialized opportunities such as New Student Orientation and Welcome Week help students form bonds with each other that will last their time spent at Anderson University and beyond.

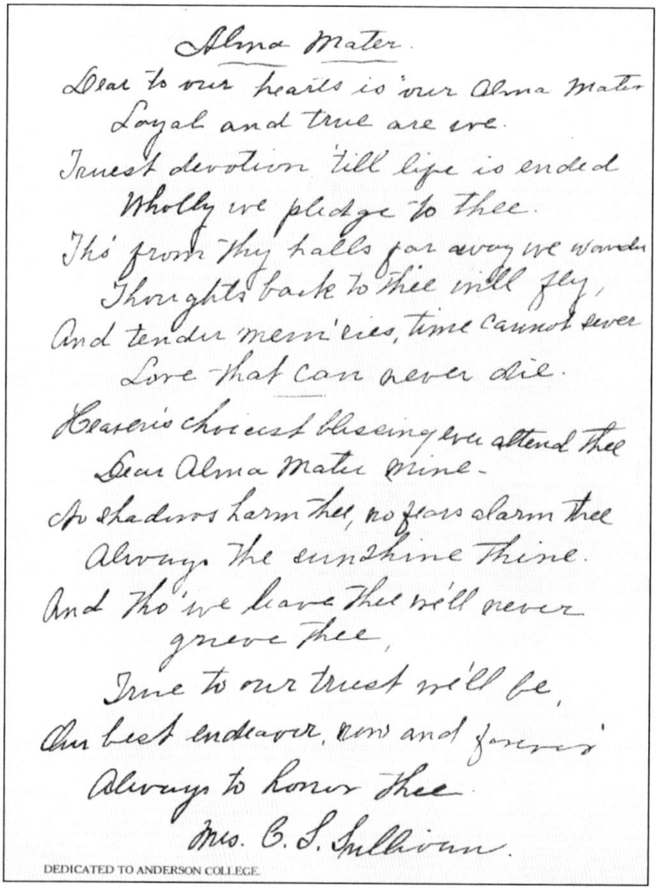

Alma Mater

Dear to our hearts is our Alma Mater
Loyal and true are we.
Truest devotion till life is ended
Wholly we pledge to thee.
Tho' from thy halls far away we wander
Thoughts back to thee will fly,
And tender mem'ries, time cannot sever
Love that can never die.

Heaven's choicest blessing ever attend thee
Dear Alma Mater mine.
No shadows harm thee, no fears alarm thee
Always the sunshine thine.
And tho' we leave thee we'll never grieve thee,
True to our trust we'll be,
Our best endeavor, now and forever
Always to honor thee.
Mrs. C. S. Sullivan.

DEDICATED TO ANDERSON COLLEGE.

Mrs. Charles S. Sullivan Sr. (Luta, below left) wrote Anderson University's first alma mater. Here is a handwritten copy from 1918. She was a loyal Anderson College supporter and was devoted to helping others in Anderson. She and her husband contributed the original president's home, which is now the Sullivan Building and is used by the campus ministries program. Their son, Charles Jr., and his wife, Coy Meeks Sullivan, were both instructors. Charles Jr. worked from 1925 to 1939, and his wife worked from the 1940s to 1959. Anderson University's centennial alma mater was penned by Johnny Mann (below right), a two-time Grammy winner and currently an Anderson resident. The new alma mater, entitled "The Sounds of Anderson," made its debut at the opening convocation in August 2009.

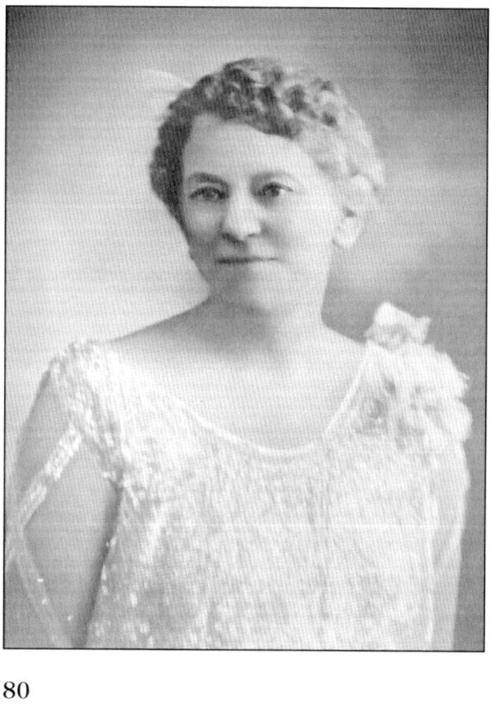

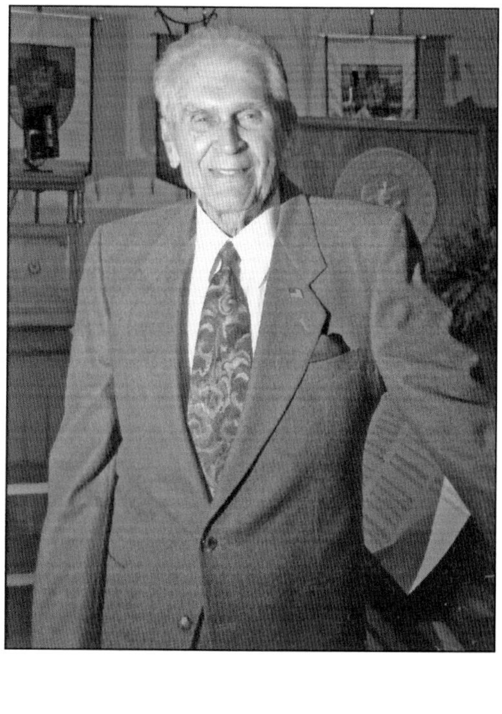

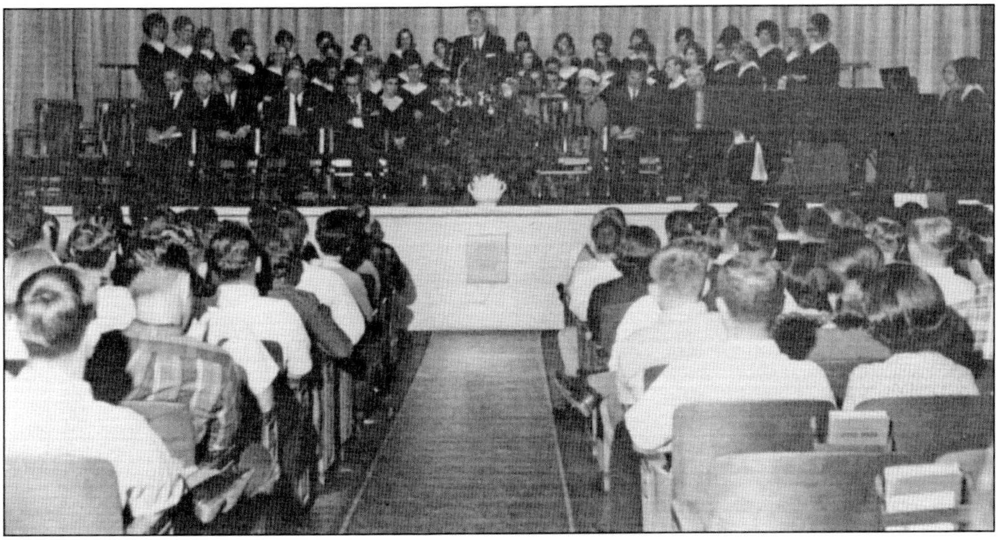

Chapel programs in the Merritt Auditorium in 1968 were characteristic of Anderson College from the beginning. A worship service or chapel was part of the daily routine of student life. For many years, chapel met every day at 10:30 a.m. By the end of the century, the number of meetings had been reduced to three times a week. Now Wednesdays are devoted to the weekly campus worship service, "The Journey." Mondays are set aside for Cultural Experience Programming, and Fridays are left for club meetings and other activities. Students are required to attend a certain number of Journey services and CEP programs each semester in order to graduate. Classes were once held Monday through Saturday, but in 1968, the Saturday class schedule came to an end.

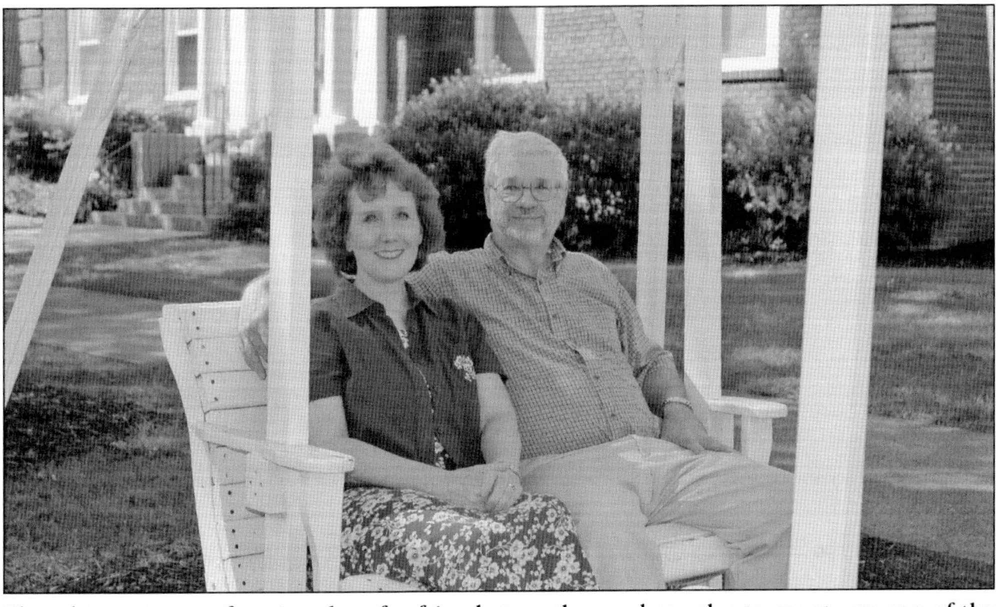

The white swings, a favorite place for friends to gather and couples to court, are one of the enduring features of the Anderson University campus. Many courtships and subsequent marriages were nurtured in the hours spent in these swings. Jacque and Doug Davison met at Anderson College as students, married, and later came back to serve as faculty. Jacque is a professor of mathematics, and Doug was a professor of English. With the arrival of computers, Doug added technology specialist to his résumé.

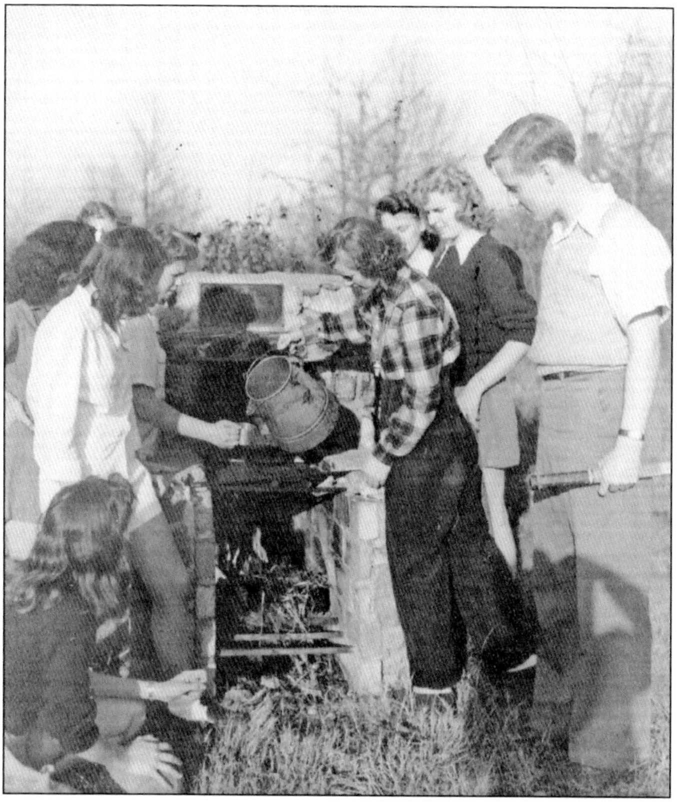

For many years, a cookout fireplace on back campus provided a convenient place for outdoor gathering and eating. This group takes advantage of a nice day to enjoy some time outside in 1944. One tradition on the calendar for many years was "October Day." On a beautiful day in October, when the students sang the October song to the president's satisfaction, she then cancelled classes, which was followed by a hike and a picnic. Students went hiking along Greenville Highway in 1930s and took buses to the mountains in the 1950s. A similar unannounced "field day" in the spring was also accompanied by a cancellation of classes, outdoor games, and a picnic.

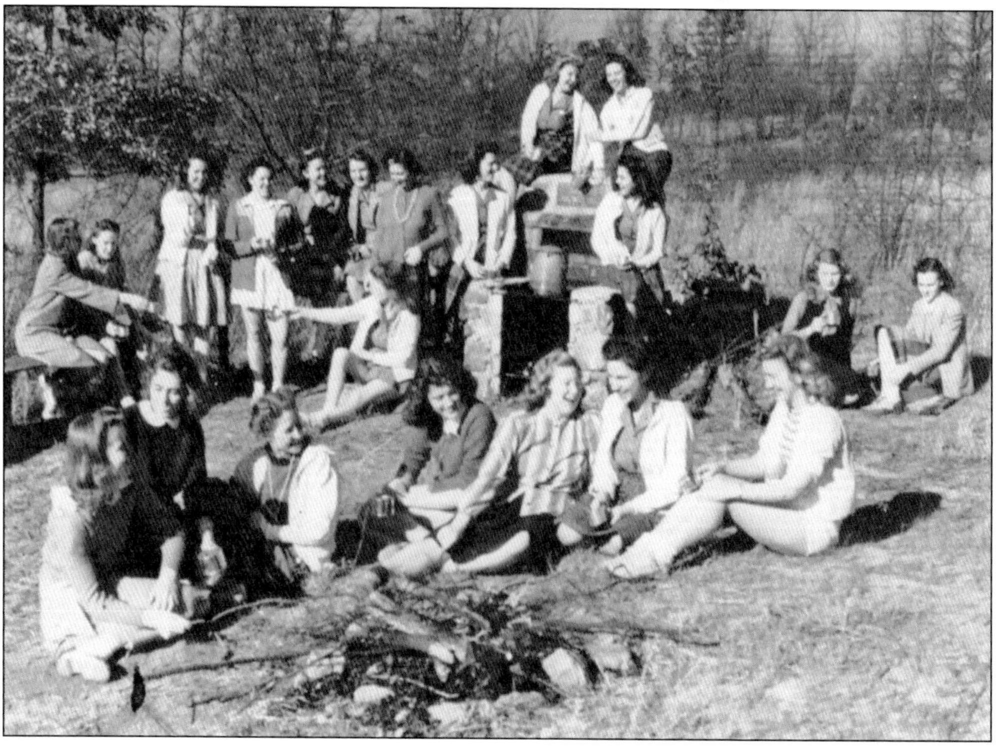

The Crook tradition originated around 1917 and was based on a local legend, which was described in a newspaper article. It was said that a student was lost in the woods behind the college and "came upon a long, white crook made of wood." It pointed her way safely home, and the hiding of the crook started as a "memento of this adventure." The photograph is from the 1926 *Sororian*, with "Bo Peep" posed by Kathryn Cannon. Though rules have changed over the years, in 1964, the sophomores started the competition and had a week to hide the crook. The freshmen then hunted for it. Once found, the freshmen hid it from the sophomores. This continued all year until commencement, at which time the class possessing the crook was considered the winner.

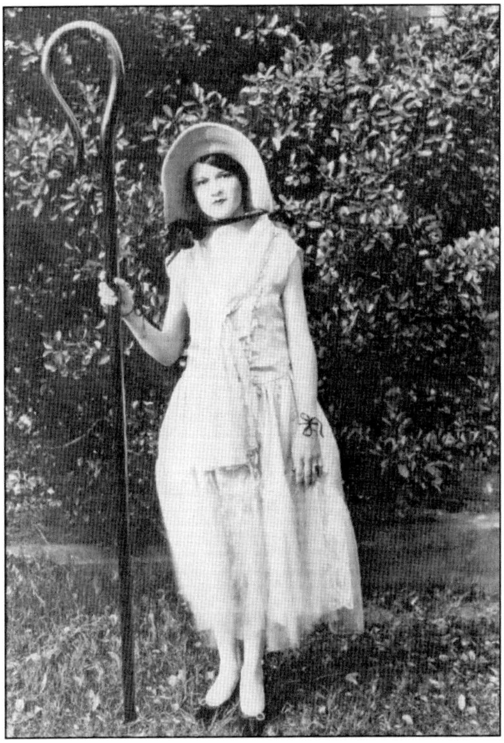

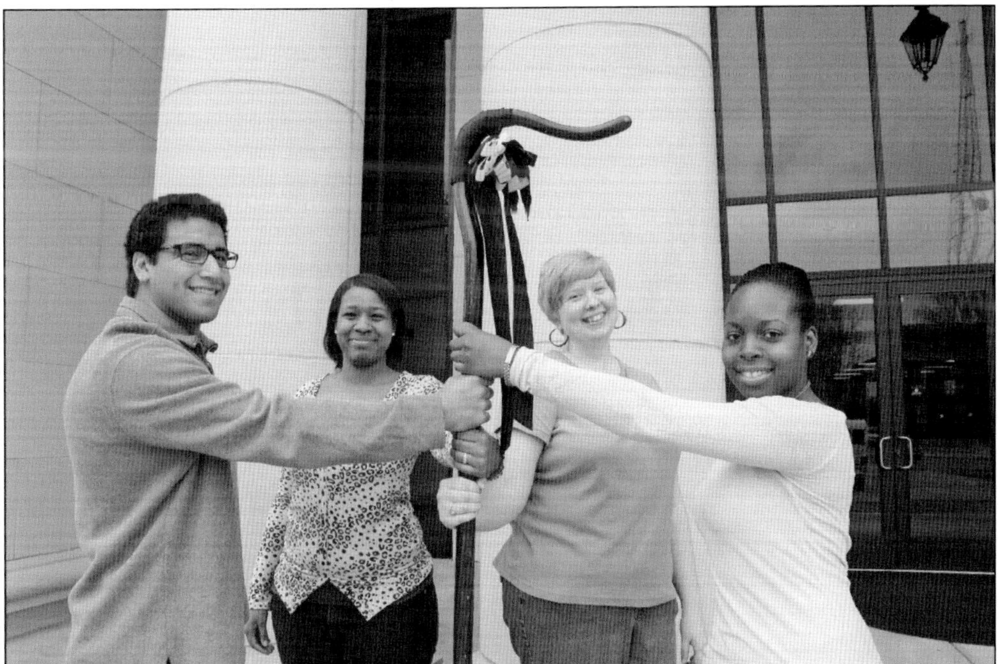

By the 1950s, the top of the crook had been broken. It is now taped together, but the upper loop is missing. From left to right, history majors Luis Audelo, J. Alyssa Stephens, Bethany Wade, and Hope Campbell, an international student from Jamaica, get an opportunity to enjoy "hands-on" history in the spring of 2010.

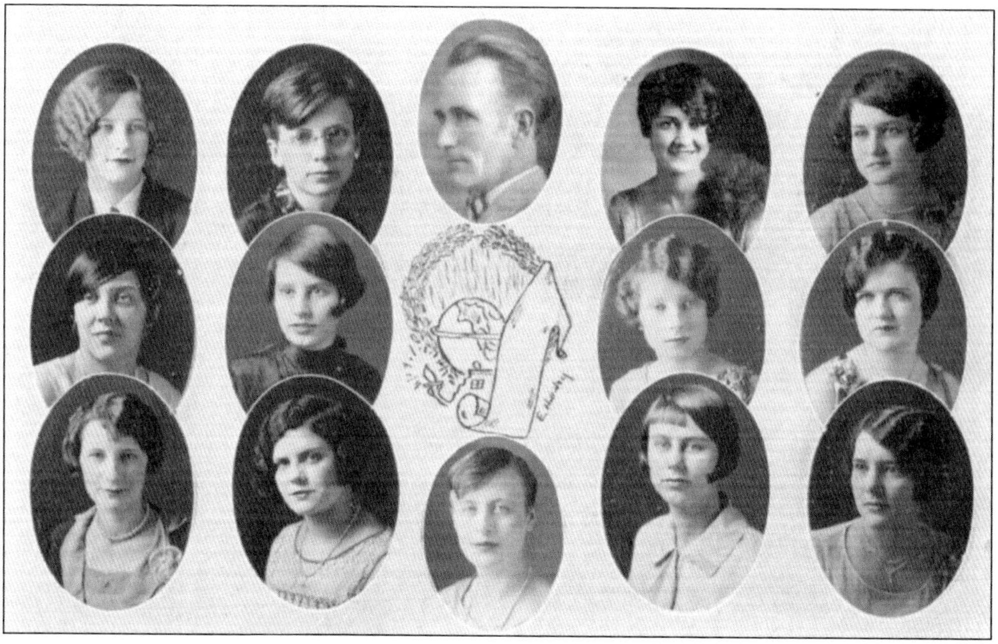

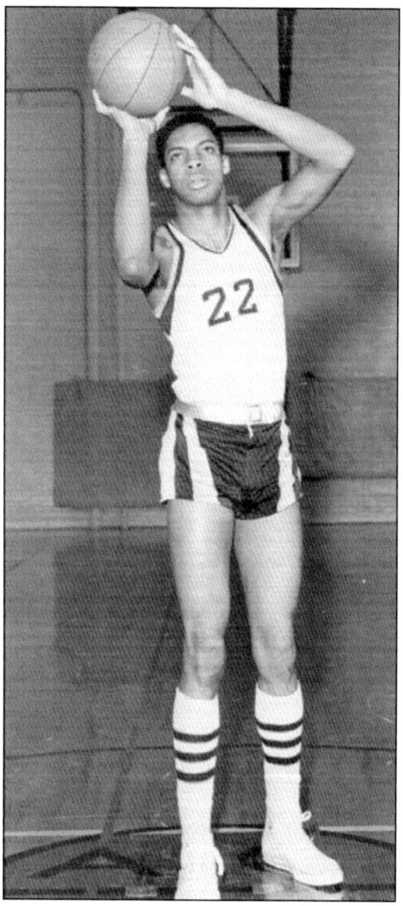

The International Club of 1927 shows that Anderson University had established a policy of diversity early on. In 1915, an immigration club attested to the students' interest in fostering the inclusiveness of immigrants at a time that much of the country was clamoring for immigrant limitation in the midst of World War I. Many nationalities attended the college, which is evidenced in yearbook photographs as early as 1930. This policy continued throughout the history of the university, except for when the school named the athletic teams the Rebels/Rebelettes and sported the traditional Confederate flag from 1962 to 1970. Despite this ugly truth, African American athlete Mack Nance played under the Conderate flag in 1967. In 1970, the school's mascot was changed to the Trojans/Trojanettes, later changed to Lady Trojans. Coaches did the first major recruitment of minority students and were later joined by the admissions office. Not only African Americans were recruited as students, but also Asians, South Americans, and Europeans. These students of different backgrounds easily blended and gave the small, provincial campus a broader scope.

Mack Nance and his cousin, Horace Clinkscales, were in the first group of the African American students to attend Anderson College.

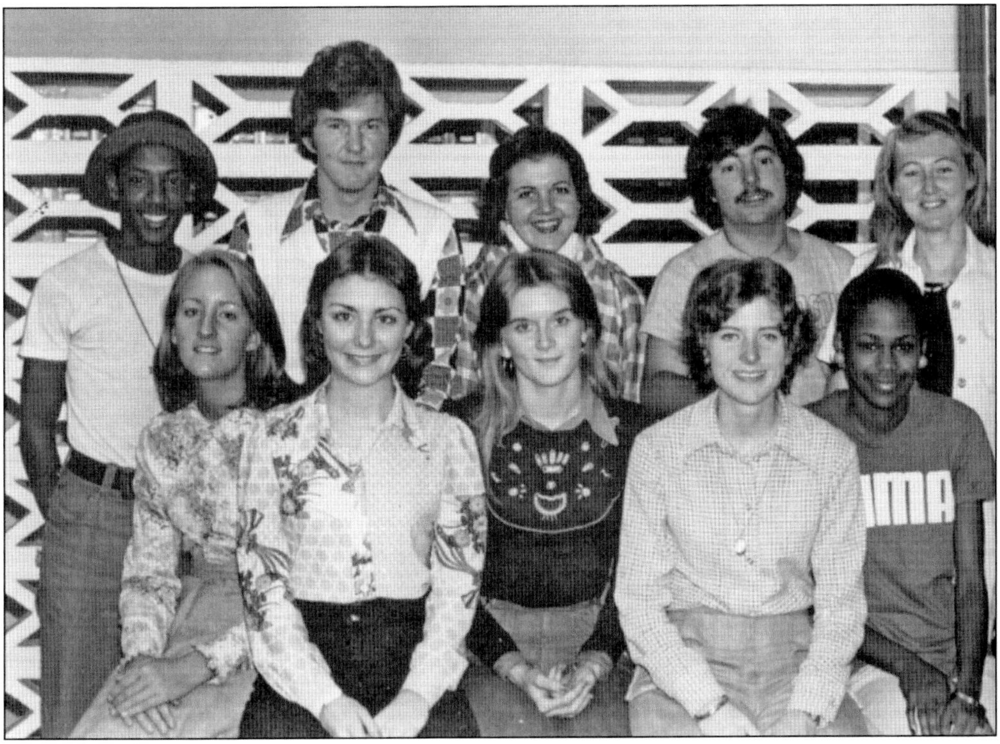

This photograph from the 1976 *Columns* of the Student Government Association Social Board reflects the diversity on Anderson's campus. The student body was greatly enriched by the addition of African American students and staff as part of the campus experience. Pictured here are, from left to right, (first row) Jane Mathis, Judy Denman, Candice Hunter, Jean Welborn, and Michelle Stevens; (second row) Stanley Greggs, Rick Ables, Lee Easley, Beatty Jackson, and advisor Lana Branham.

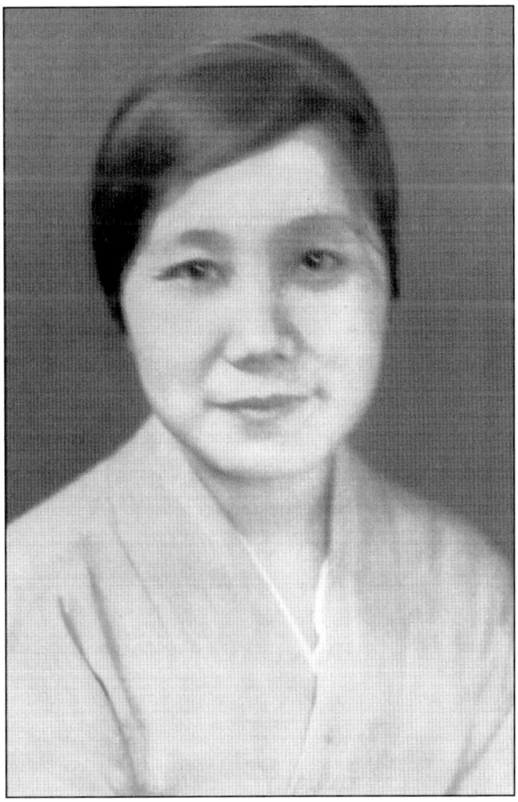

Tomeko Uno San was featured in the 1930 edition of the *Sororian* as "Most Popular." Her story was highlighted by Dr. Annie Dove Denmark for her eagerness to grow. She was led to Anderson College to study by an alumna, Myra Anderson, who taught in the business department of the Hiroshima Girl's School in Japan.

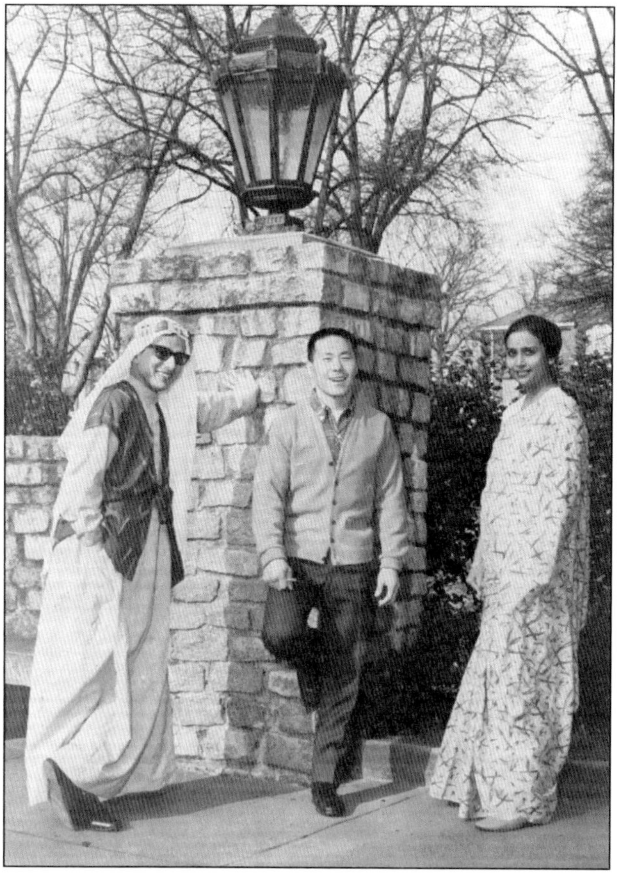

By 1967, a variety of nationalities were represented among the students of Anderson College. Pictured here from left to right are Nabil Kabbani from Aleppo, Syria; "Billy" Hong Ung Hyong, a Tae Kwon Do expert from South Korea; and Sudha Yennemadi from India, who followed the example of her cousin, Sanjivi "Raj" Natarajan, who attended from 1959 to 1960.

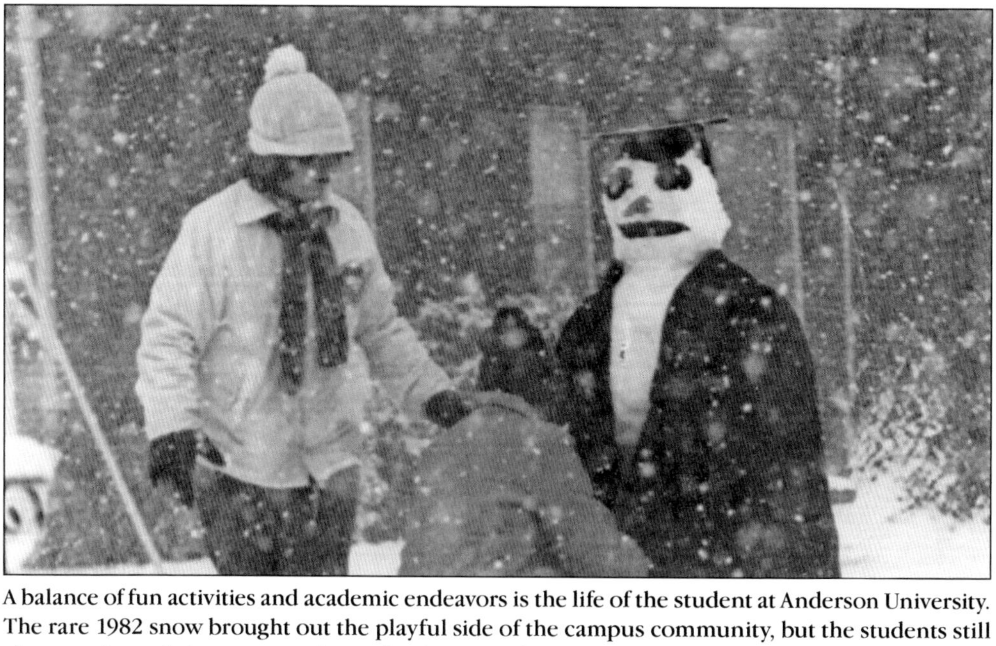

A balance of fun activities and academic endeavors is the life of the student at Anderson University. The rare 1982 snow brought out the playful side of the campus community, but the students still chose to dress their snowman in academic cap and gown!

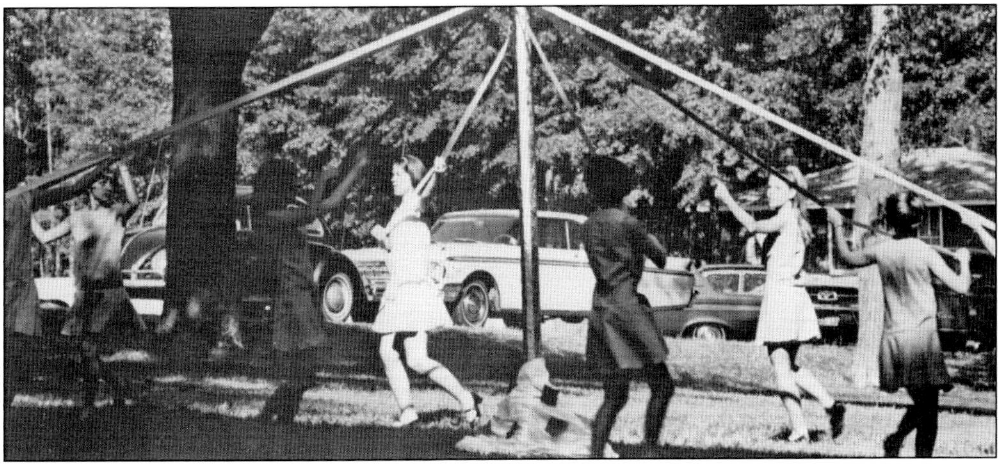

A dance around the maypole was included as part of the May Day celebrations. At that time, spring final examinations took place at the end of May, with classes having started in September. This photograph is from the 1970 *Columns*, and sadly, by the 1980s, this charming custom had faded away.

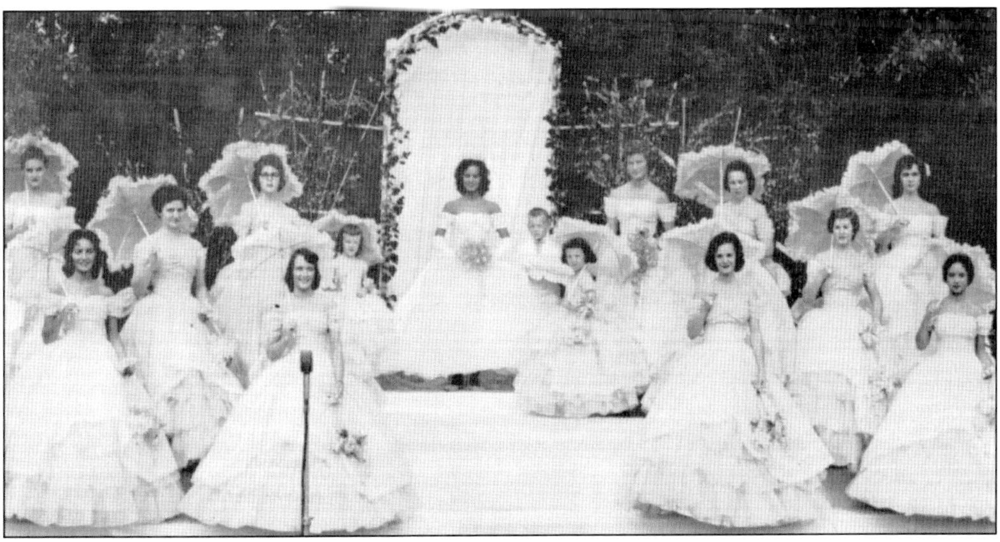

May Day 1958 was planned by the Anderson Athletic Association. The May Queen and her court reigned over the campus, which was transformed for a day.

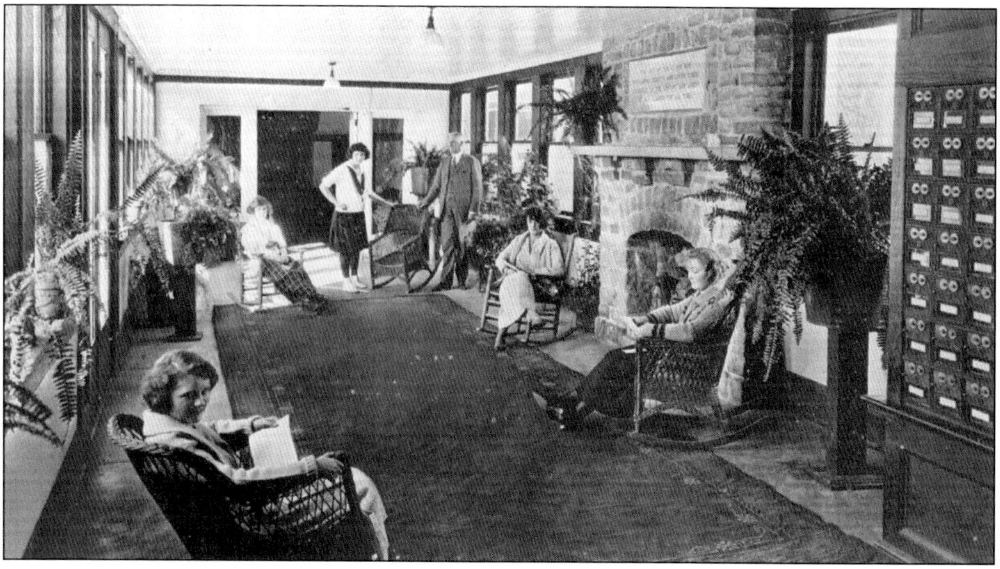

In the 1920s, students are relaxing in the attractive loggia, called the "sun parlor," connecting the West Building (now Denmark Hall) and the Administration Building. Note the mailboxes in the foreground. The fireplace was used for many years as the location of the lighting of the Christmas Yule log.

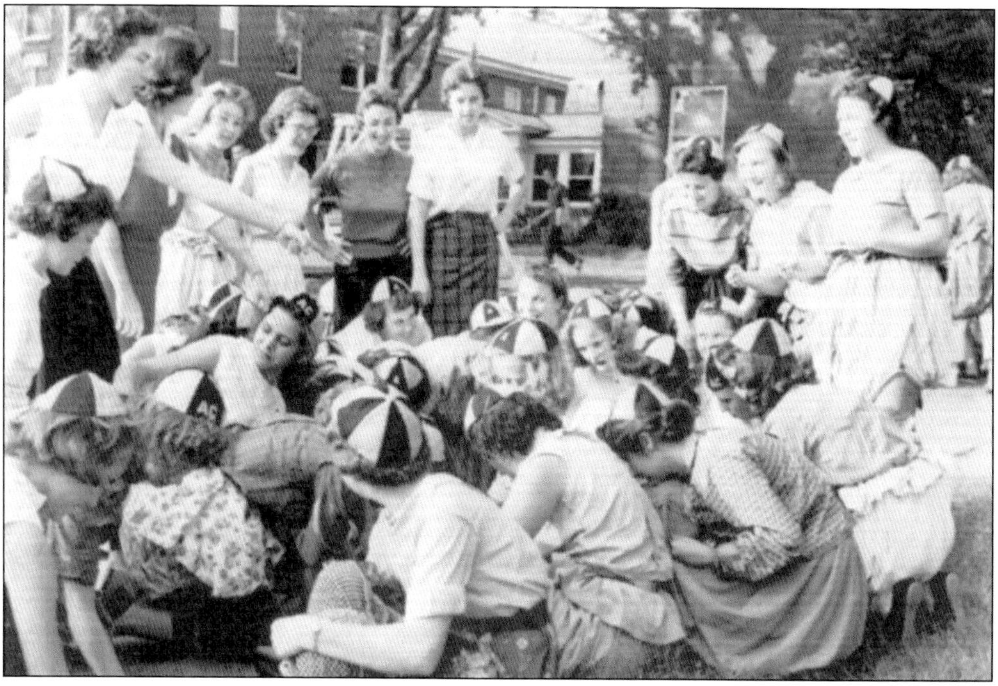

During the 1960s, many campuses required freshmen to wear special hats, "beanies," in the first days on campus. The experience helped identify the new folks on campus; at the same time, it gave freshmen the chance to form bonds quickly among their classmates. The tradition had once required freshmen to wear these "rat hats" until Thanksgiving. In the fall of 1964, the custom was reduced to one week, "Rat Week," with restrictions implemented. Such practices faded during the 1970s.

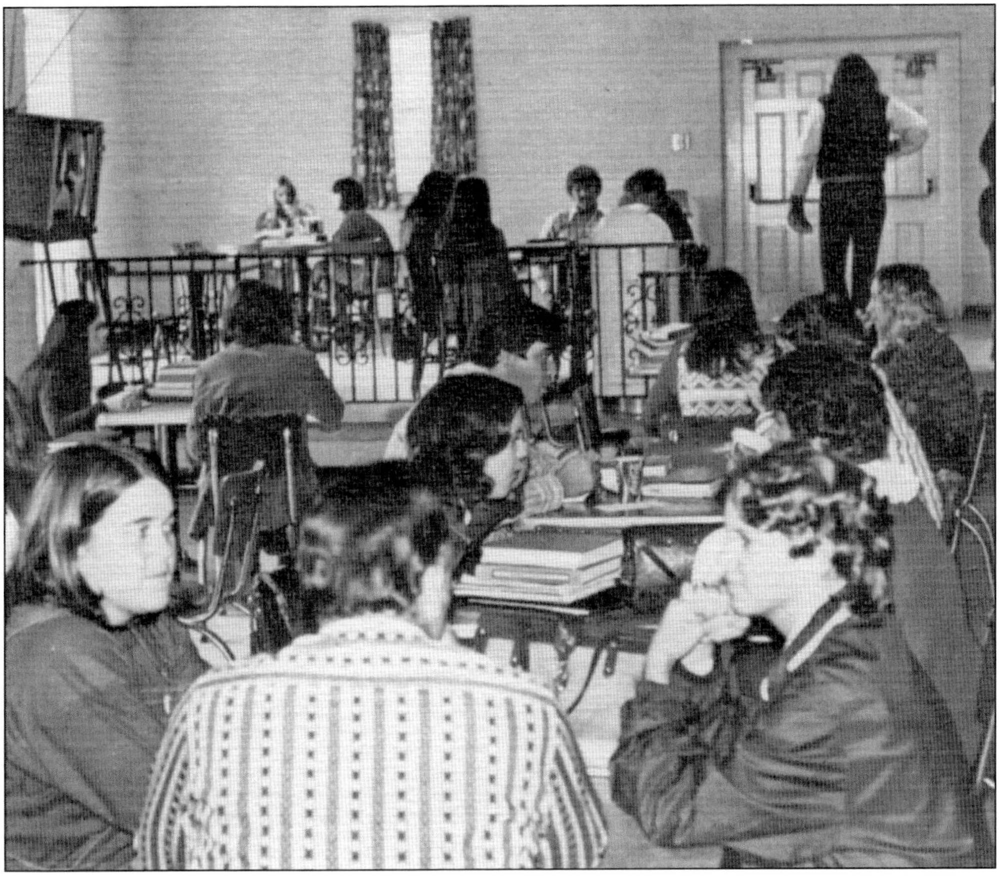

Students are relaxing in the student center between classes in 1973. The original canteen, post office, and bookstore were all located in the building now known as Vandiver Hall. A new student center was constructed in 1965, allowing for a greater expansion of services to the student population.

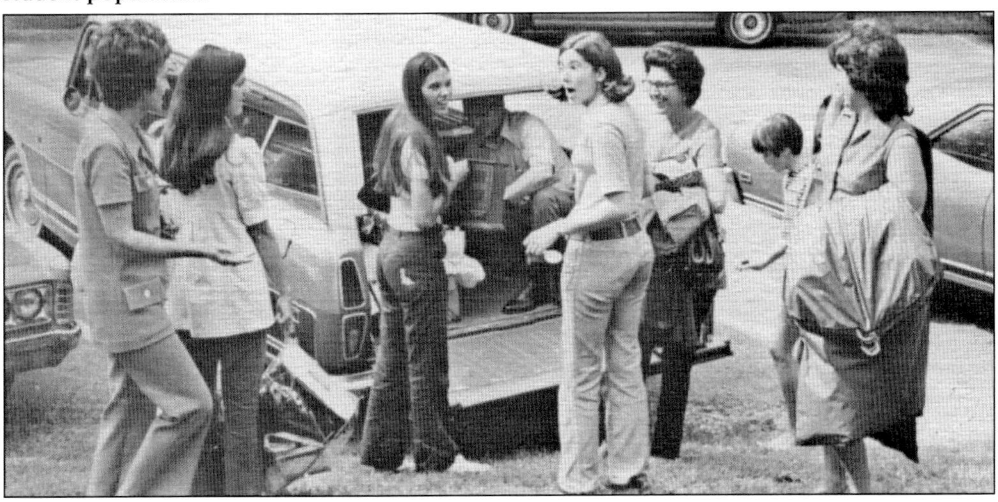

The ritual that begins each school year is move-in day. As seen in this photograph from 1973, it was clearly a family affair.

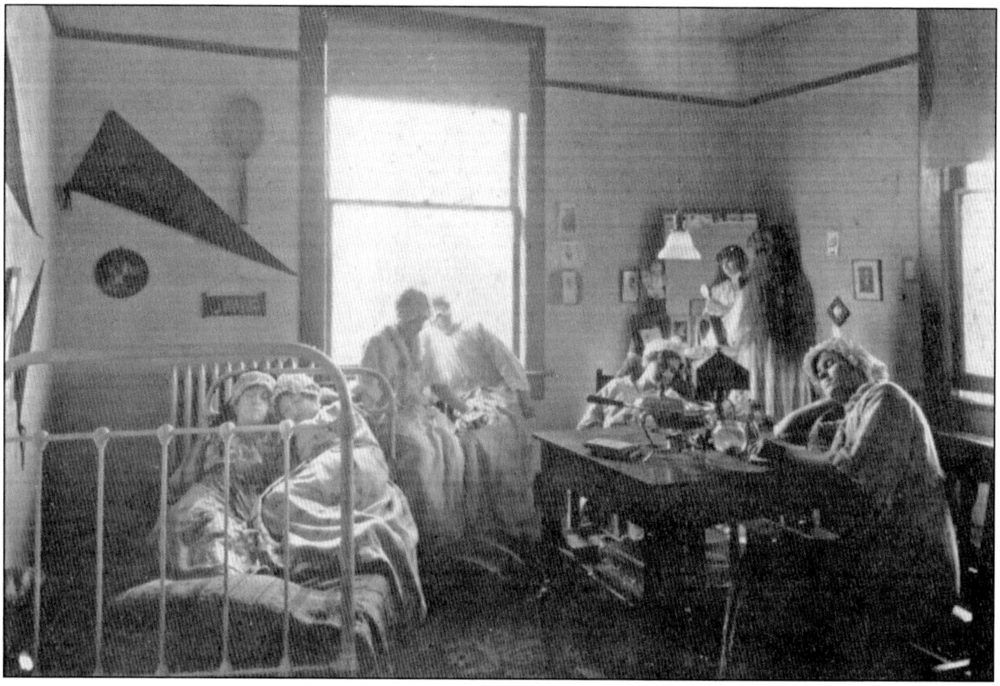

Entitled "Worshipers of Morpheus," this photograph from the 1915 *Sororian* gives a peek at the dorm room of the day. The iron bedsteads were used until the mid-1950s, when they were replaced with wooden furniture.

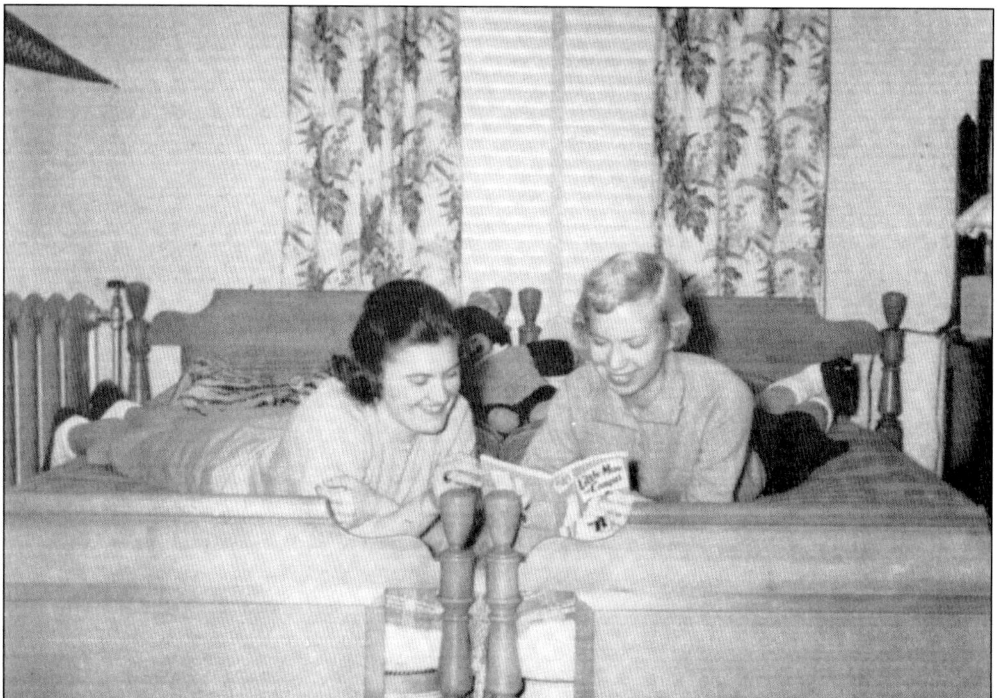

Dormitory life was improved with the purchase of new furnishings. The winners of the 1959 superlative "Wittiest," Sarah Ellen Martin (left) and Penny Clements, are pictured here.

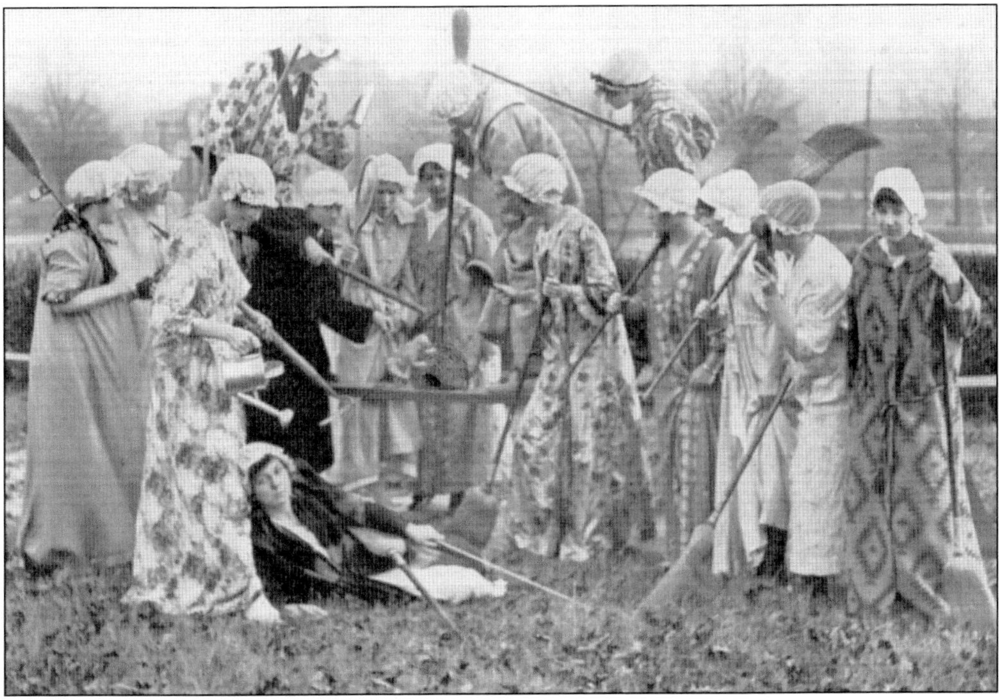

Woe unto any untoward creature threatening these capable and determined ladies in a photograph entitled "Reptile Police Force" in the 1916 *Sororian*.

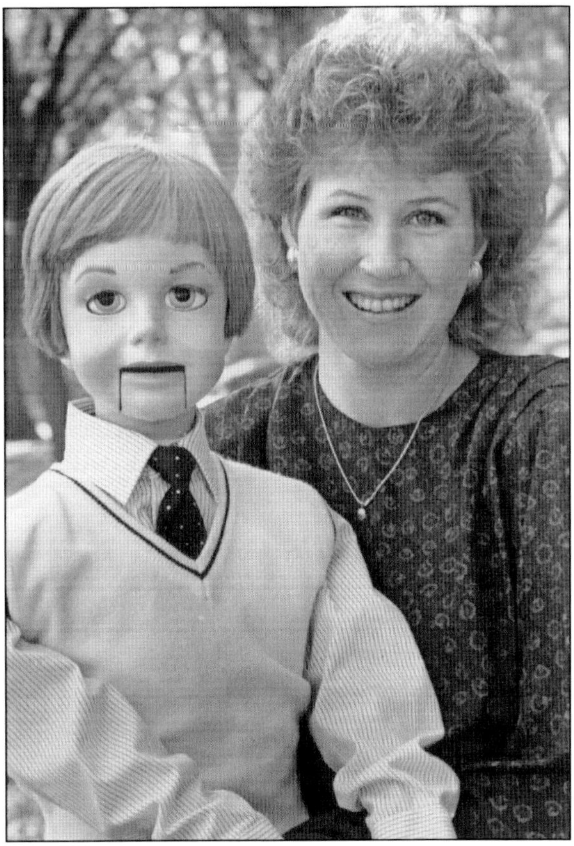

"Students" came in many forms! Pam Bryant and "Freddy" came as students in 1977 and were a vital part of the campus and community outreach. They returned to the campus in 1983, when she was a college representative in the Campus Ministries Area working with Journey Teams. Members of these Journey Teams traveled and promoted Anderson College. Bryant's duties as an admissions counselor were later augmented by the role of head softball coach. In 1996, she became director of admissions.

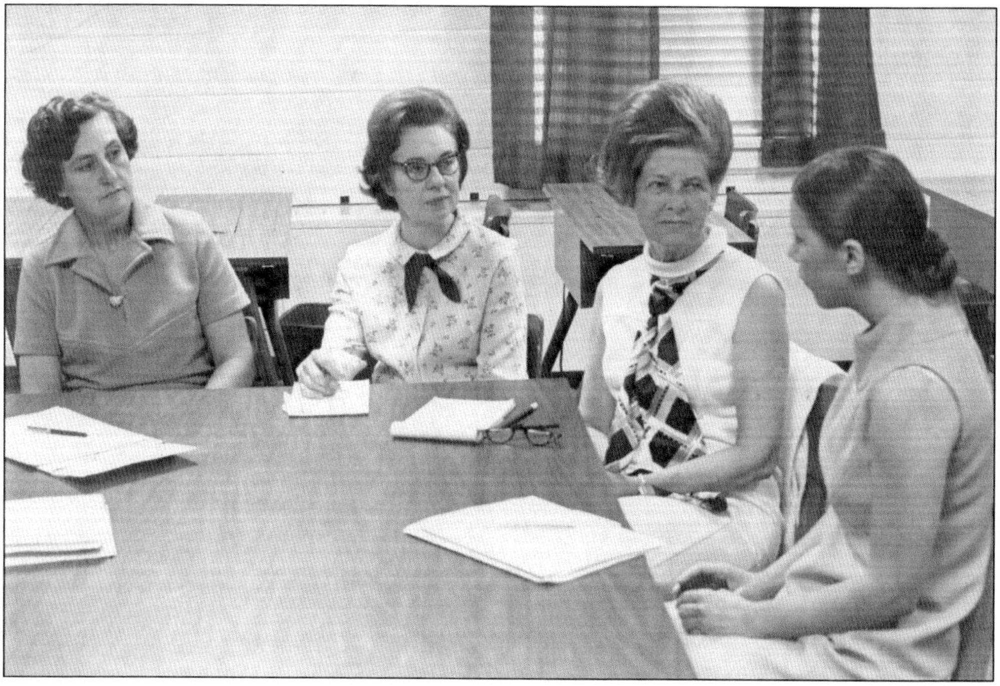

Ada Powell Meeks '30, located second from right, was the social secretary for the campus for many years. Here she is shown as part of a committee interviewing a student for the Altrusa Club. The others are faculty member Mary Martin (left) and staff member Agnes Raney (center).

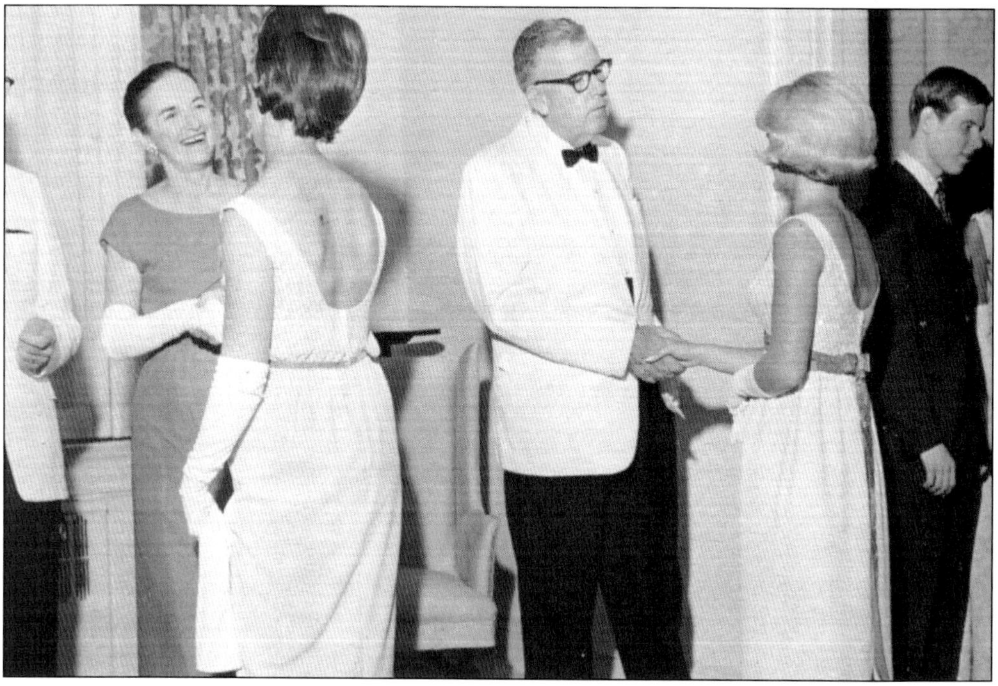

A welcoming reception has become the traditional way to open the fall semester. Here President and Mrs. Rouse greet students in 1966 in a very formal setting. By the 1980s, the reception had changed to a more casual tone and moved outdoors to the front yard of the president's home.

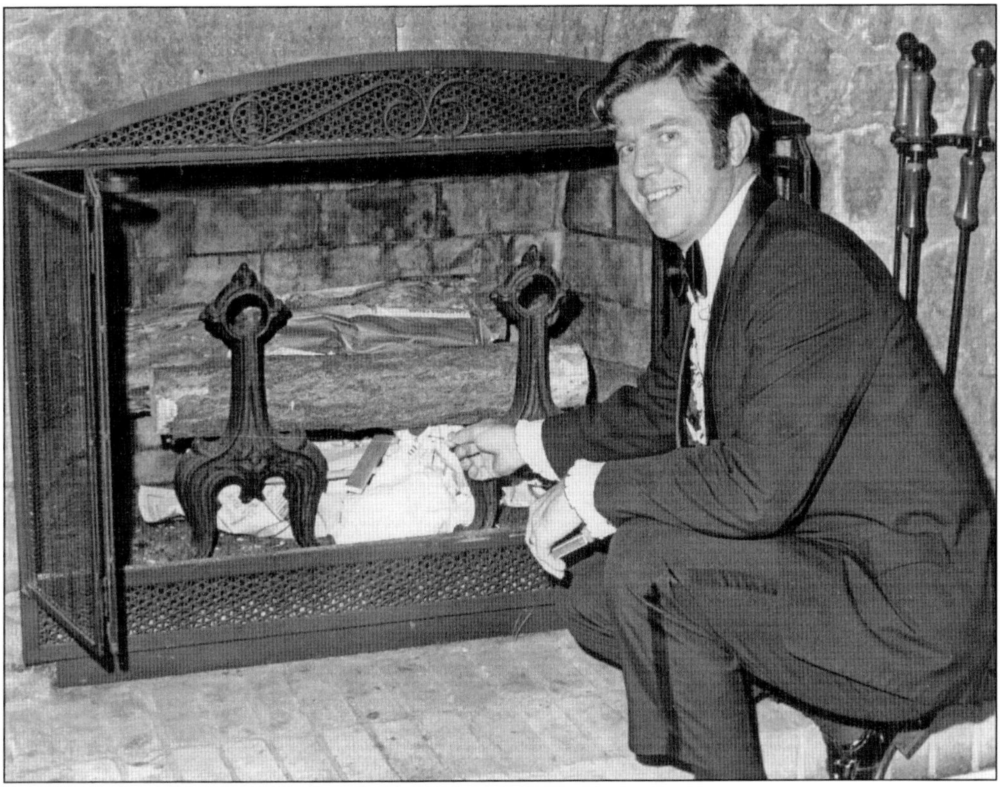

Dr. Cordell Maddox is lighting the Yule log for Christmas First Night on December 4, 1973. This ceremony was first mentioned in the *Yodler* in the December 1937 issue.

Christmas First Night in the 1950s was a day that students were excused from classes to decorate the campus for Christmas. In the evening, a banquet was held requiring formal dress, followed by entertainment provided by the choir or other campus groups. The Yule log was then lit in the fireplace in the colonnade, located between Denmark and the Administration Building. The evening ended with refreshments, including the (non-alcoholic) wassail bowl, in the Merritt Parlor. Today the event starts with a major musical production in Henderson Auditorium, followed by the formal lighting of the Yule log outdoors and singing of carols by students, parents, and members of the local community.

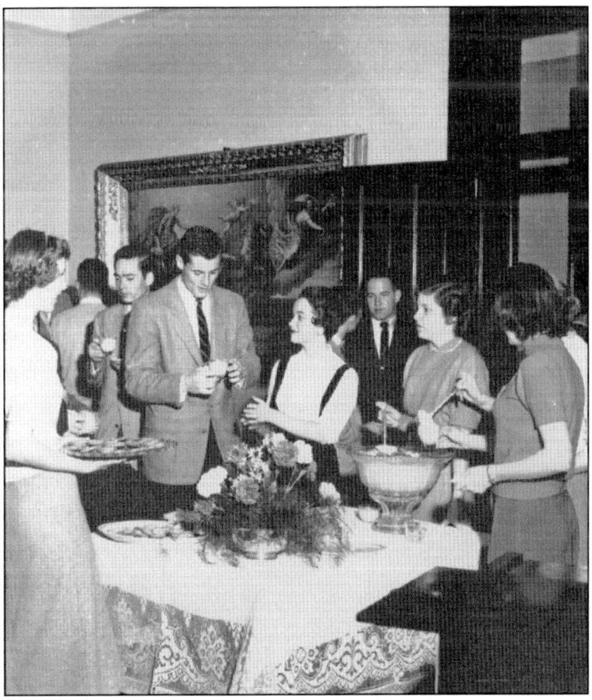

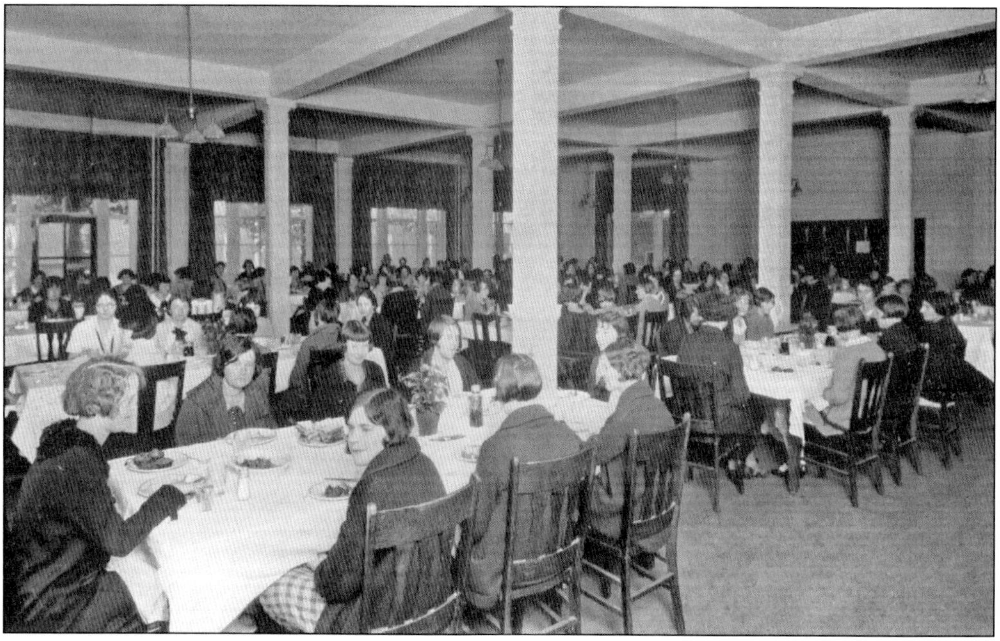

In the dining hall in 1927, meals were served family style, with a faculty host or hostess and seven students at each table. The students would be rotated every two weeks to a month so that everyone would get to know each other. Students were required to be present for lunch and supper; breakfast was optional. It was dedicated as the Dr. T. Willis Martin Dining Hall in 1968 and renovated and redecorated in 1997. The view below was photographed in 1985.

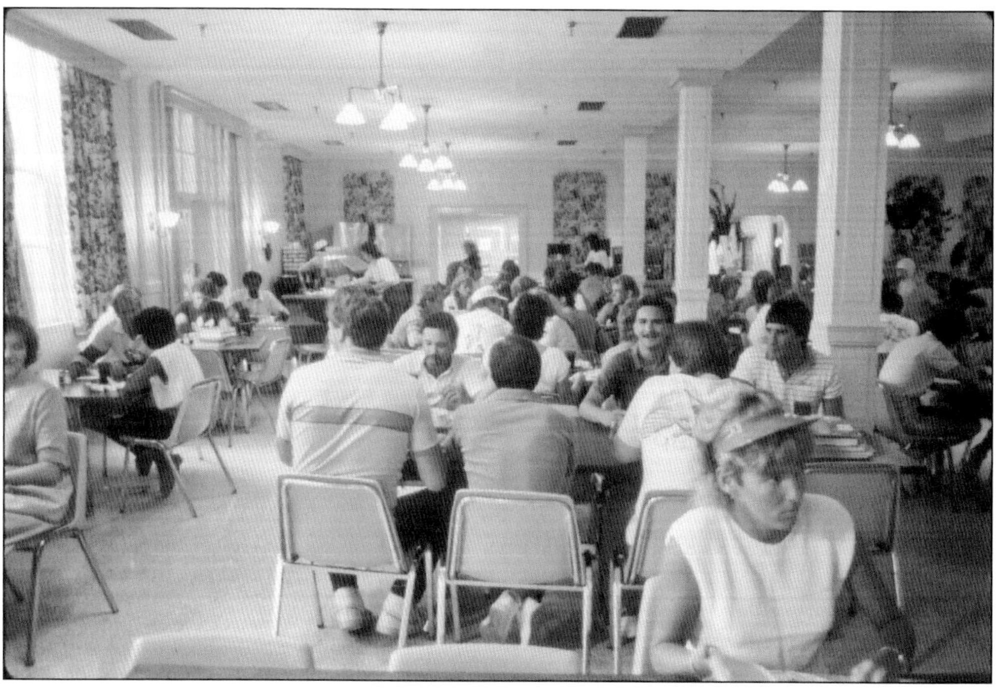

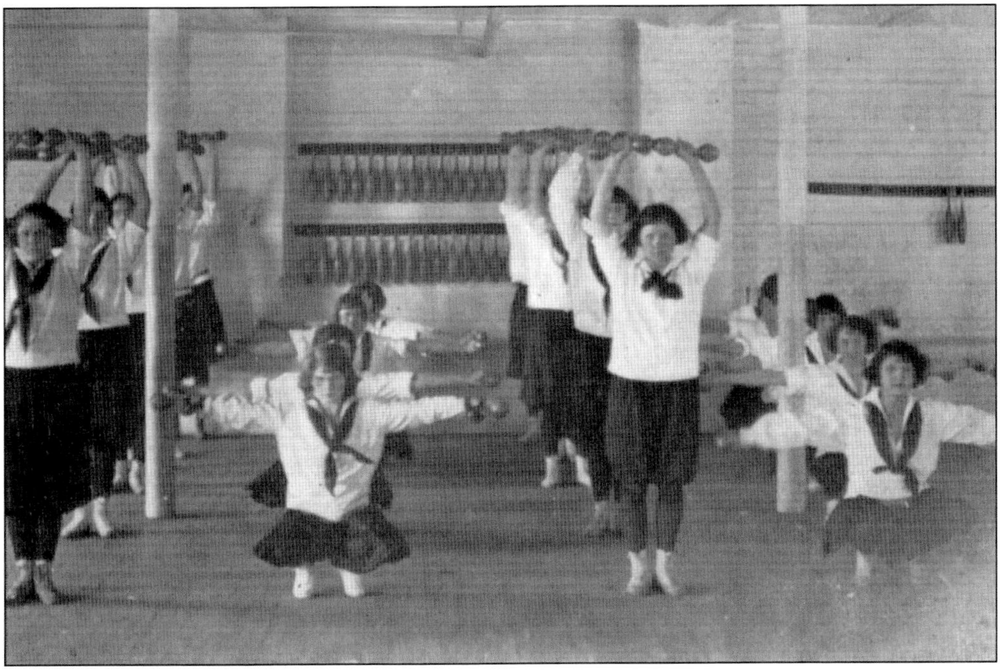

The original gym was in the basement of Pratt. The back area of the basement was the location of the business department in the late 1950s. The building also housed for many years the offices of the dean of women, the personnel director, the art studio, the infirmary, and the voice studio.

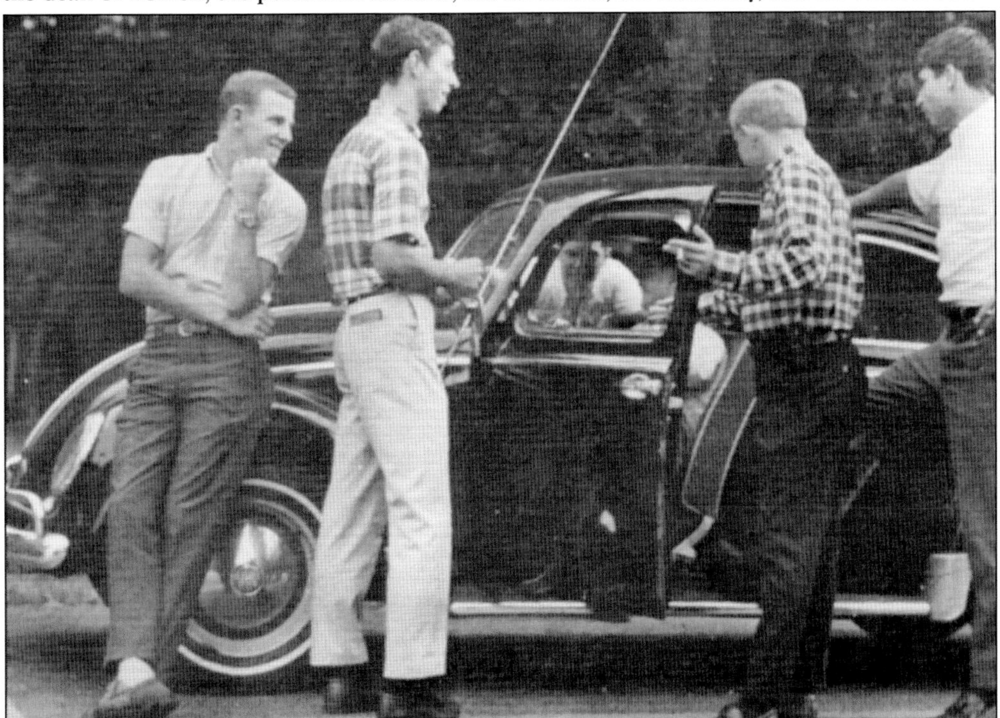

A fad of the 1960s was Volkswagen "stuffing." Is this 1967 group of students considering the possibility?

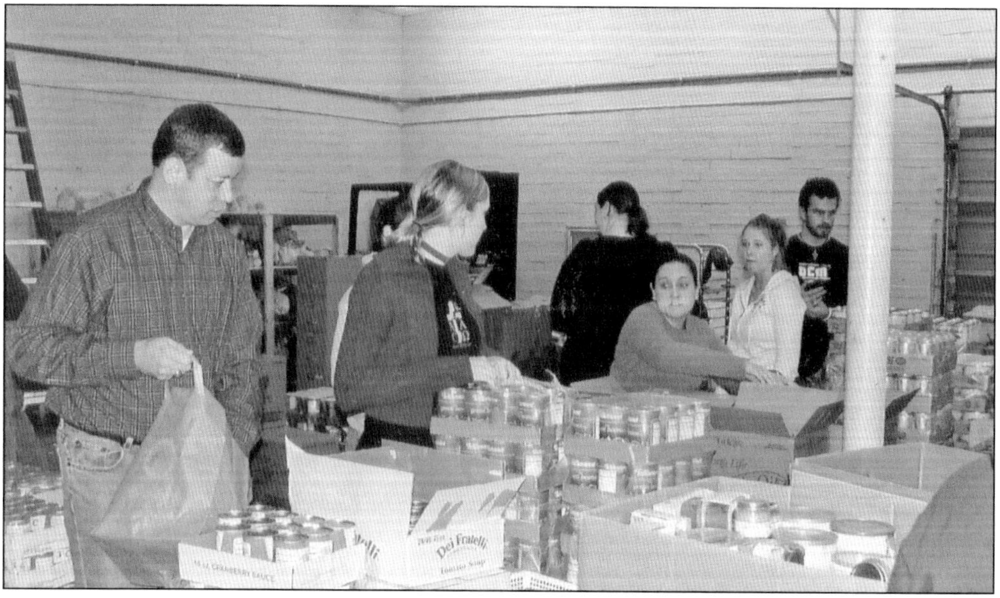

Campus Minister Greg Allgood and students volunteer their time to help at the AIM food pantry. The Martin Luther King Jr. "Day of Service" provides the entire campus community an opportunity to participate in activities ranging from reading to students in elementary schools to cleaning up various parks and other community service locations. The day ends with a program featuring a community leader as speaker; in 2002, the speaker was Dr. Julius Scipio. His innovative efforts to help at-risk children have garnered him numerous national awards. (Courtesy of David Korn.)

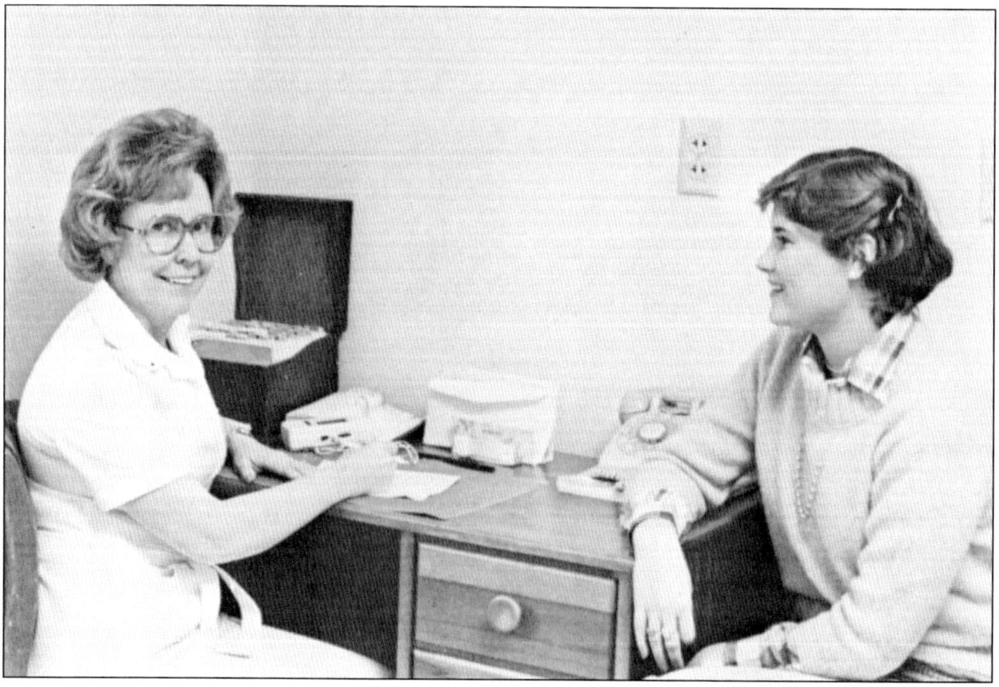

From the beginning, health care was an important part of the services provided to enhance student life. Rice Infirmary was to provide a hospital-like setting for ill students. Here Nurse Betty Cathey meets with a student in 1980.

When the campus opened, there was just one telephone, but many more followed. Sarah Westmoreland was the operator of the central switchboard and the "voice" of the college for many years.

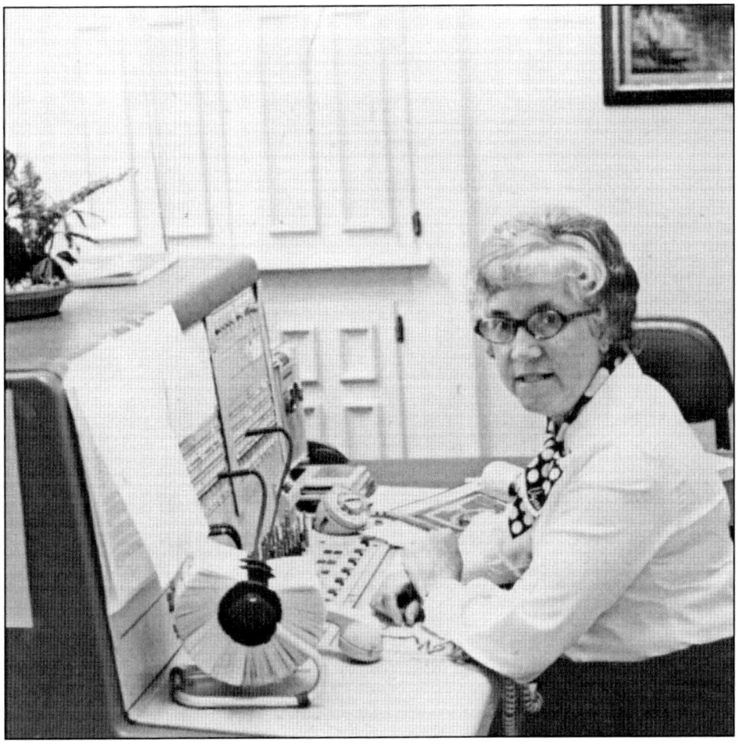

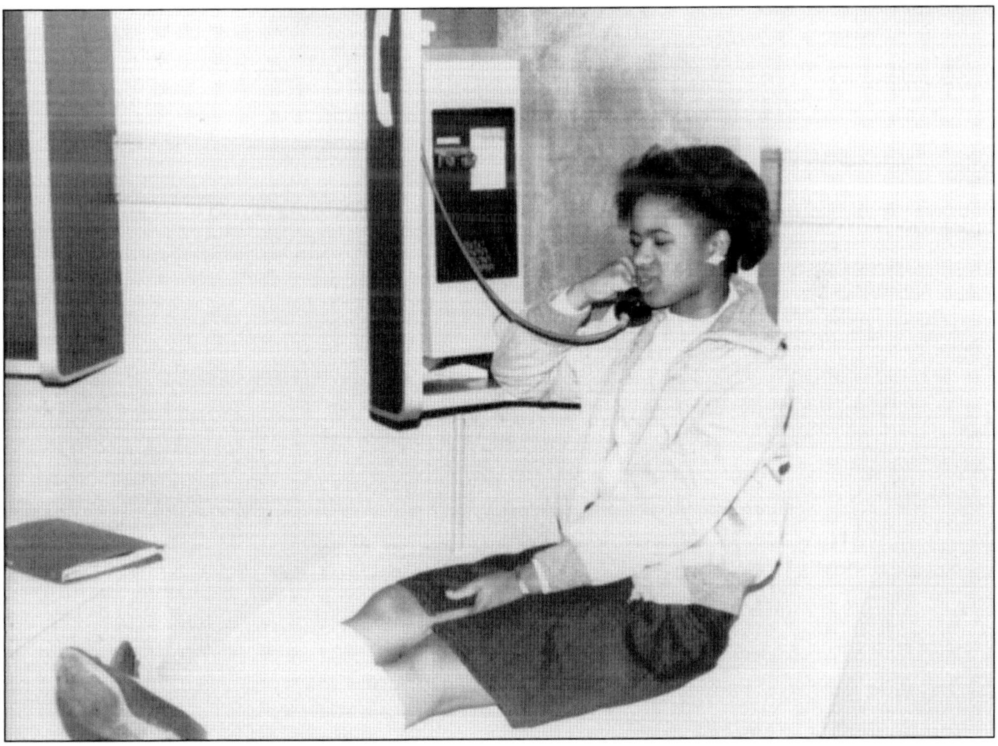

Until the mid-1980s, students had access to only one phone on the hall. Phones soon became available in each room, as well as cable television.

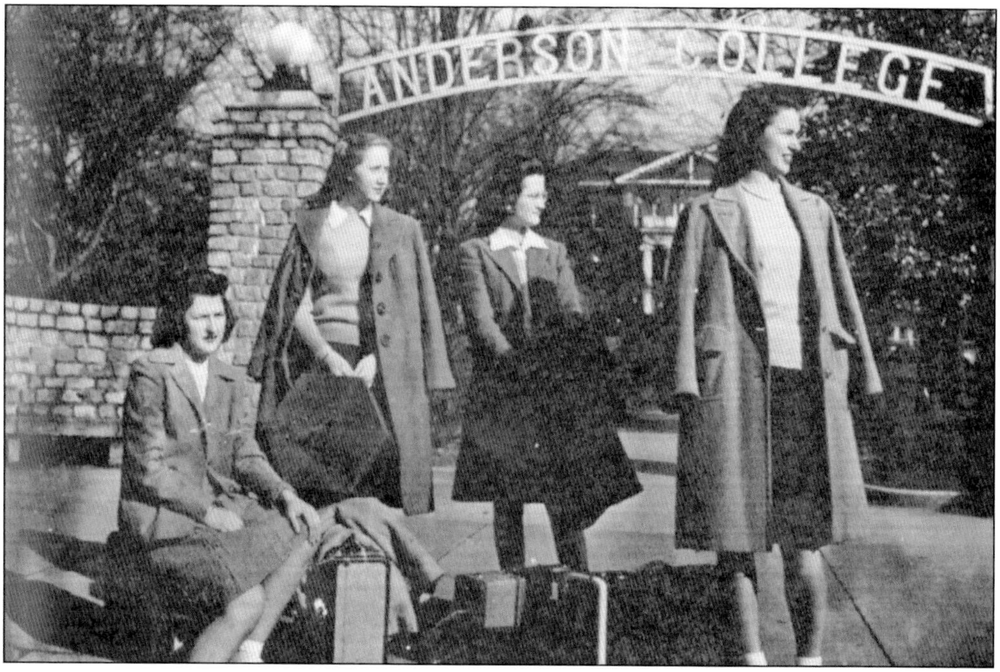

Baptist Student Union conventions provided opportunities for off-campus trips. This group of students is leaving to represent Anderson College in Columbia in 1945. The named archway first appears in photographs in the 1930s.

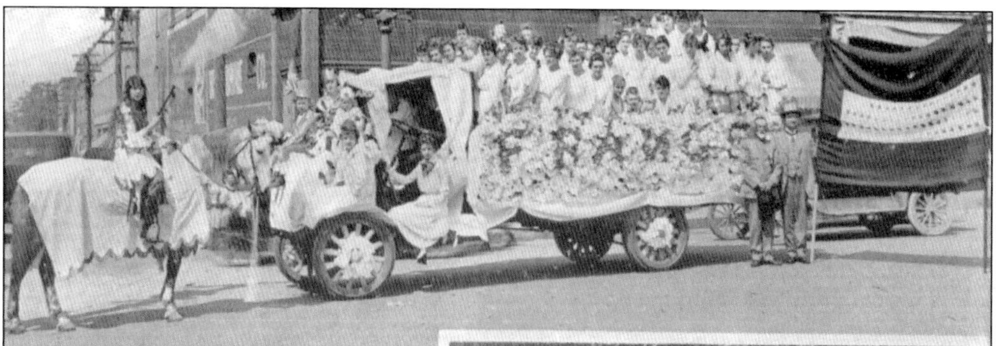

Here a group of students shows its support for the United States war effort during World War I by decorating a float in 1917 for what was most likely a bond fund-raising parade. Notice that France is spelled out in flowers on the side.

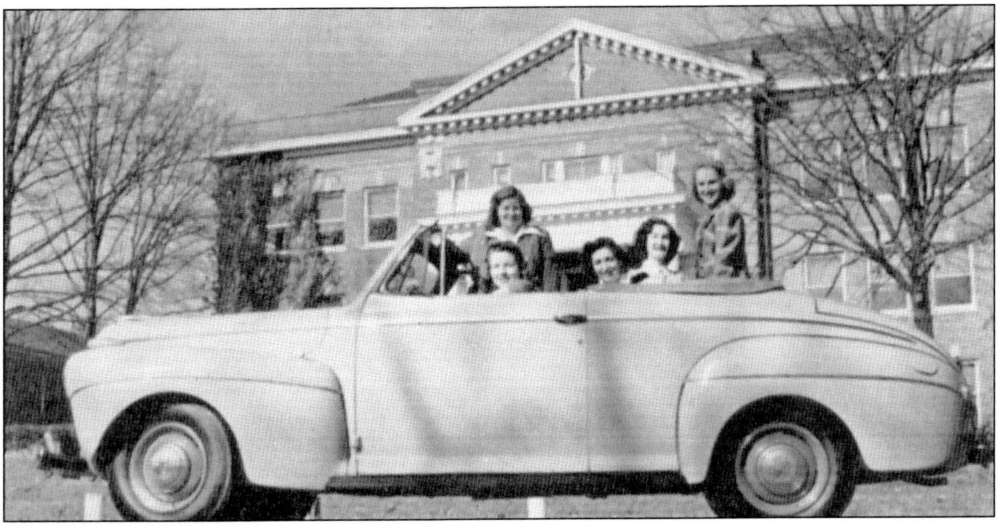

In 1942, it was still rare for students to have a car on campus. This group has happily found a roadster and is putting it to good use. Keys were turned in to the dormitory host or hostess when not in use. The 1960 students are waiting in the parlor dressed for dates. Dating was an important part of student social life, but it had many rules, which included signing in and out and having curfews as early as 10:30 for freshmen and 11:30 for sophomores. Dates had to also meet a college dress code.

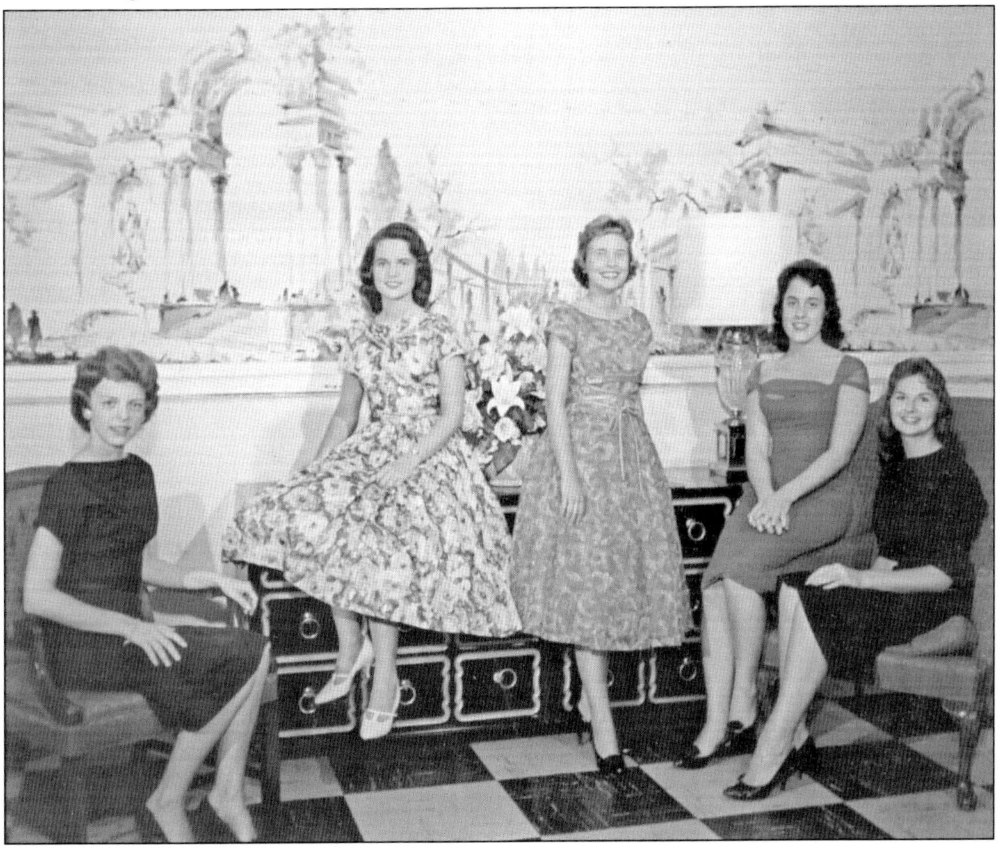

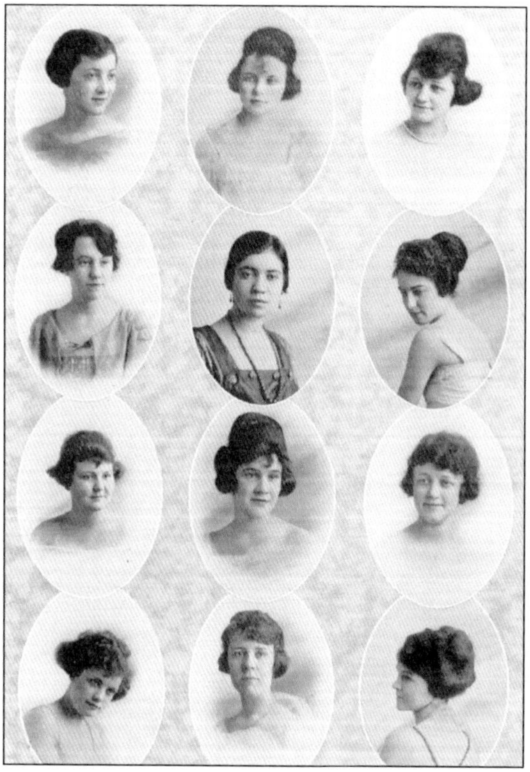

Among the earliest campus clubs were Greek lettered social organizations. The Pan-Hellenic Society of 1920 is pictured here. These Greek organizations faded from the scene when the institution moved from a baccalaureate to junior college status. They have since returned but are now honorary and professional organizations. One example can be seen in the 1987 group portrait of the members of Omicron Iota Kappa, the Fashion Merchandising and Interior Design organization.

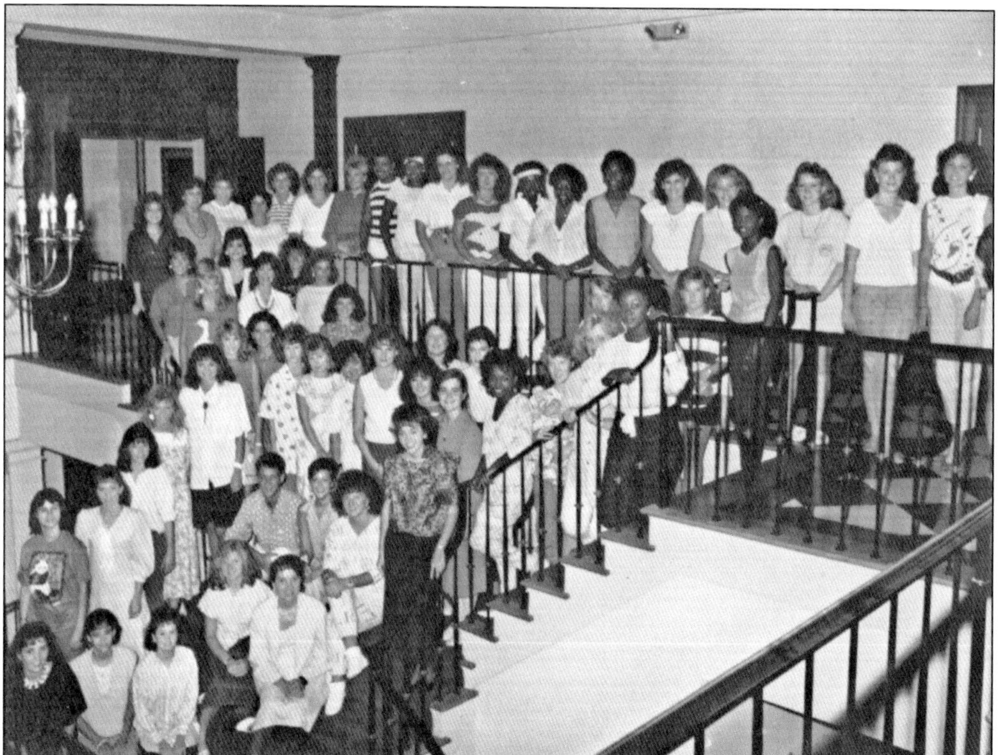

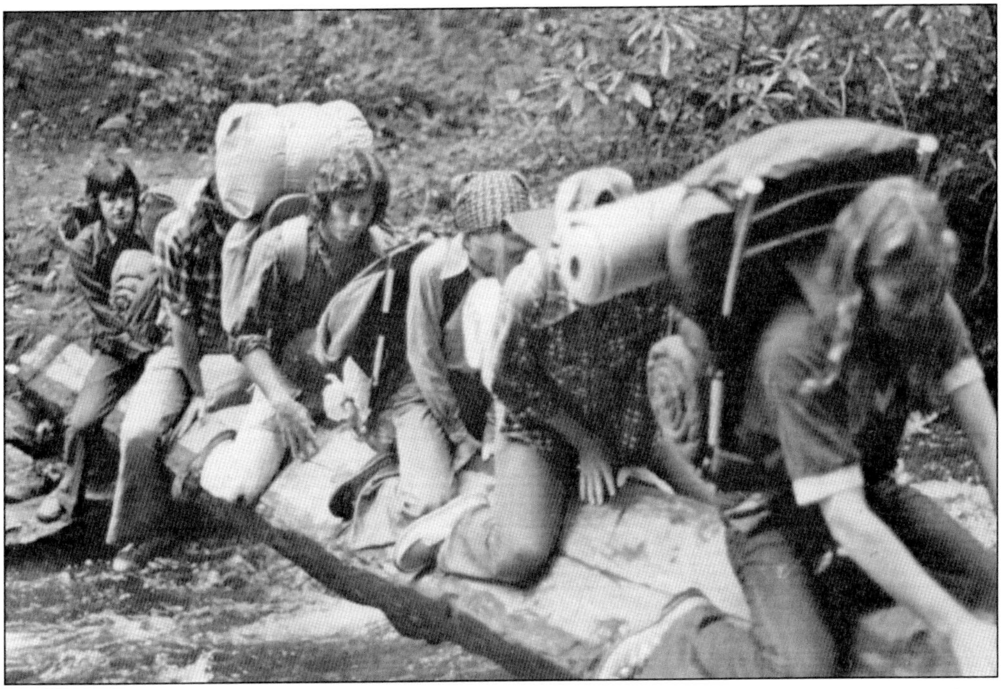

Among the different variety of clubs offered over the years was a hiking club. Here members cross over fast water in the mountains. Dennis James, an English instructor, was the leader for this group in 1976.

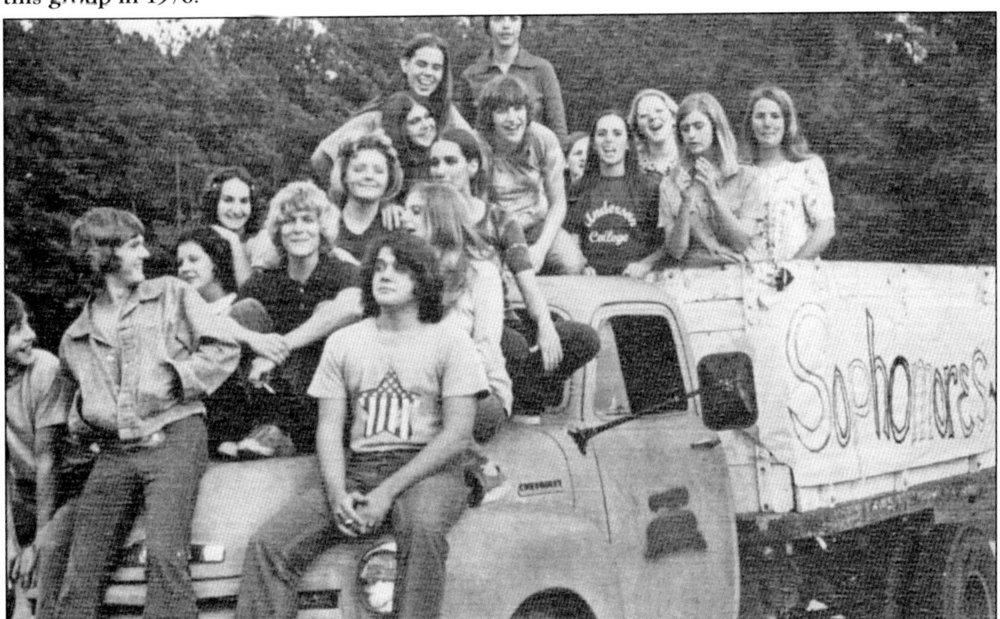

Intramural competition continues to be a popular part of campus life. Part of the fun involves devising creative names, such as the women's powder-puff teams in 1950 that chose the "Wet Hens" and the "Dead Pigeons." According to the vice president for student development, Dr. Bob Hanley, around 700 students in the 2009–2010 academic year participated in these various events.

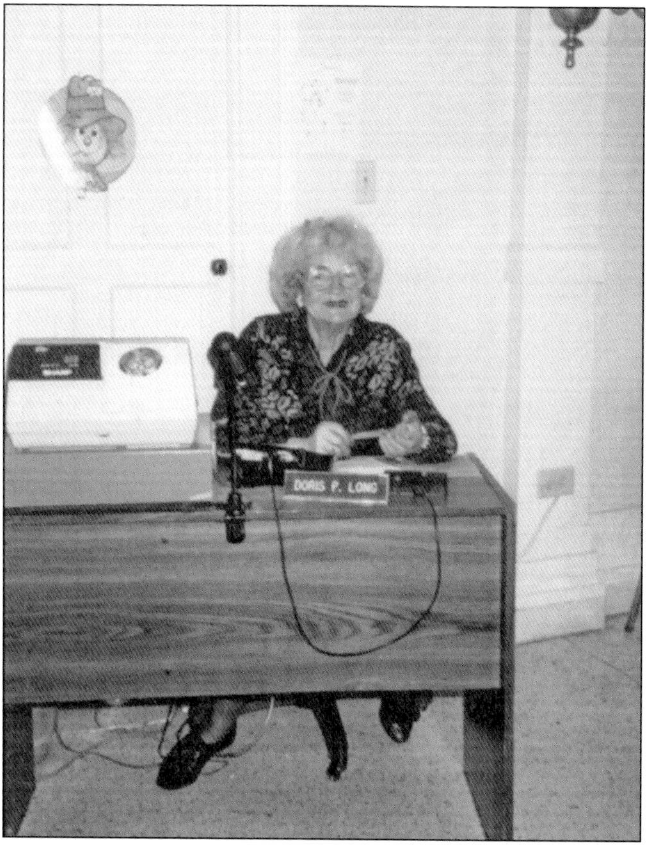

Equally important in the lives of students are members of the staff with whom they often interact each day. Here longtime cafeteria workers Pauline Hedden (below) and Doris Long (left) have a smile and a cheerful word for each student who comes to the cafeteria.

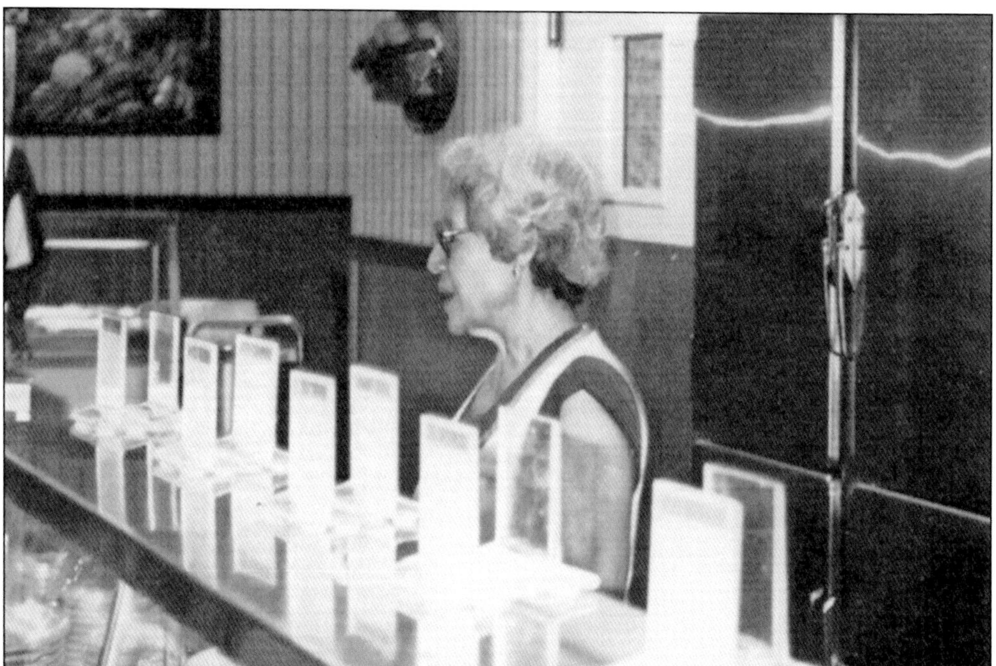

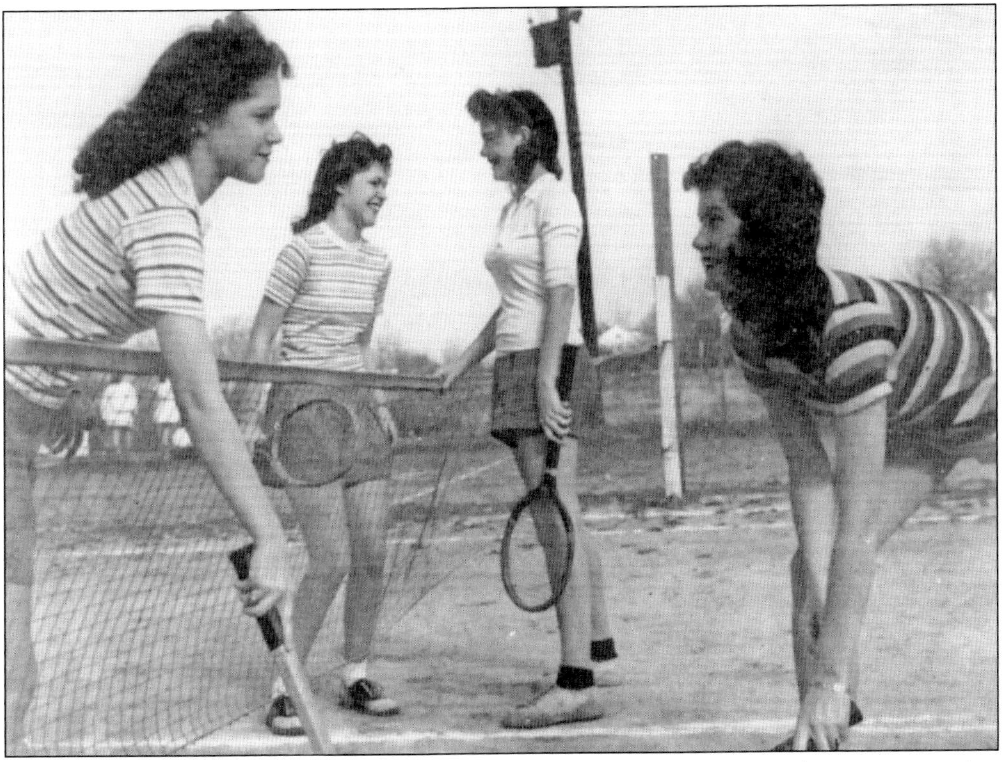

In 1943, 2009, and 2010, identical twins made following athletic competitions far more interesting than usual. The unidentified group of twins above is playing tennis in 1943. Below, the five sets of twins in 2009–2010 participated in tennis, soccer, track and field, and cross country. Pictured are, from left to right, Laura and Lisa Gorman, tennis, and Nigel and Nick Reynolds, Andrew and Derrick Driver, Jessica and Ashley Kleinberg, and Joelle and Kathryn Purinton, soccer.

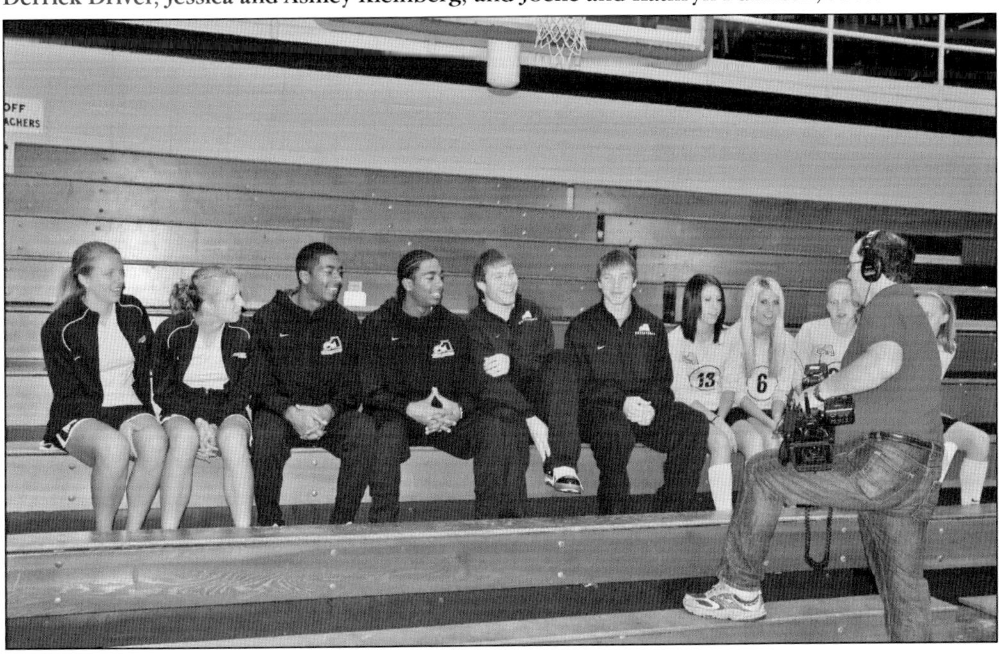

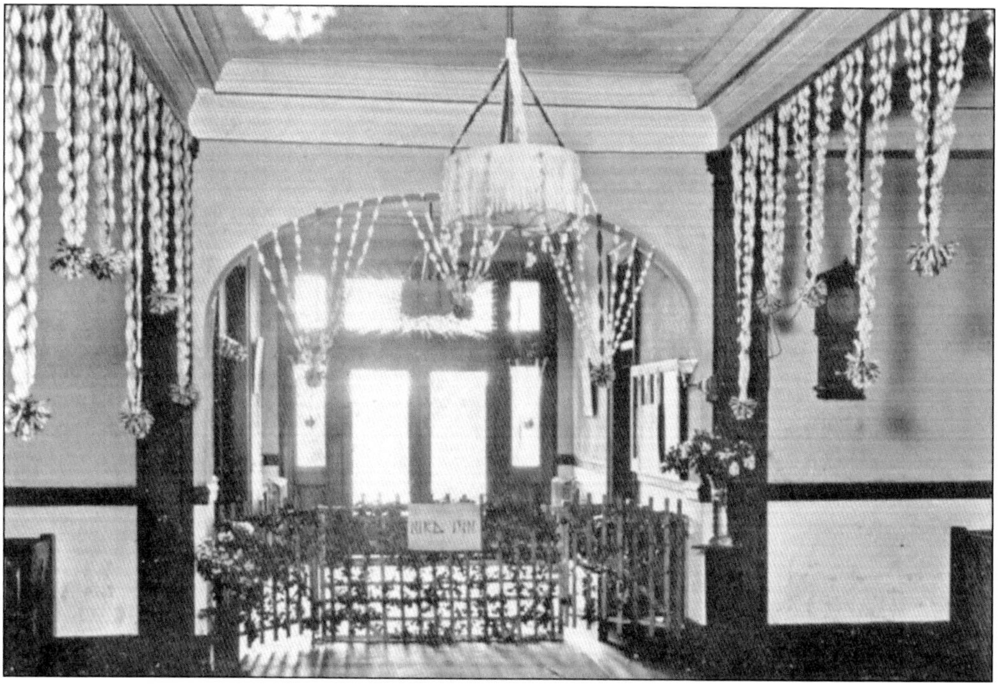

The milestones of accomplishment continue to be celebrated. These two photographs from the 1923 *Sororian* display the preparation for the 1922 Junior-Senior Reception. The foyer and the dining room are shown. The building where it took place is what is now called the Merritt Administration Building.

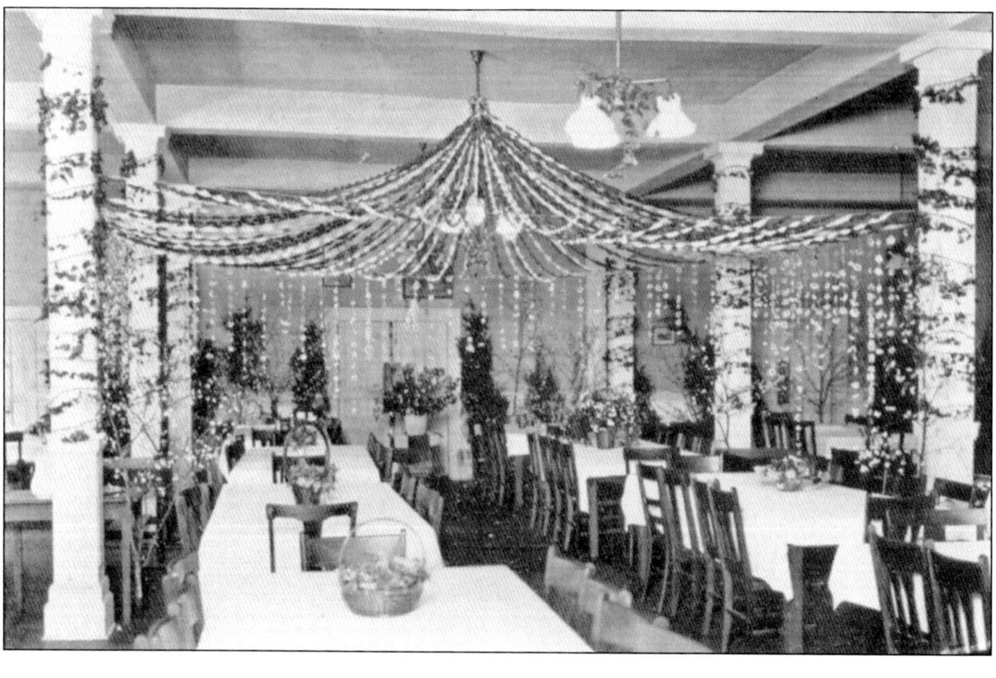

Six

Athletics

Based on the premise that a liberal arts education includes good physical health, the institution has fostered participation in athletics since its inception. In the early years, activities were primarily intramural sports or club participation, but beginning in the 1960s, the university moved to competitive programs. These early years were limited to games with neighboring junior as well as senior colleges and no membership in athletic conference associations. James "Red" Hill was the first director of athletics at Anderson College. In 1963, he was instrumental in getting Anderson College in the Western Carolina Junior College Conference, later known as Region X, for men's sports.

The university found itself a viable force. Women participated in the Association of Intercollegiate Athletics for Women (AIAW) from the 1960s until 1977, when they began competing in Region X. In 1974, 1975, and 1976, women captured the national crown in basketball under the coaching of Annie Claire Tribble and, in 1977, under Frankie Porter. From 1968 to 1978, men's basketball, coached by Jim Wiles, compiled an incredible record of 248-5 while winning eight consecutive conference titles and posting three undefeated seasons. For a total of five times, Wiles was named Coach of the Year in the Western Carolina Junior College Conference and Region X. He also guided AC to the National Junior College Athletic Association (NJCAA) Tournament five times, reaching the Final Four in 1978. Men's tennis under Max Grubbs garnered much honor for the institution in the 1960s and 1970s, and teams under coach Jim Boykin in 1986 and 1987 and coach Ned Caswell in 1992 won the National Championship.

The university athletic offerings grew from the 1980s to 2010 to include golf, table tennis, women's tennis, softball, baseball, wrestling, men and women's soccer, cross country, track and field, and volleyball. Additionally, Anderson moved to the NCAA in 1996, Division II in 2000, and the Carolinas Virginia Athletic Conference, later called the Conference Carolinas. In 2010, Anderson moved to the South Atlantic Conference, and it continues to compete at a championship level.

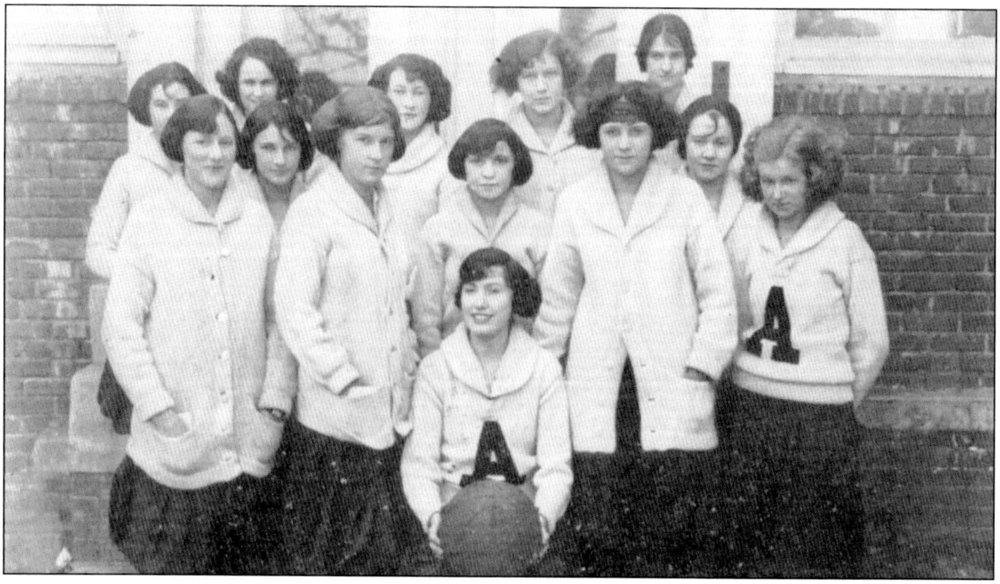

One of the earliest competitive sports on campus was women's basketball. The varsity squad of 1923 played a season of games with women's college teams from Charleston, Columbia, and Newberry. In the 1930s and the 1940s, off-campus travel for competition was quite limited, and competition did not resume again until the 1950s. AC was able to use the YMCA gym on Greenville Street for their games until the Whyte Gym was constructed in 1960.

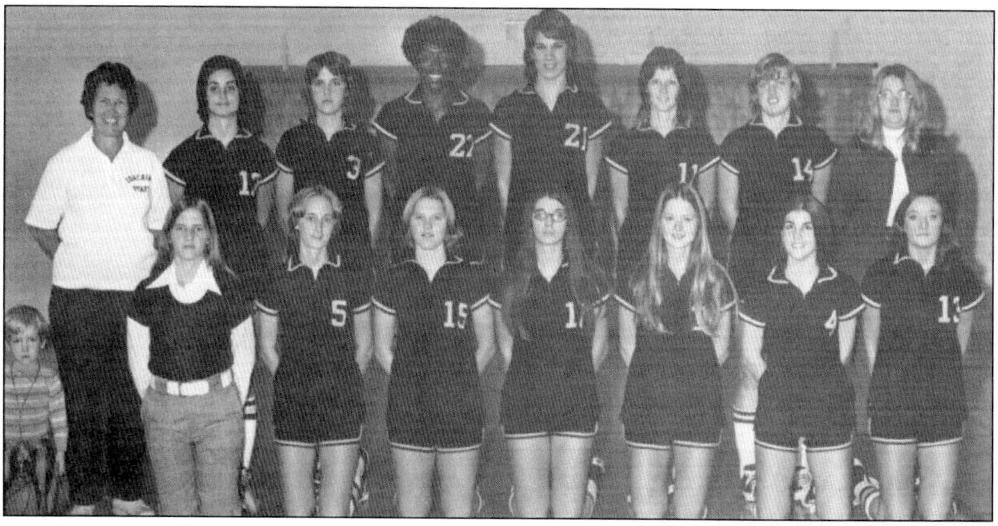

Coach Annie Tribble was a member of the women's basketball team when it did not lose a single game in the 1963 season. She came back to become coach for that team and led it to the AIAW junior college national championships three years in a row: 1973–1974, 1974–1975, and 1975–1976. The members of her first national championship team are, from left to right, (first row) Donna Kay, manager; Sherry Caldwell, Marilyn Felkel, Vickie Burton, Brenda Paulk, B. J. Shell, and Dale Campbell; (second row) Andy Tribble, mascot; Annie Tribble, head coach; Libby Mullinix, Doll Eadon, Janie Ruth Lee, Susan Neal, Laura Lawton, Grace Lyle, and Pam Watkins, manager. Janie Ruth Lee was the first African American female to play for Anderson and was a member of the national championship teams for both seasons she was on campus. Both Tribble and Lee were among the first inductees for Anderson College's Hall of Fame on May 15, 1999.

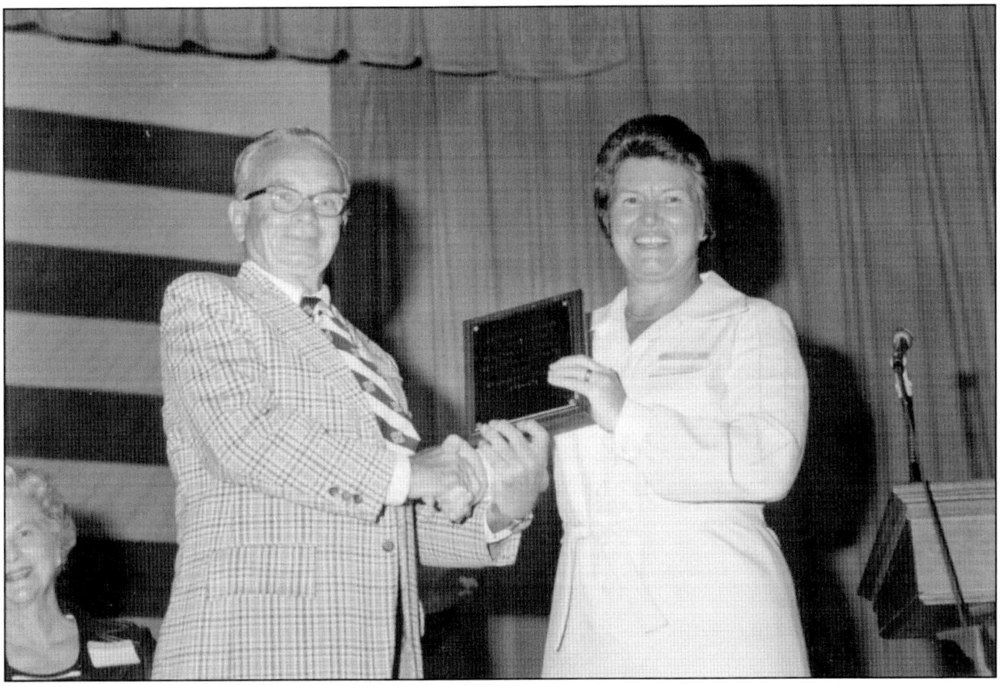

Athletic director and tennis coach Max Grubbs and Annie Tribble, pictured here, were inducted into the South Carolina Athletic Hall of Fame in 1981 and in 1994, respectively. Coach Grubbs's tennis teams had "only one losing season in 20 years," according to Ernie Trubiano in *South Carolina Sports Legends*.

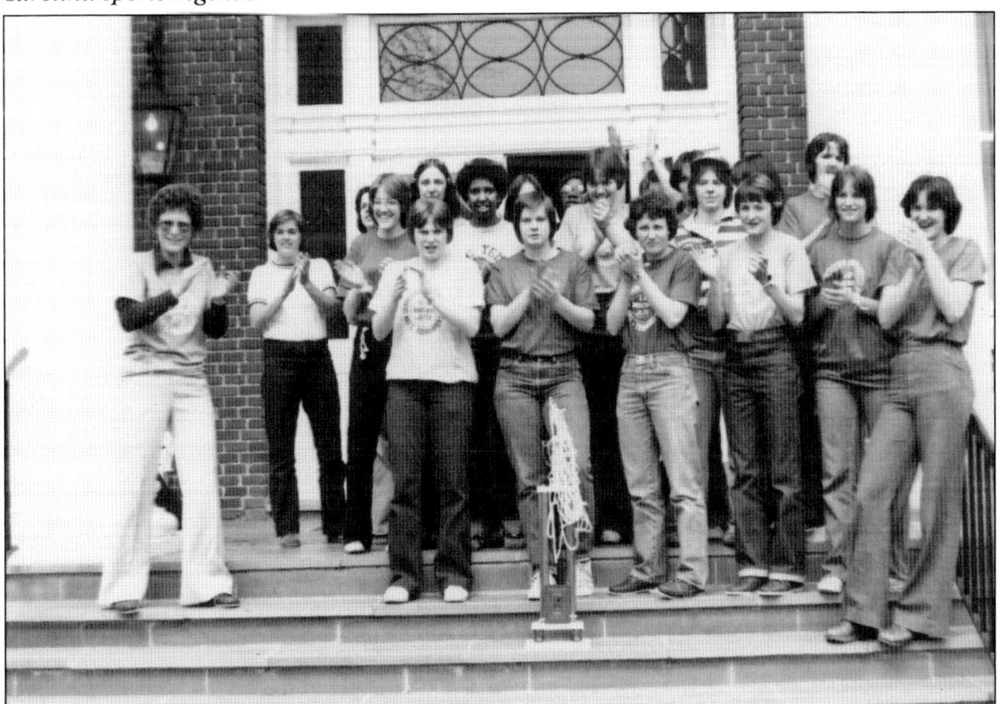

Women's basketball coach Frankie Porter and the team celebrate their national victory in 1977.

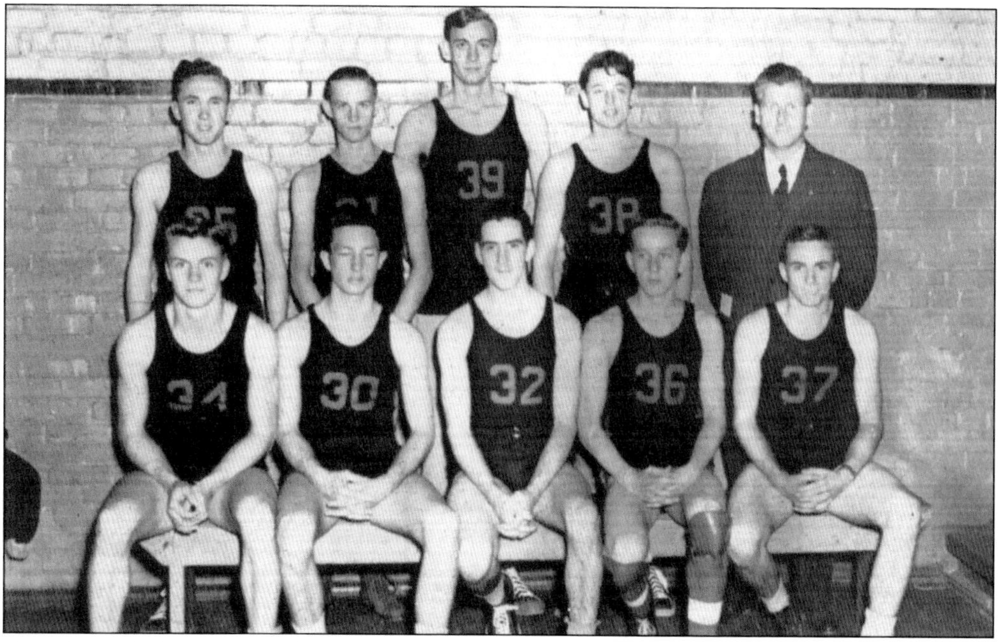

Men's basketball came to Anderson College as seen in this 1947 photograph. The team members were, from left to right (first row) Charles Hart, Jack Kilgore, Ray Ellis, Cecil Buchanan and Fred Whitten; (second row) Loriane Shore, Harold Rogers, Wesley Bruce, George Coleman, and Chick Evans, coach.

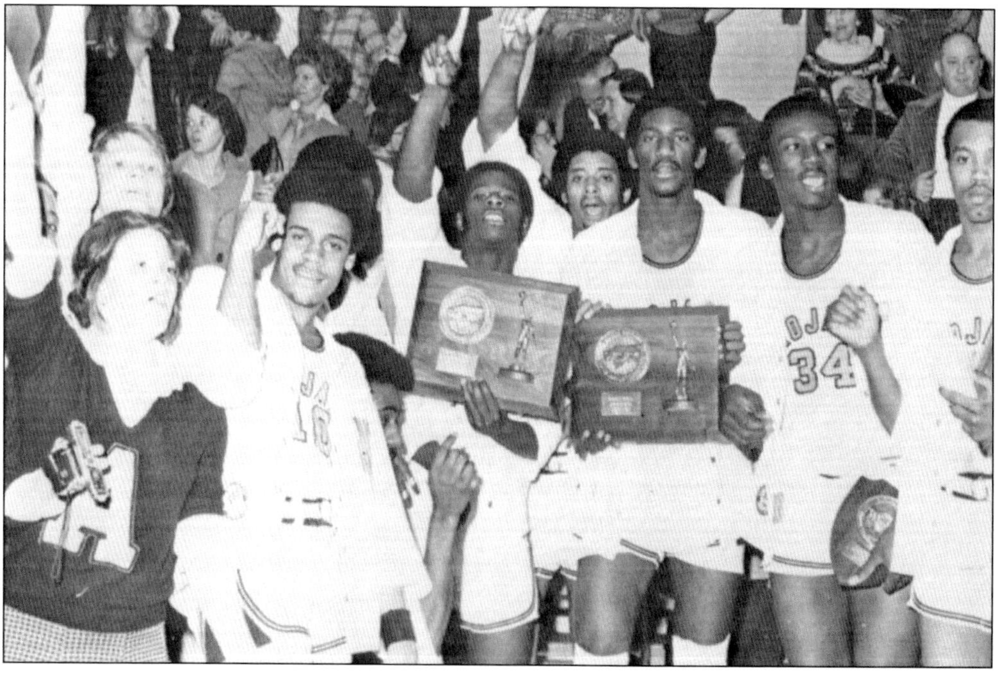

From 1968 to 1978, basketball coach Jim Wiles led his teams to eight consecutive conference titles and three undefeated seasons. Here the team celebrates its achievement in 1978. Pictured are, from left to right, Carter Ridenhour, Billy Hovis, Vince Brooks, Larry Wilson, Anthony Harris, Reggie Small, Tom Wimbush, and Ron White.

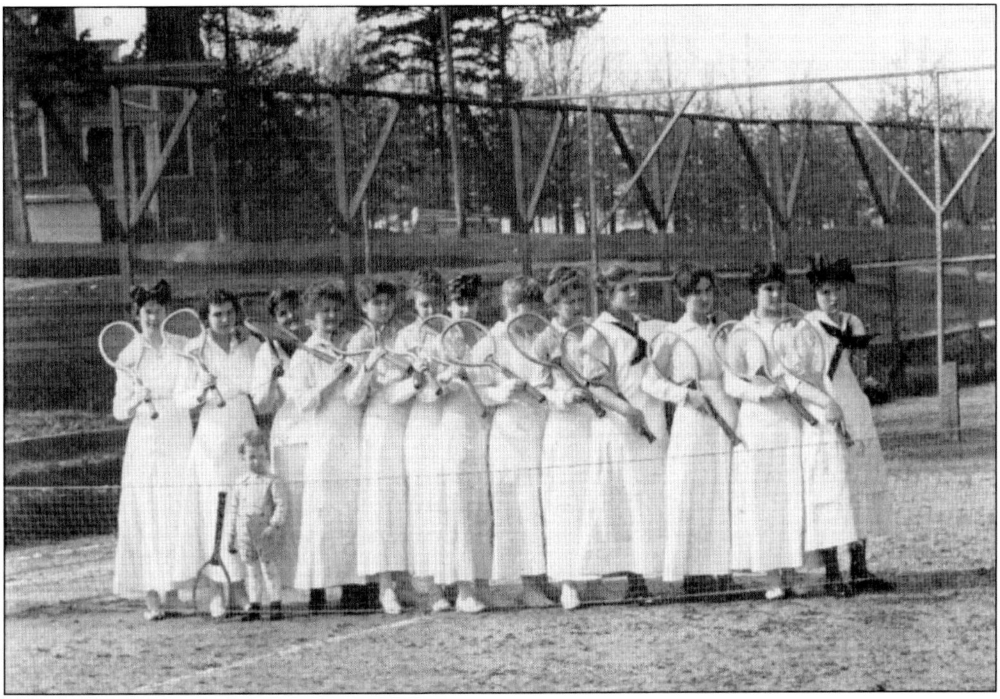

Tennis was another of the earliest sports on the Anderson campus. The tennis club lines up with their mascot in this photograph from 1916.

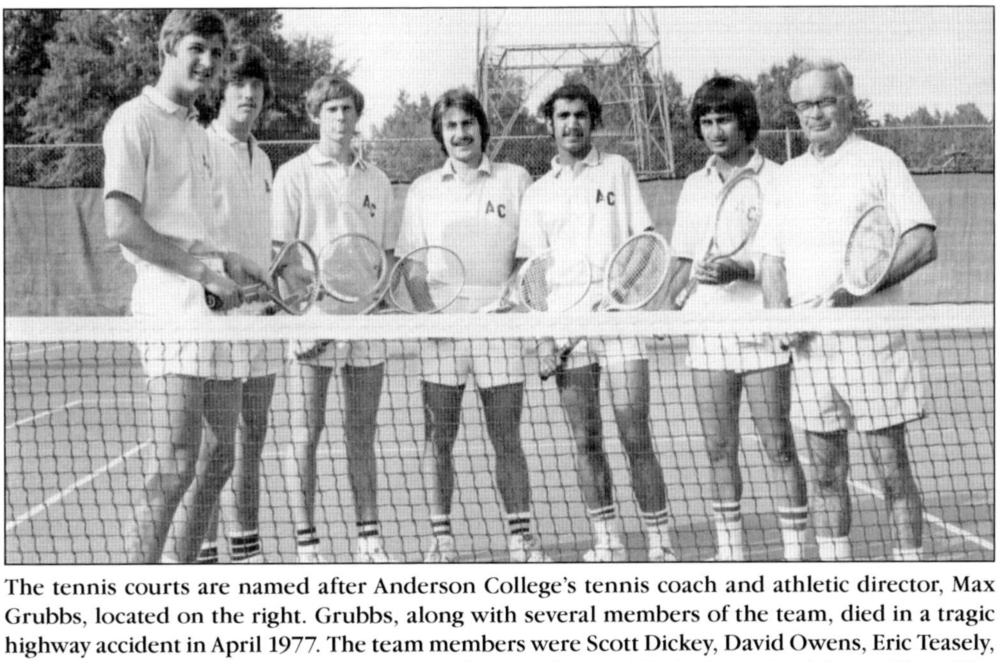

The tennis courts are named after Anderson College's tennis coach and athletic director, Max Grubbs, located on the right. Grubbs, along with several members of the team, died in a tragic highway accident in April 1977. The team members were Scott Dickey, David Owens, Eric Teasely, Donnie Pankin, Fazal Khan, and Dhiren Rathad. Dickey and Rathad survived the accident. The team, the first to include international students on its roster, was nationally ranked at the time.

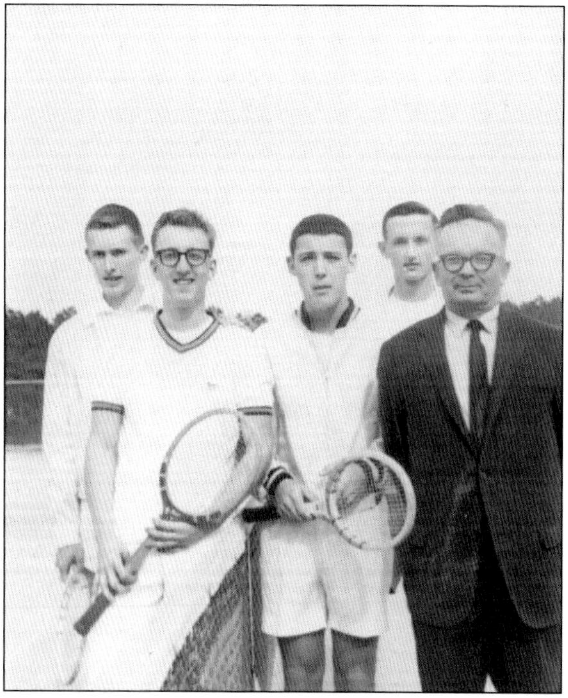

Terry Poore and John Burden were ranked second in the nation in doubles in 1963–1964; as singles players, they never lost a conference match. Pictured in the team photograph from left to right are John Burden, Peppy Holtzendorff, Terry Poore, Albert Cox, and Max Grubbs.

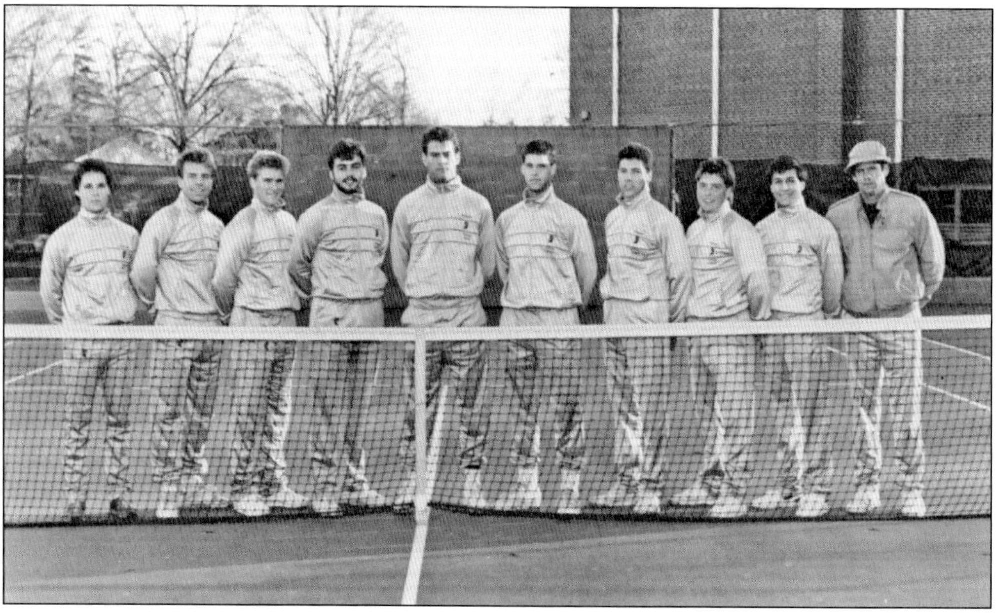

The first men's tennis team to reach the national championship, in 1986, is pictured here. Members are, from left to right, David Jenkins, Mat Malmberg, Robert Woods, Pat Pfuhl, Rex Terwilliger, Tawn Harden, Bobby McPherson, Owen Casey, Juan Balbontin, and coach Jim Boykin. Coach Boykin was inducted into the NJCAA Hall of Fame in 1994 and the Anderson University Hall of Fame in 2000. He was also named Coach of the Year twice (1986 and 1987) in the NJCAA and 12 times in Region X. Coach Sam Shrivastava led the men's tennis team to a national championship in the National Christian College Atletic Association (NCCAA) in 1996, which was also their first year of competition on the four-year level.

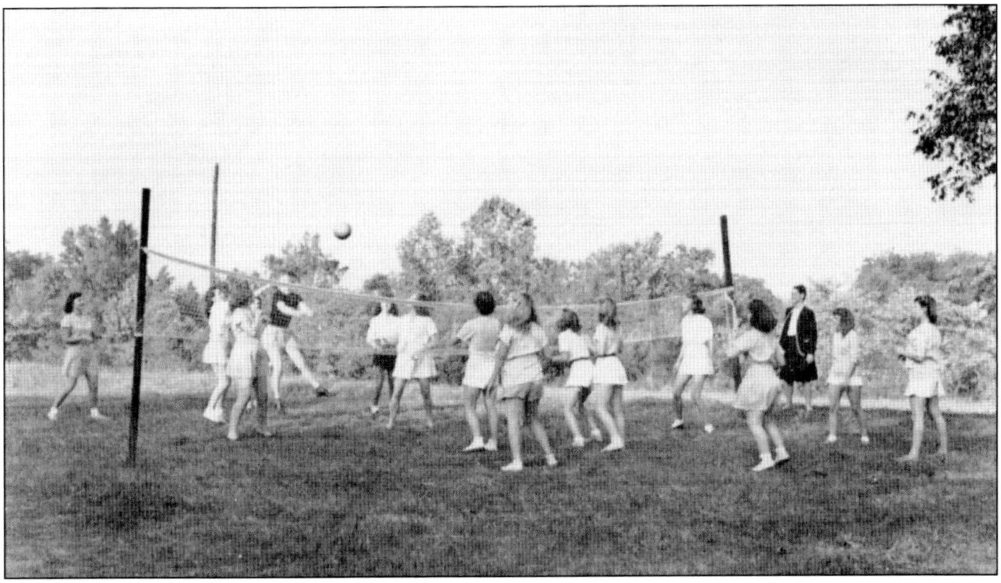

Volleyball had an early presence on campus, which is visible in this photograph from 1947.

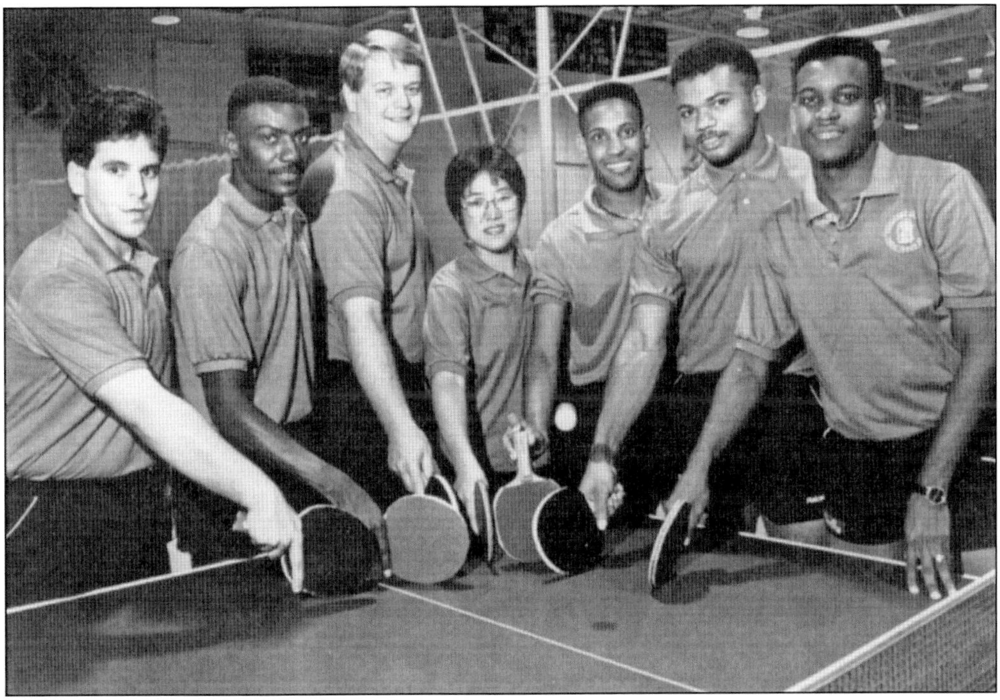

The table tennis team in 1992 included Michael Hyatt, who participated in the 1992 Barcelona Olympics. Michael and his brother Robert were from Jamaica. Team members include, from left to right, Julian Millan, Gregory Riley, coach and director Richard McAfee, head coach Amanda Chai, Michael Hyatt, Nigel Christopher, and Robert Hyatt. Amanda Chai was on the Chinese table tennis team that played for Pres. Richard Nixon's visit to China in 1972. The only other AC student to qualify for the Olympics up to that time was Owen Casey, a tennis player, who represented the Irish Republic in 1988.

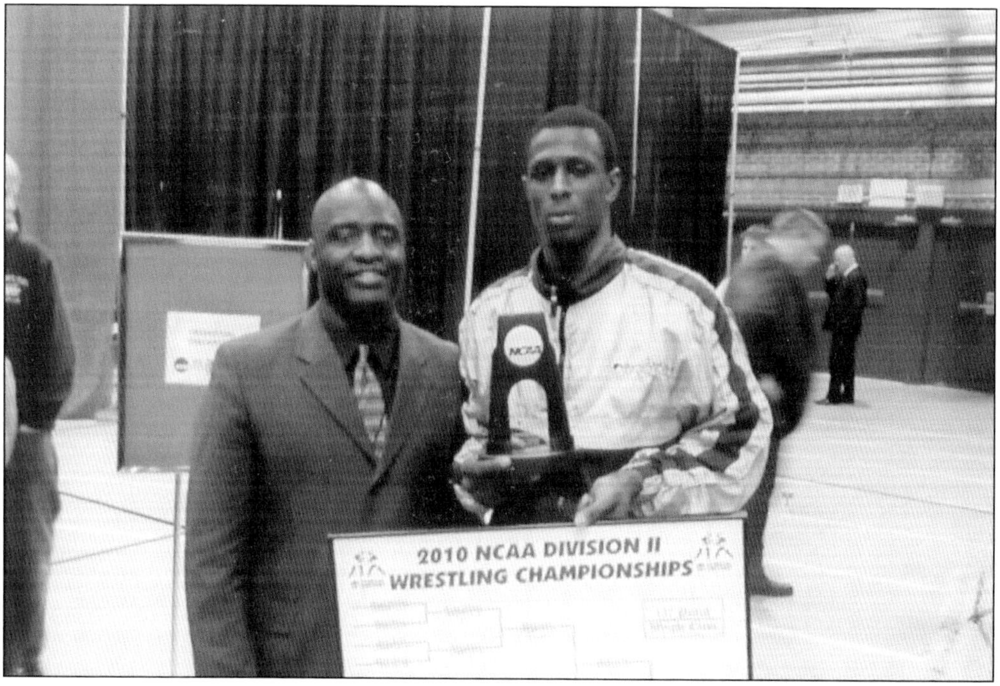

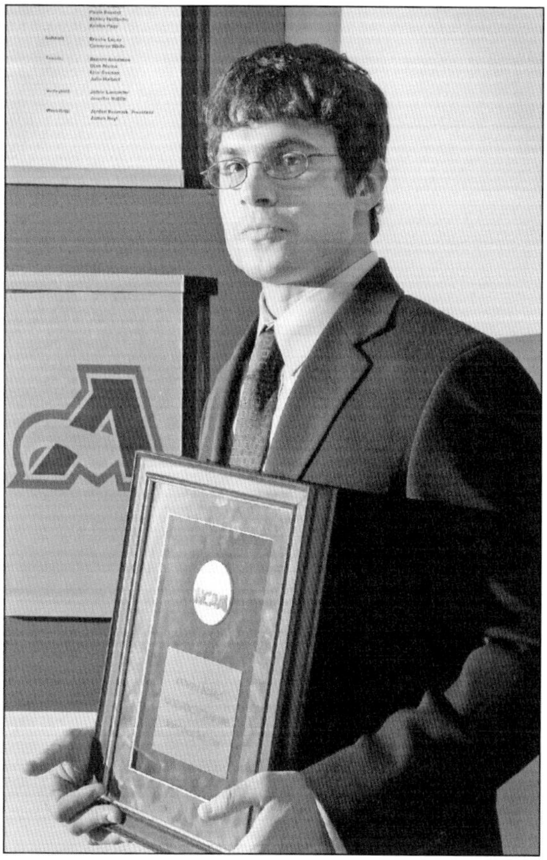

Wrestling was added to the athletic roster in 1992. Careef Robertson won the first national championship in wrestling in 2005. The second national championship was won by J. J. Jackson (top right) at the 2010 Division II Wrestling Championship at the University of Nebraska-Omaha. To the left of Jackson is AU wrestling coach Dock Kelly. Anthony DiCarlo (left) lost a match because he refused to press an advantage over an injured competitor. This outstanding example of integrity and sportsmanship made him winner of the Conference Carolinas Sportsmanship Award, and he went on to win the 2009 NCAA National Sportsmanship Award, as well as the Division II Award. He was honored at the AT&T National Sportsmanship Awards in St. Louis on November 21, 2009, which was aired on CBS.

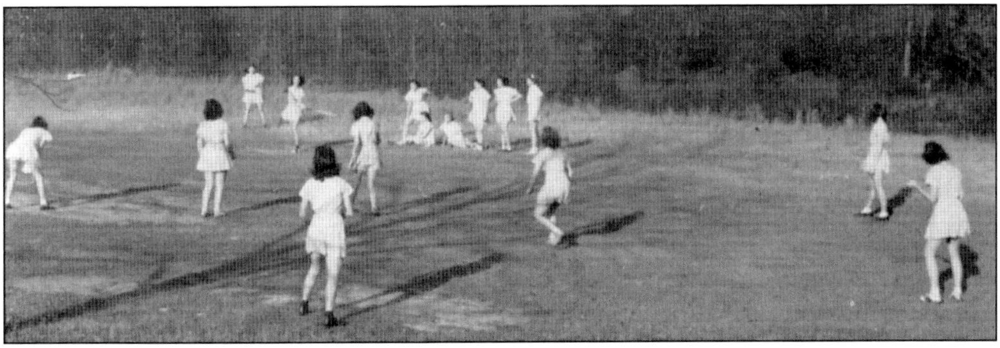

By the 1940s, softball had joined the ranks of options for the active Anderson College woman.

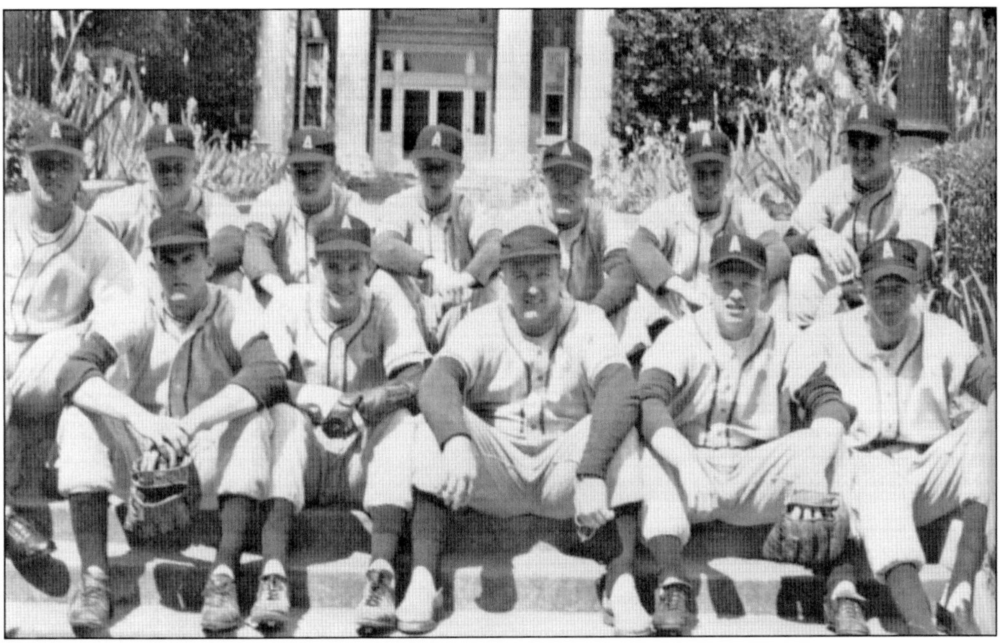

The creation of the first baseball team 1959 is an example of the expanding opportunities for men's athletics. The baseball diamond occupied back campus and was also used for outdoor graduation ceremonies. With the building of the Abney Athletic Center removing some of that space, baseball was suspended from 1978 to 1983, when an agreement with the City of Anderson allowed the team to use community facilities for baseball practice and games.

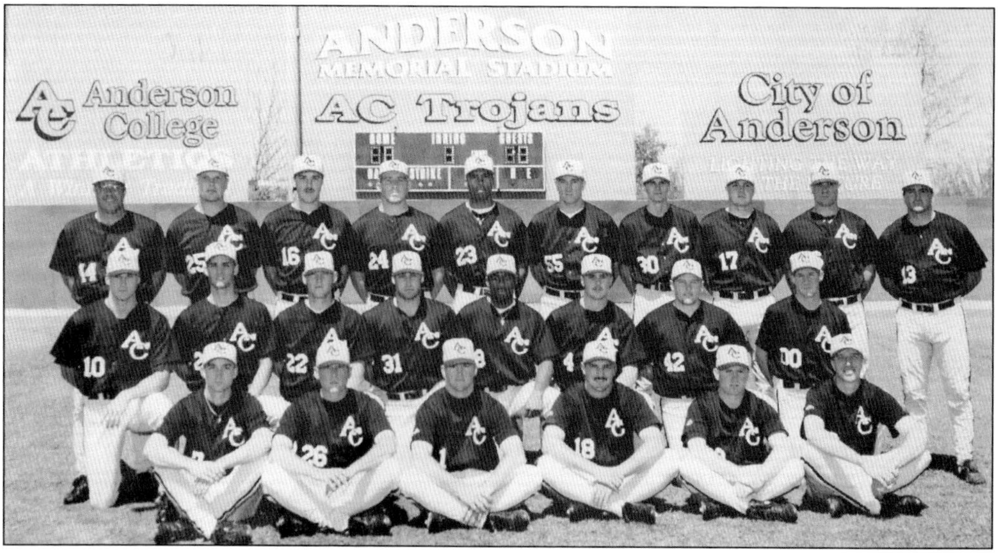

The baseball team that won the NCCAA World Series national championship on May 5–7, 1994, included, from left to right, the following: (first row) Kenny Schilling, Scott Jackson, Billy Coons, Wesley Williams, John Keenan, and Kevin Carroll; (second row) Chad Nelms, Bobby Beliveau, Steve Dickerson, Bryan Futch, Tony Cammon, Kevin Atkins, Jay Wickeri, and Brendan Donohue; (third row) coach Bobby Beville, Tom Alert, Brian English, Todd Williams, Jim Dolfinger, Robby Stanifer, Mark Huntsberger, Tony Young, Doug Beard, and coach Todd McCormick. Bobby Beville '76 returned to coach baseball when the sport was revived on campus in 1983. (Courtesy of Chad Nelms.)

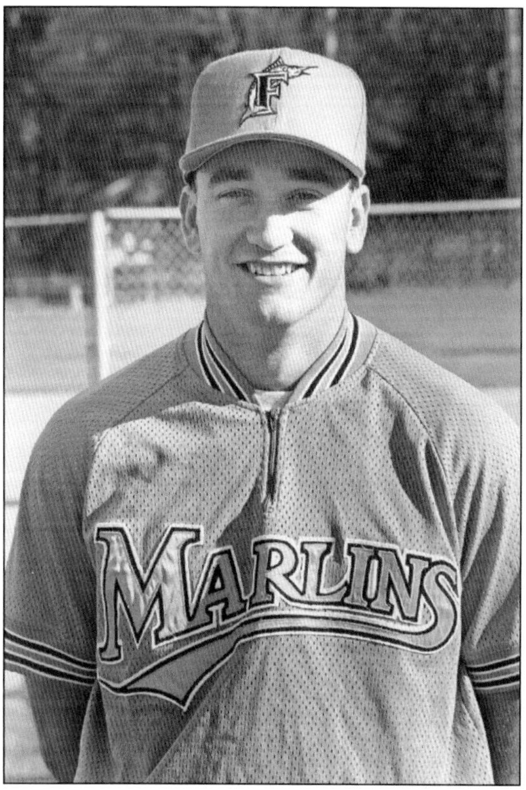

Baseball standout Robbie Stanifer '95 was drafted by the Florida Marlins in 1994 and was part of the team when it won the World Series during his first year in 1996. Other players with larger opportunities included Jeff Twitty '77, who played for the Kansas City Royals. Others such as Kenny Dickson and Chris Hawkins, who played from 1983 1984, were also draft candidates, as well as Don Brock, who was drafted by the Giants. David Buffamoyer, class of 1977, went on to the New York Yankees' minor league teams for four years and was inducted into the AU Hall of Fame in 2000. David Mattox, a pitcher for AC in 2000 and 2001, received the Sterling Award as the New York Mets minor league pitcher of the year in 2002. Blair Carson '09 was drafted by the Cincinnati Reds in the 42nd round in 2009.

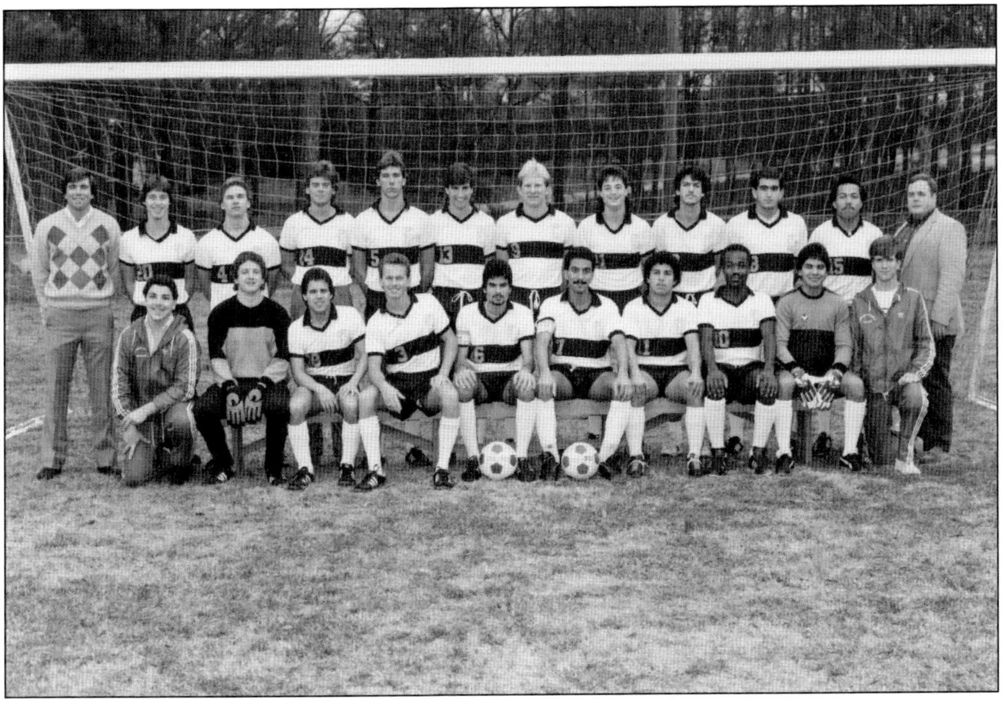

Men's soccer was a club on campus until 1982. Rick Wright served twice at Anderson College as coach, for five years beginning in 1982 and again beginning in 1992. Members of the 1984–1985 team are, from left to right, (first row) Nick Plakis, Matt McGonegal, Miguel Zabriskie, Steve Huff, Darrin Lewis, Ihab Ahmad, Rogoberto Bruce, Cliff Simmons, Greg Dobbs, and trainer Cecil Marrett; (second row) coach Rick Wright, William Jennings, Steve Butler, Wyatt Lewis, Todd Heebner, Rob Moody, Nick Shady, Scott Brown, Gene Bishop, Mark Nasim, Carlos Morales, assistant coach John Willis. Wright and a number of the players were from Bermuda.

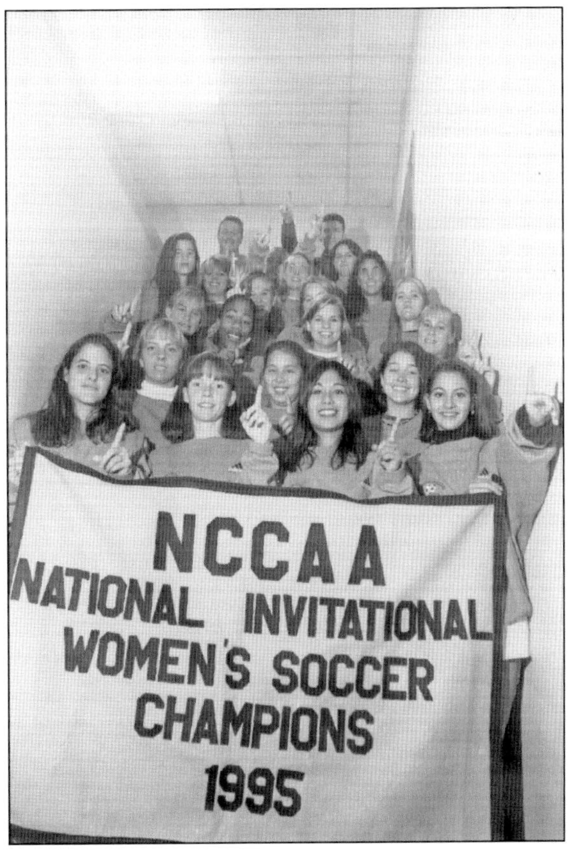

Women's soccer won the NCCAA national championship in their first season of competition at the four-year level in 1995.

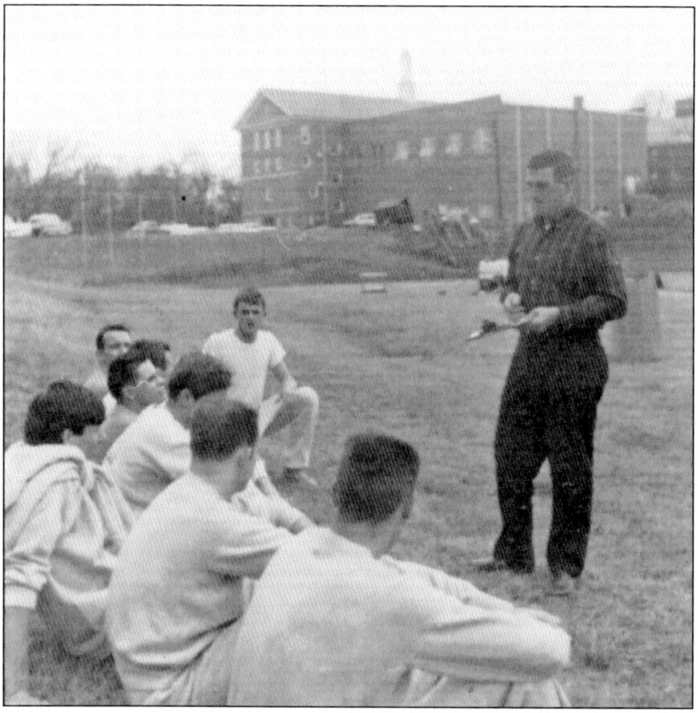

Track and field and cross country came to Anderson College under coach Howard Bagwell. He launched programs for men and women in 1963 before he went to what is now Charleston Southern University. His stellar coaching career there from 1965 to 2000 garnered induction into the Big South Hall of Fame and the South Carolina Athletic Hall of Fame. By the 1980s, the sport had been dropped, but it returned around 2000. Outstanding athletes, such as runner Whitney Bishoff 2009–2010, have brought more attention to the sport.

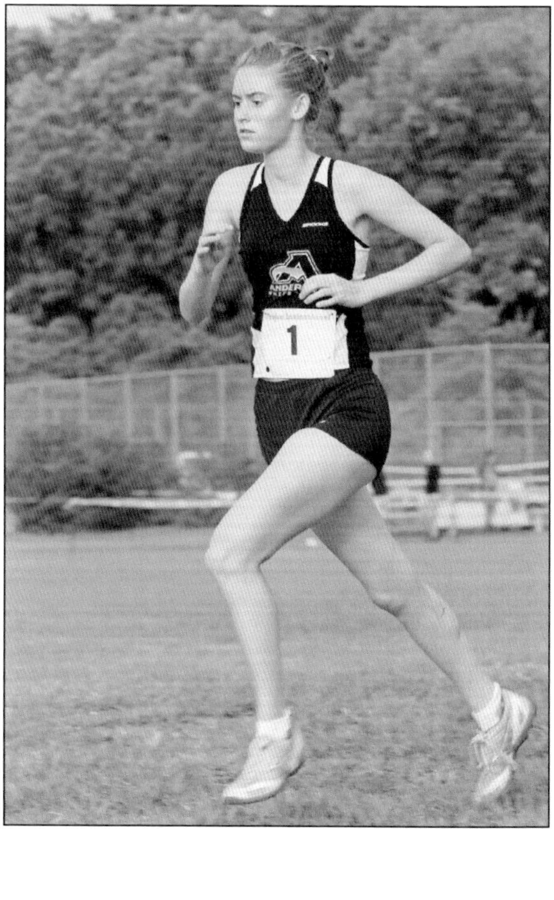

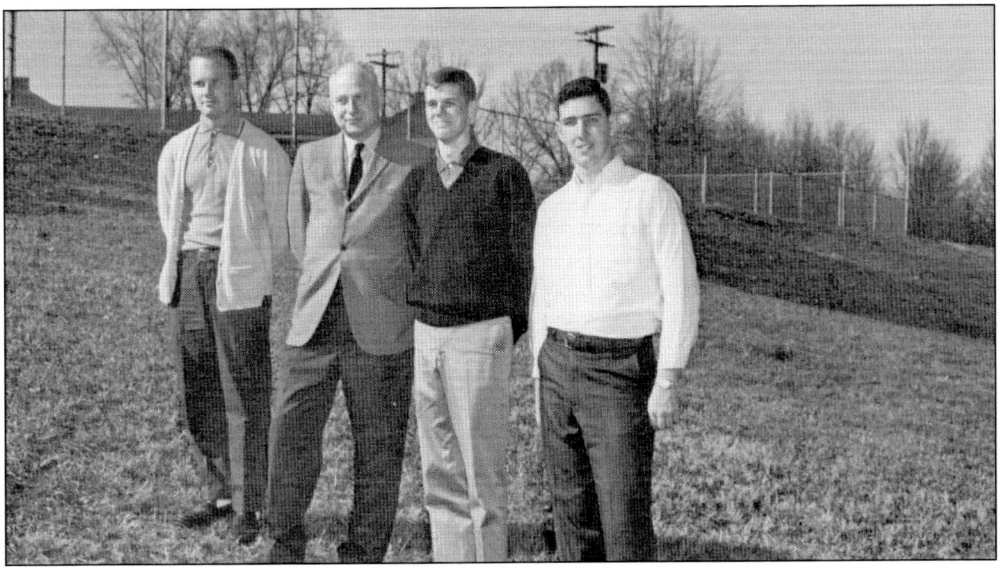

In 1964, golf was added to the roster of campus sports. Members of the first men's team are, from left to right, Lawrence Thompson, coach King Pushard, Luther Rickenbaker, and Skipper Maynard.

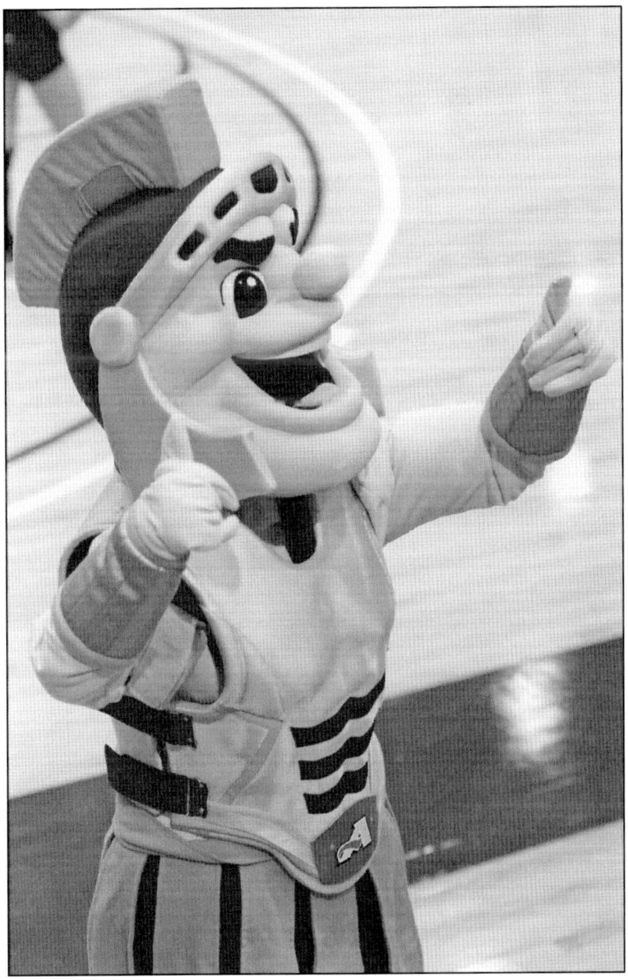

Troy the Trojan, the Anderson University mascot, was unveiled in 2009.

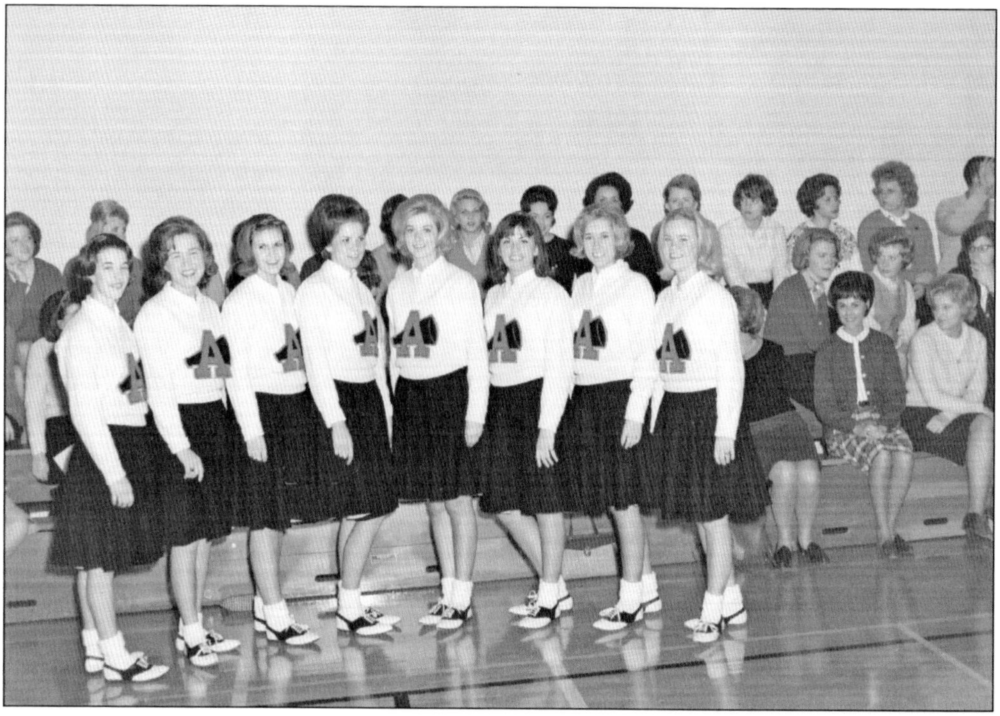

Athletic competition was enhanced with the addition of cheerleaders in the 1940s. Today's cheerleaders are accompanied by a dance team.

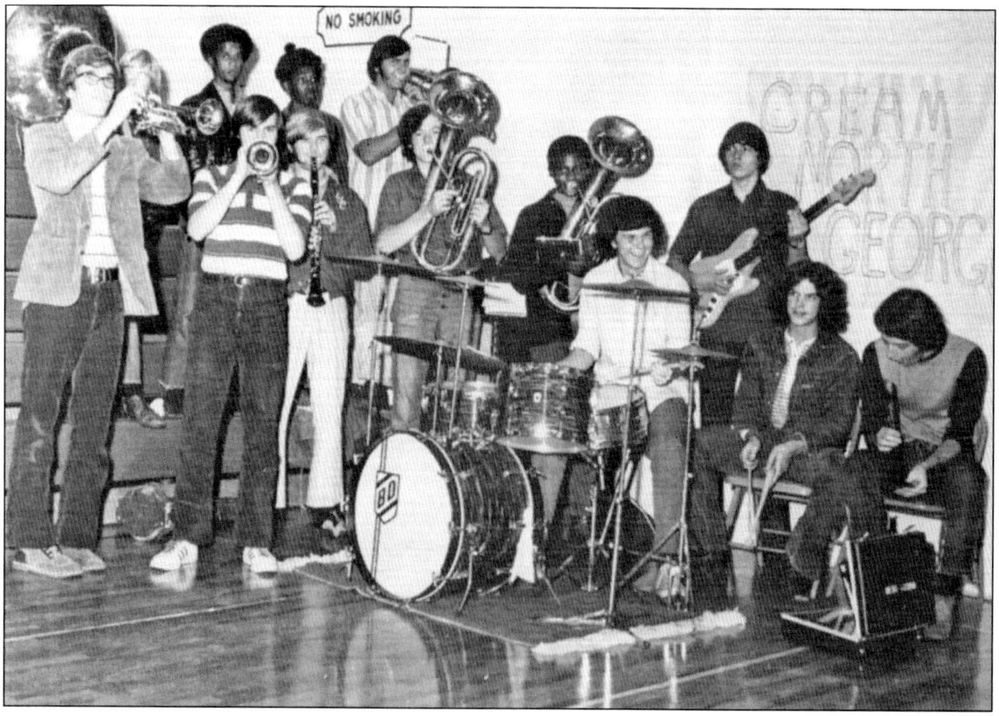

At times, pep bands were created to help stoke enthusiastic support at ball games. Here is the band in the gym in 1972.

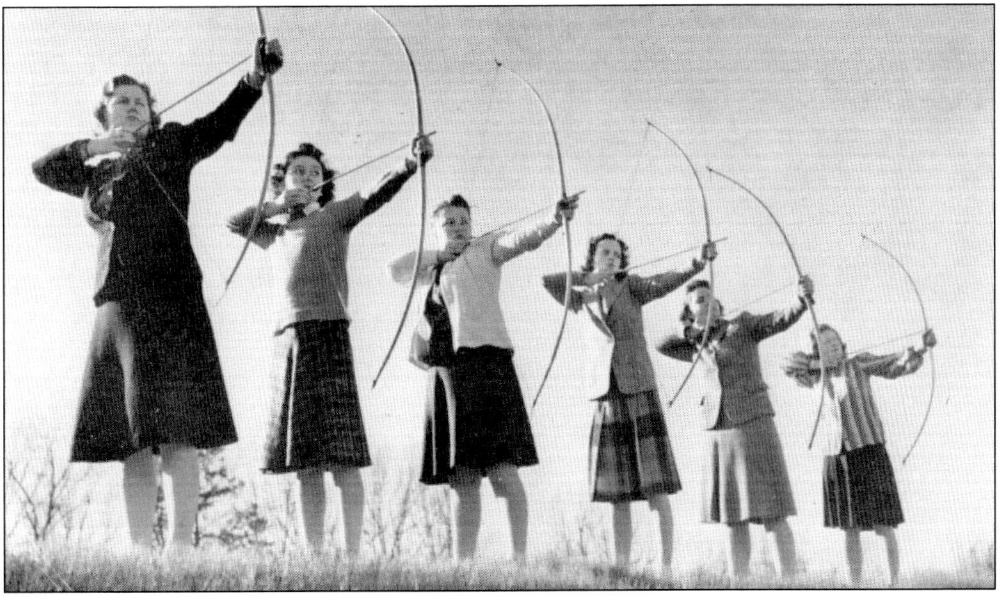

Archery was once available at Anderson College. Here the sport is seen in a 1942 photograph.

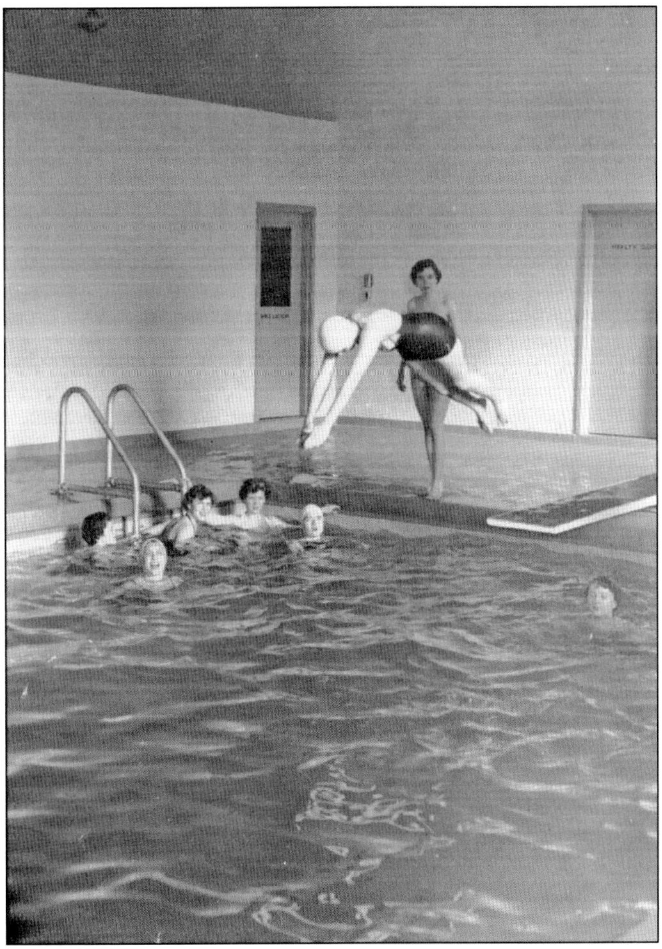

Though the campus never had its own pool, swimming was a course offering for students from time to time between 1918 and 1975. From the 1950s to the 1970s, students were able to use the facilities at the YMCA on Greenville Street to take these classes. These students are enjoying the pool in 1955. The YMCA also provided space for college basketball games and dances.

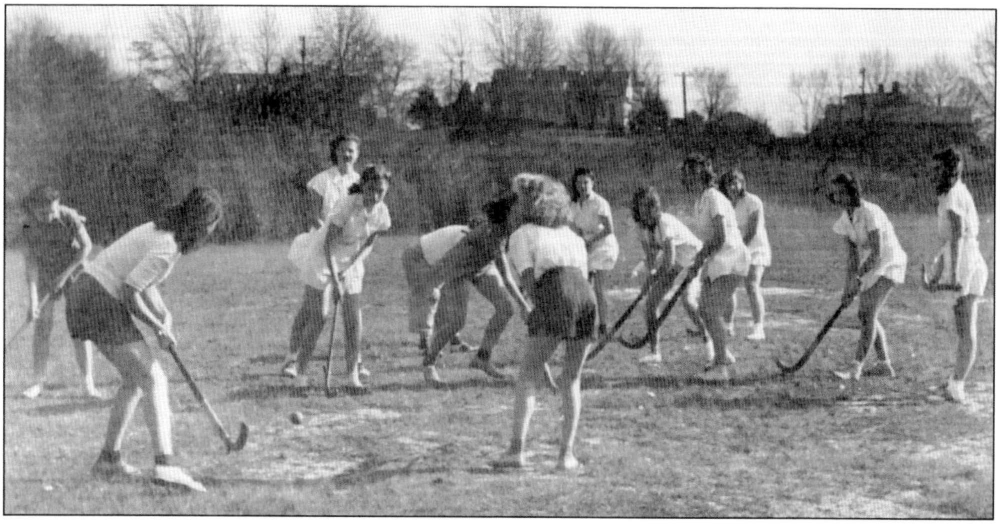

Though the campus was now coeducational in 1943, women's opportunities were not diminished. Here students play field hockey in a photograph captioned, "Goalie . . . Beware!"

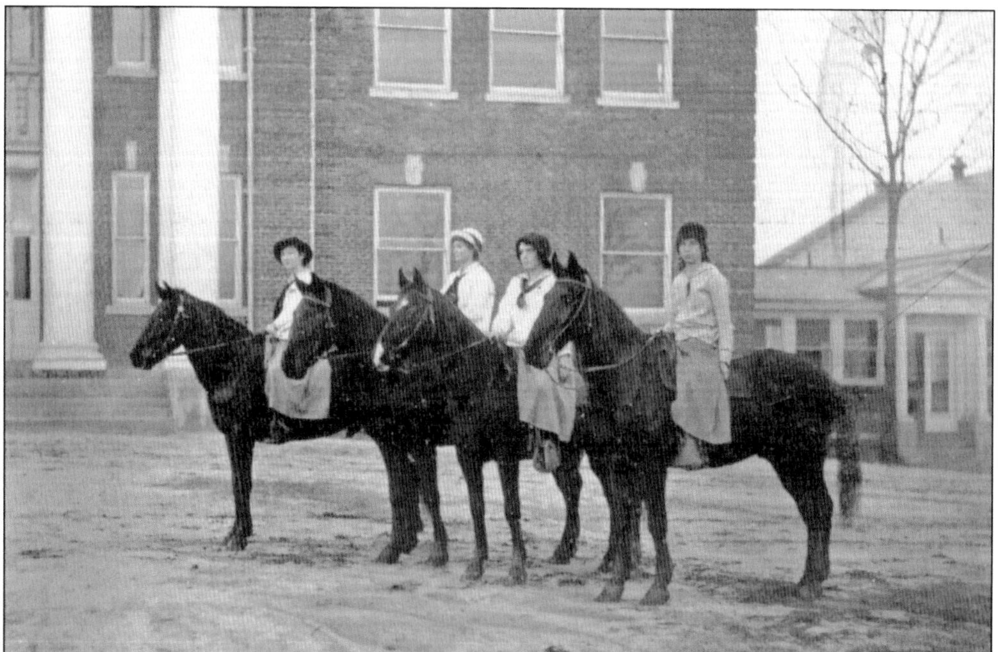

Another sport offered on several occasions over the years was horseback riding. This group of 1915 students, Helen Harris, Lou Nell McGee, Lola Dell Ramsay, and Sara Frances Stephens, called themselves "The Rough Riders."

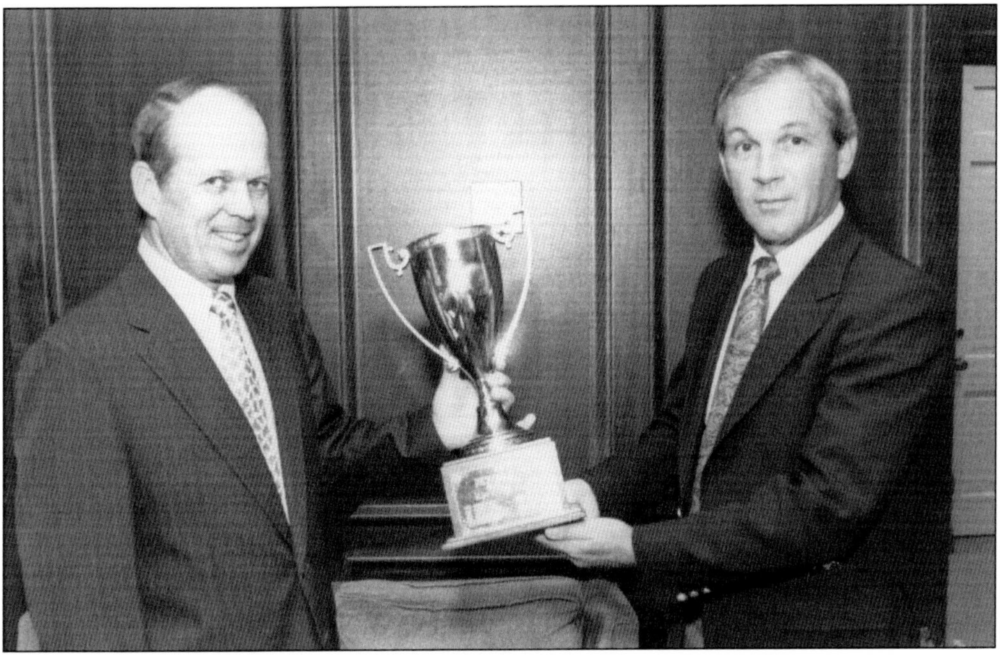

Pres. Mark Hopkins and athletic director and basketball coach Steve Lytton hold the Dickerson Cup in 1990. AC had earned the cup in the last six out of seven years. This cup was awarded annually to the school that performed the best in the Region X Tournament competition. The Dickerson Cup was established in 1979 to honor longtime Lees-McRae coach Fred I. Dickerson.

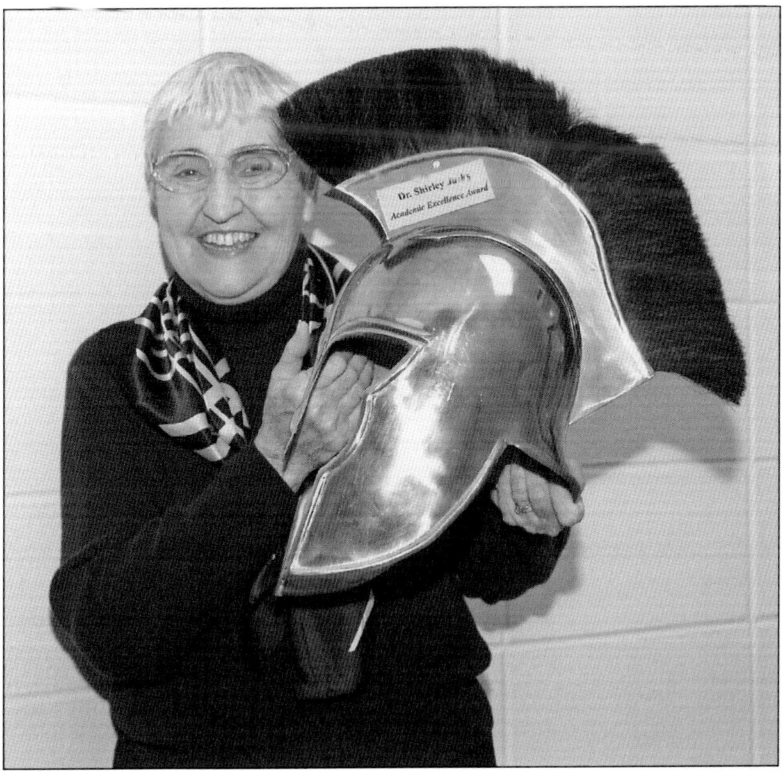

The Shirley Jacks Academic Award was created to honor the longtime professor of French and avid Trojan supporter. It is awarded each semester to the team with the highest GPA and is placed in the winning coach's office. The first team to win the award was the softball team in the fall of 2007.

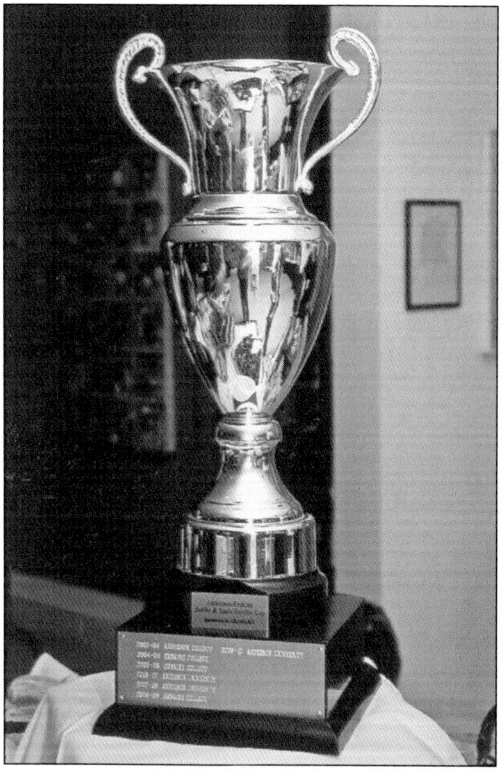

The Beville Cup, originally known as the Anderson/Erskine Cup, is presented to the winner of the competition between Erskine and Anderson's athletics programs. It was established in the fall of 2003 and is sponsored by ARAMARK in order to promote and enhance the rivalry between the Trojans and the Flying Fleet, whose campuses are separated only by 20 miles. Anderson University won the cup in 2004, 2007, 2008, and 2010. In 2007, the name of the cup was changed to the Susie and Bobby Beville Cup in honor of Anderson's former athletic director and his late wife, who both attended Anderson and Erskine.

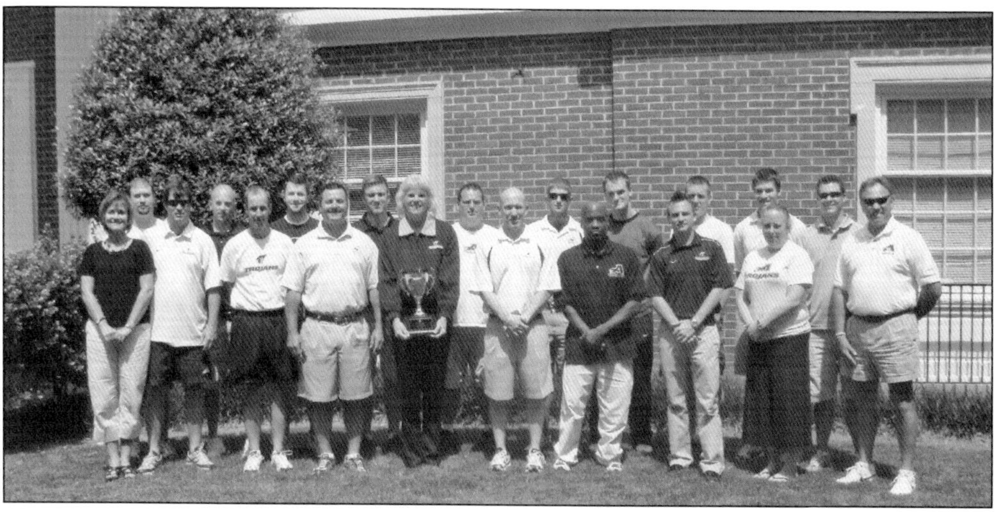

The athletic staff celebrates the winning of the Conference Carolinas all-sports trophy, the Joby Hawn Cup, for the second time in 2008. AU ended its participation in Conference Carolinas in 2010 by winning this coveted cup for the fourth year in a row. The Hawn Cup, awarded each year in honor of former Commissioner H. C. "Joby" Hawn, goes to the league member who shows the highest rating of excellence in all conference-sponsored sports. It was also the fourth time a South Carolina member of the conference claimed the honor. AU was the first South Carolina member to win the Hawn Cup and is currently the only member of the league to have won both the Hawn Cup and the John D. Messick Sportsmanship Award in the same athletic year (2006–2007). Anderson first received the prestigious Messick Award in 2004.

Seven

EPILOGUE

As Anderson University launches into its second century, the horizon glows brightly as many changes transform the institution and its outreach. During the last decade, much of it under the administration of Pres. Evans Whitaker, the institution changed its status from a college to a university in 2006, saw dramatic expansion in programs and degrees including the university's first six graduate programs, the largest gift in the university's history, the refurbishment of numerous facilities, the construction of Thrift Library and three residence halls, and the implementation of the most important technological advances in the university's history, which involve online and mobile learning. These changes were accompanied with an equally dramatic 56-percent growth in enrollment and a significant increase in selectivity and prestige. Under Whitaker's leadership, Anderson was named for the first time to the top tier of Southern universities by *US News & World Report* and received national recognition as one of "68 Up and Coming Universities in America" for its advancement and innovation.

Among the most visible of those changes was the physical expansion of the campus from 68 to 271 acres in 2008 by the Pracht gift and the purchase of the former county fairgrounds, now known as the Athletic Campus. The latter now houses many athletic activities as well as the Physical Plant and provides many opportunities for development in the future.

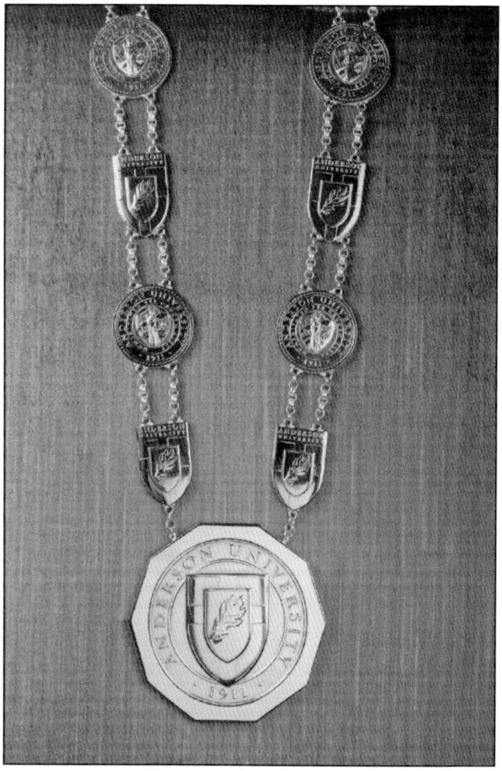

One new tradition is the Anderson University Chain of Office, worn by the president on ceremonial occasions, which was a gift from alumni, friends, and the class of 2007. The silver and gilt collar has a medallion with the university's coat of arms, which features the cross and an oak leaf and acorn. The eight sides represent the institution's eight stakeholder groups. The cross represents Christ as the center of the institution; the oak leaf and acorn represent the oak trees on the Alumni Lawn and also the oak's qualities of strength, courage, learning, stability, wisdom, and endurance. The seal is centered on the figure of a woman who represents the institution's first years as a women's college. She "holds the torch of knowledge on her right arm and wears a chain from which hangs the symbol of Christianity. The shield is encircled by a band that contains the Latin words *Humanitatem per Crucem Alere*, meaning 'Serving humanity through the Cross.' Outside parallel circles contain the name of the institution and its founding date," according to *Anderson University Magazine*.

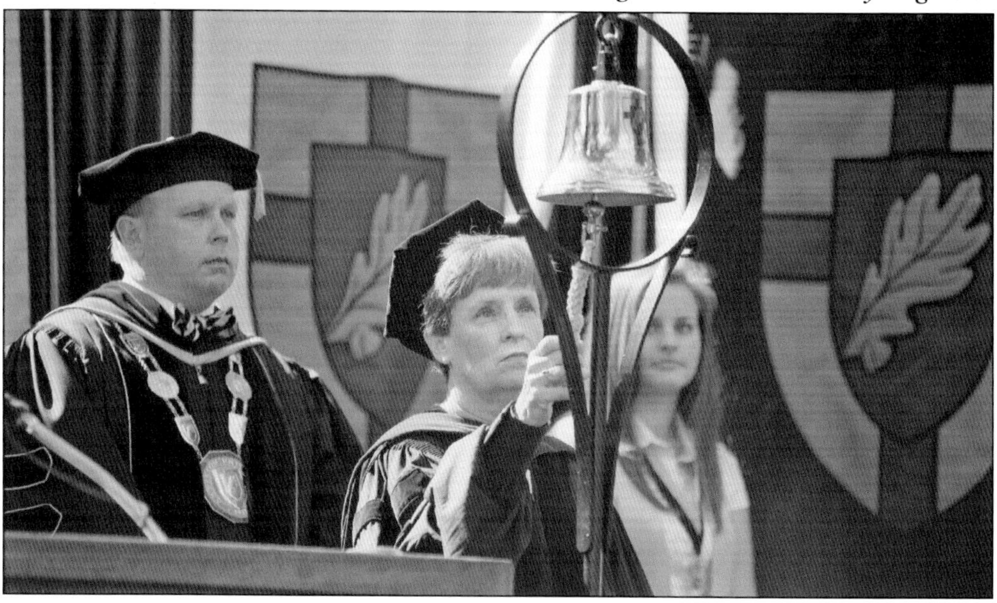

Since May 2002, the May commencement exercises have been held on front campus. A new tradition, ringing in the hour, has been included, performed by the faculty member who carries the mace. The bell is rung eight times symbolizing the eight stakeholder groups, which the university strives to serve. In 2010, Dr. Margaret Wooten, professor of English, had the honor. Behind Dr. Wooten, President Whitaker and a graduation marshal hang banners that represent each of the university's colleges by color, emblazoned with the university crest.

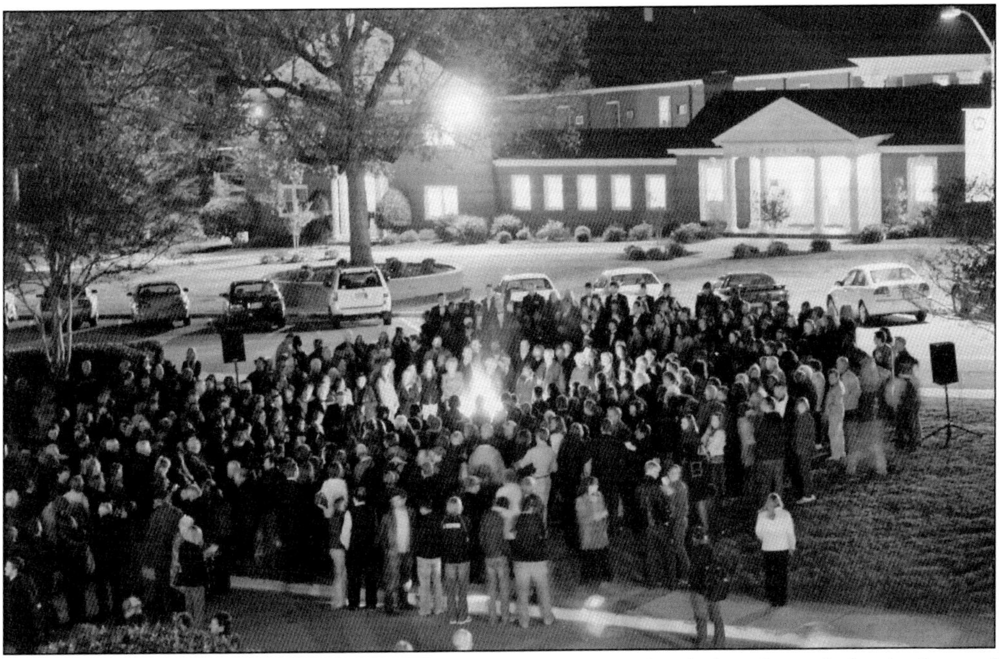

During the first week of December in 2009, President Whitaker lights the Yule log in front of Henderson Auditorium following the performances celebrating Christmas First Night. This traditional festivity opens the Christmas season. The many different campus musical ensembles provide the sacred sounds of Christmas.

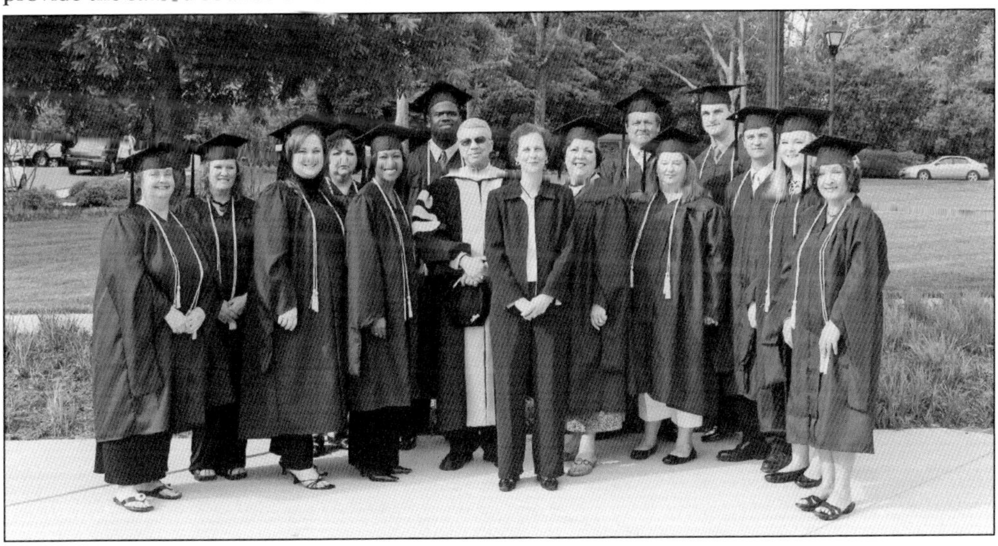

In May 2008, the first graduate class received the master of education degree. Those pictured are, from left to right, Terry Ann Snipes; Wendy Batten; Teresa Culpepper; Elizabeth Cannon; Shiela Hadden; Selynto Anderson; Dr. Chuck Wooten, dean of the College of Education Graduate Studies; Brenda Gray, graduate studies coordinator; Pamela Thomason; Sammy Franks; Terri Smith; Stewart Hudspeth; Russell Gray; Jennifer Smith; and Martha Hartwig. Graduate program offerings continue to grow, including now a master of arts in teaching, master of business administration, master of ministry, and the Command College of South Carolina at AU, which is a graduate-level program for management in criminal justice fields.

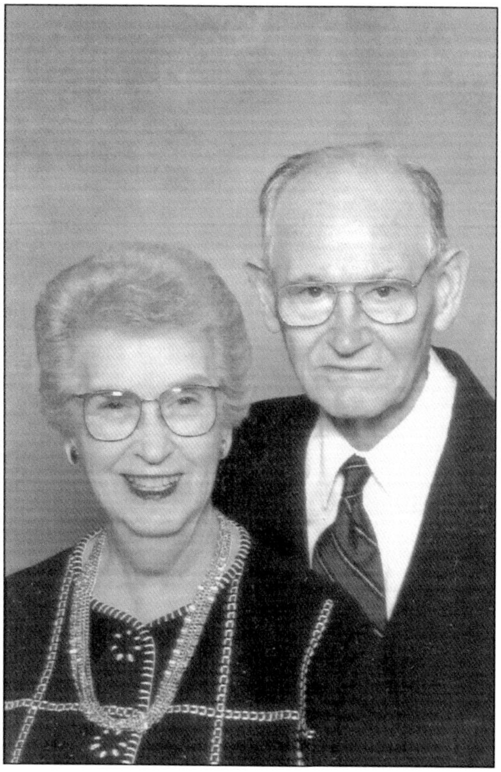

In May 2008, the Graduate School of Christian Ministry was formed by the board of trustees vote and was subsequently joined by Dr. Michael Duduit as founding dean. At the May commencement in 2009, the largest gift in the university's history, an $8-million estate gift from David Clamp, was announced by his wife, Jane. The graduate school was renamed the David T. Clamp Graduate School of Christian Ministry and became part of the College of Christian Studies, created in 2009. The Clamps, pictured here, were awarded honorary doctoral degrees at that commencement. Mr. Clamp's was awarded posthumously.

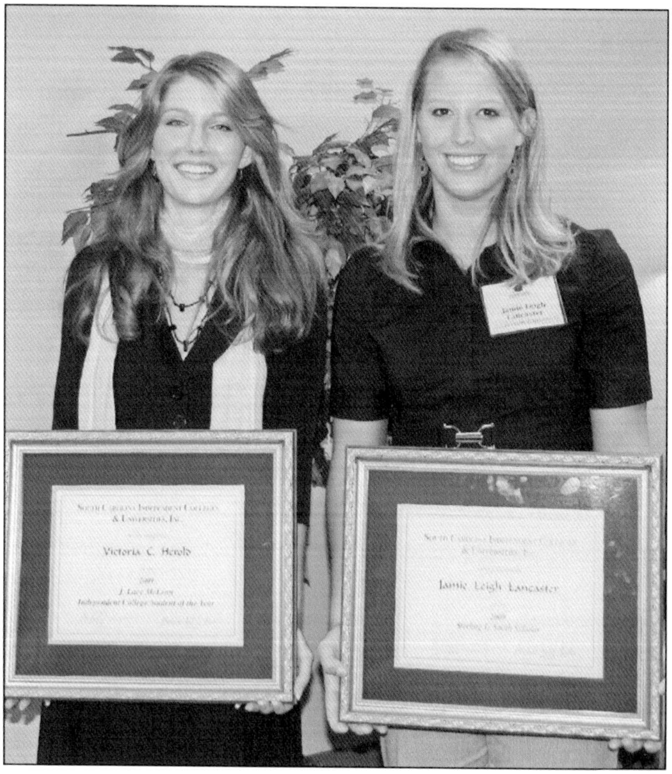

At the end of its first century and at the beginning of its second, Anderson University is increasingly recognized for the excellence of its students. In 2009, for only the second time in its history, the South Carolina Independent Colleges and Universities selected the two most outstanding students in South Carolina from Anderson University. Pictured are Victoria Herold (left) and Jamie Lancaster (right). Lancaster, a volleyball player, was also recognized as the most outstanding student-athlete in the Conference Carolinas, winning the Murphy Osborne Award in 2010.

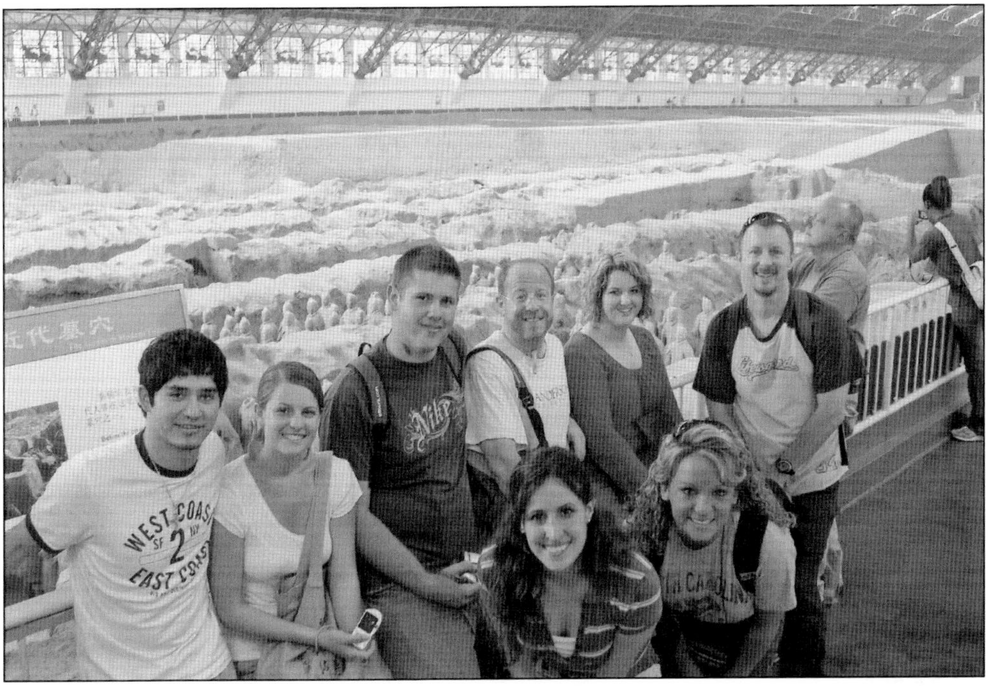

International study programs and mission opportunities continue to expand with the development of the Quality Enhancement Plan (QEP) and an AU semester in Australia, which began in the fall of 2010. The 2008 business in China class is pictured in front of the terra-cotta warriors near Xi'an, Shaanxi Province. Members are, from left to right, (first row) Kristine Fikes and Adrian Allen; (second row) Andrew Deal, Valerie Zenoni, Walter Sutherland, Dr. Joe Spencer, Kerry McJunkin, Dr. Bill Liang, and unidentified.

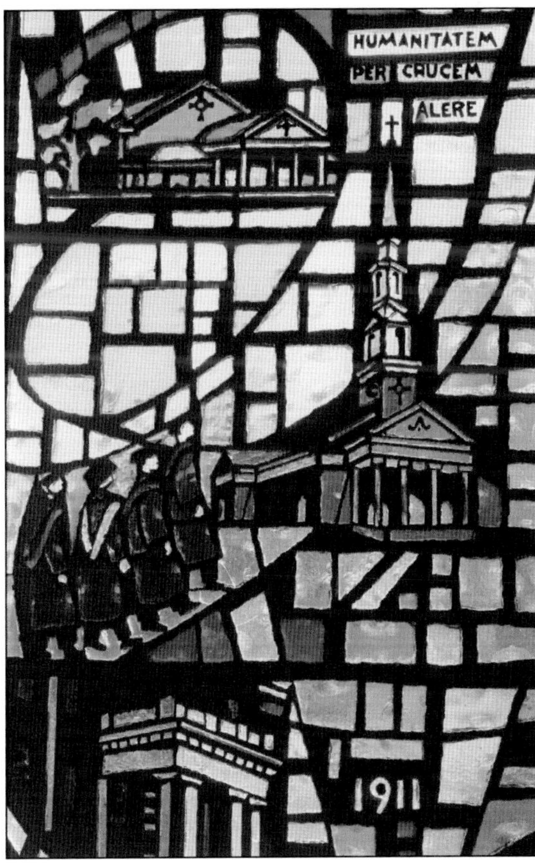

This stained-glass window from the Rainey Fine Arts Center epitomizes the path taken by Anderson University in its first 100 years and also sets the direction for its next 100 years. New programs, new traditions, and new opportunities flourish in tandem with a new century.

www.arcadiapublishing.com

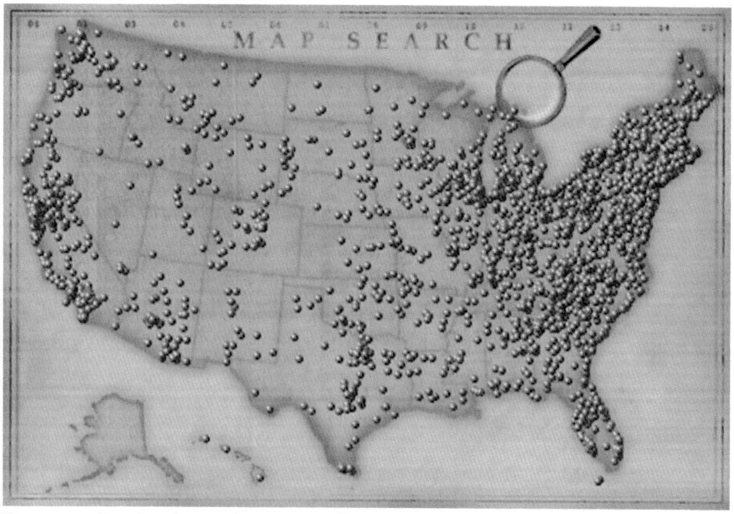

Discover books about the town where you grew up, the cities where your friends and families live, the town where your parents met, or even that retirement spot you've been dreaming about. Our Web site provides history lovers with exclusive deals, advanced notification about new titles, e-mail alerts of author events, and much more.

MADE IN THE USA

Arcadia Publishing, the leading local history publisher in the United States, is committed to making history accessible and meaningful through publishing books that celebrate and preserve the heritage of America's people and places. Consistent with our mission to preserve history on a local level, this book was printed in South Carolina on American-made paper and manufactured entirely in the United States.

This book carries the accredited Forest Stewardship Council (FSC) label and is printed on 100 percent FSC-certified paper. Products carrying the FSC label are independently certified to assure consumers that they come from forests that are managed to meet the social, economic, and ecological needs of present and future generations.

FSC
Mixed Sources
Product group from well-managed forests and other controlled sources

Cert no. SW-COC-001530
www.fsc.org

Find *Your* Place in History.